£3-50

ENGLISH FURNITURE

an illustrated handbook

A. ARMCHAIR of gilded wood, upholstered in crimson brocaded silk with gold fringe. About 1675. One of a pair listed in the seventeenth-century inventories of Ham House as 'sleeping chayres'. The back is adjustable by means of iron ratchets. Height 4 ft. 7 in. *Ham House, Surrey.* *See page 45*

ENGLISH FURNITURE

AN ILLUSTRATED HANDBOOK

by

MAURICE TOMLIN

FABER AND FABER
3 Queen Square
London

First published in 1972
by Faber and Faber Limited
3 Queen Square London WC1
Printed in Great Britain by
Robert MacLehose & Co Ltd Glasgow

ISBN 0 571 08381 1

ACKNOWLEDGEMENTS

The illustration of a piece of furniture in the Royal Collection at Hampton Court Palace (Plate 50) is reproduced by gracious permission of Her Majesty the Queen.

I should also like to express my thanks to the following for permission to illustrate items from their collections or for the use of their photographs: His Grace the Duke of Northumberland; the Earl Spencer; the Trustees of the Chatsworth Settlement; the Victoria and Albert Museum; the Rijksmuseum, Amsterdam; Temple Newsam House, Leeds; the Glasgow School of Art; the National Buildings Record; the Council of Industrial Design; Conran and Co. Ltd; David Bartlett Designs Ltd; Fratelli Fabbri, Milan; Goods & Chattels Ltd; Hille of London Ltd; Lupton-Morton Mail Order Ltd; Merrow Associates Ltd; and Race Furniture Ltd. The appropriate acknowledgements are shown below the photographs. Figures 1, 2, 3, 4, 6, 7, 9, 16, 18 and 19 were drawn by Michael Young, A.R.I.B.A, A.R.A.I.A.

I am grateful to my colleagues in the Department of Furniture and Woodwork at the Victoria and Albert Museum for their help on many occasions during the preparation of this work and to Mrs. Judith Bumpus for her helpful comments on the last chapter.

CONTENTS

ILLUSTRATIONS

COLOUR PLATES

MONOCHROME PLATES
at the end of the book

FIGURES
in the text

INTRODUCTION

The aim of this book is to provide a comprehensive guide to the characteristics of English furniture from the Middle Ages to the present day incorporating brief details of important designers and makers. The author does not claim to be producing remarkable new discoveries but has rather sought to present the known facts in a compact volume in the hope that it will serve as an introduction to those new to the subject and be a convenient source of reference.

The book describes ordinary pieces that were typical of the furniture in fashion in their day as well as a number of items that were exceptional in either design or quality. The reader should bear in mind that the dates given for the currency of styles refer to the approximate periods when they were in fashion and that there was always, until recent times, a considerable time lag in the remoter country districts where furniture continued to be made in styles no longer favoured in London.

Each period style is dealt with in a separate chapter, each – except for the chapter on modern furniture – beginning with an introduction in which the general characteristics are described. After that, the different types of furniture have been arranged in the following order for easy reference:

(1) SEATS AND BEDS
(2) TABLES (sideboards, which derive from the side-table, have been included here, as well as other items in which the word 'table' occurs, even where they are largely intended for storage)
(3) CASE FURNITURE (i.e. furniture designed mainly for storage)
(4) MISCELLANEOUS

Terms such as 'settee' and 'sofa' that have alternated in fashionable usage are for convenience treated as synonymous, though in fact the latter term, introduced about 1700, often implied a form of seating especially suitable for reclining. 'Mirror' and 'looking-glass' are similarly interchangeable, although the former was probably reserved until the nineteenth century for a hand mirror or one made of polished metal. 'Candle-stand' has been used throughout in preference to the French words *torchère* and *guéridon.*

I

MEDIEVAL AND EARLY TUDOR

Comparatively little furniture of this period still exists, due not only to its inevitable disappearance during the course of time but also to the fact that very little existed in the first place. The population was small and ordinary people lived in hovels, their interiors not containing much that was worthy of the name of furniture. Even castles and manor houses were sparsely furnished in the Middle Ages, such small suggestions of luxury and comfort as they might contain being created by means of painted decoration on ceilings, on walls and on the simpler pieces of furniture together with hangings of silk, velvet or other textiles. Fortunately our knowledge of Gothic furniture is not restricted to what we can learn from surviving pieces but can be supplemented by reference to contemporary illuminated manuscripts and paintings.

Socially it was a time of great insecurity and unrest, the wealthy and powerful living in the strongly fortified castles and manor houses. Their aspirations to comfort and luxury were stimulated by the return of the Crusaders, who brought with them news of the luxury to be found in the Middle East as well as fine damasks and silks that they had acquired. In general, England lagged behind developments on the Continent owing to difficulties of communication so that new ideas and methods took some time to reach this country, particularly the northern and western parts. England's comparative isolation also played a part in establishing certain national characteristics in the arts. Despite this, the Gothic style was widely diffused and it is not always possible to determine the country of origin of a piece of furniture, particularly as many pieces in use here were undoubtedly imported. The most that can be said is that certain characteristics were more often in evidence in one country than in another.

Carved decoration was almost entirely based on the forms and motifs of Gothic architecture and included such features as roundels resembling plate tracery, pointed arches and arcades. They were at first executed in low relief and later in openwork carving. Finials and buttress-like forms were used too. Shortly before 1500, a distinctive type of carving known as linenfold because of its resemblance to hanging draperies was introduced from Flanders, becoming widely used for the decoration of panels (Plate 1). Early in the sixteenth century, Renaissance motifs such as profile heads in medallions (known as Romayne work) were brought in from the Continent as well and sometimes appeared on furniture that was otherwise completely Gothic in conception. The introduction of these Renaissance decorative forms was largely the result of Henry VIII's encouraging Italian artists and craftsmen to come and work here – up to the time of his break with Rome in 1534.

In England, as in other countries of Northern Europe, most furniture was made of oak, which was the commonest wood and also the most serviceable, because of its hardness. Elm, yew and fruitwoods were sometimes used and a small amount of sycamore and walnut was available for furniture-making towards the end of the period, these trees having been introduced in the fifteenth century.

In addition to being carved, much of the furniture, like the walls and ceilings, was painted in bright colours, often with the addition of gilding; the paint served to brighten the rooms as well as being a preservative for the wood and traces of it can sometimes be seen today. Occasionally wood was painted and grained, generally in imitation of walnut.

The earliest and most primitive form of construction, used for chests, was the hollowing out of a tree trunk which would then be bound with iron bands, a method that continued to be employed on occasion until the end of the fifteenth century. In the twelfth or thirteenth century, carpenters adopted a method of construction by which broad, stout planks were fastened together at the angles with wrought-iron nails or wooden pegs. The mortise and tenon joint, secured with oak pins, came into use in this country in the thirteenth century. It was just before 1500 that the panelled construction known as wainscot was introduced, though it did not become generally adopted for nearly a century. This skilled work was done by a joiner. The framework was fitted together with mortise and tenon joints, and the panels were set fairly loosely into grooves on the inside edges to allow for the shrinkage and warping of the various parts. The method made for lighter furniture and wasted less wood. Although the joints of the framing were brought together at an angle of ninety degrees, mitres set at an angle of forty-five degrees were cut into their mouldings.

Wrought-iron was used for the mounts on medieval furniture, and these included iron strengthening bands and, from the fourteenth century, locks, hinges and carrying handles. Locks usually had a flush metal plate behind which the works were sunk into the chest front; locking was effected by means of a hasp hinged from the top. Small iron hinges were in use as well as wooden ones from quite an early date and became generally used about 1300. Strap hinges appeared in the fifteenth century. Carrying handles consisted of a bar attached on a swivel at each end.

Little is known about individual craftsmen at this time. One of the earliest references is to a joiner named William Grene who supplied Henry VIII with a close stool in 1547.

Much of the best furniture was made for ecclesiastical use and many of the pieces that survive today, particularly the chests, come from churches or monasteries.

SEATS AND BEDS

The usual seat for one person was the stool. It consisted, in its simplest form, of a circular top – probably a section cut from a tree-trunk – into which were slotted three turned legs set at a slight angle to one another to give stability. Another type common to the whole of Europe had three vertical legs linked by stretchers at the sides and jointed into a triangular seat-rail, the seat itself being made of either wood or rushes. A primitive form of 'backstool' was evolved later, in which one of the legs continued upwards and was fitted with a bracketed cross-bar for the sitter to lean against.

Also in use in the fifteenth century was the slab-ended stool. The rectangular seat was supported by a splayed slab or plank at each end, tied to the seat by a vertical underframing which might be nailed to the supports or slotted through them and secured with wedges. The slabs were cut at the bottom, often in an ogee arch shape, thus dividing them into separate feet; cusping or similar decoration derived from architecture would be used to decorate the lower edge of the underframing (Plate 2). Occasionally a stretcher near the base was used to link the end slabs. Exactly the same construction was used for some benches (Plate 3).

Folding stools with curved or straight legs of X form were also in use in England in the Middle Ages. They would have had seats of cloth or leather; from the fourteenth century, brass-headed nails were used for attaching the upholstery to seats. In some X-frame stools the cross-pieces were extended high enough for the rails linking the front to the back to serve as arm-rests.

The chair was an exceedingly rare item of furniture in the Middle Ages, being reserved for the use of persons of exalted rank. The earliest surviving examples are ecclesiastical but chairs of a similar type would have been used at the high table on the dais in the medieval Great Hall where the family and guests of honour would be seated overlooking the less important guests and retainers in the main body of the room. One of the best examples of these throne-chairs is the fourteenth century Coronation Chair in Westminster Abbey, made for Edward I to contain the Stone of Scone. Its reliance on architecture as a source of decoration can be clearly seen and it was originally painted in bright colours. Chairs such as this were often very high and provided with canopies surmounted by finials and crockets. The earliest examples, dating from the thirteenth and fourteenth centuries, were made of slabs of wood, tenoned and pegged; they had little or no carving as they were draped with a 'dorcer' or 'dosser' for the back, made of rich damask or velvet, and the seat was provided with a cushion or 'banker'.

Another cushion served as a footstool. These chairs, though comparatively immovable objects owing to their weight, would sometimes be dismantled to accompany the owner on his progresses about the country.

Towards the end of the fifteenth century chairs of panelled construction, known as box chairs and made by a joiner, came into use. Chairs of this type, which had panels in the back, front and sides, would be for the master of the house (Plate 1). The box-like receptacle was generally reached by means of a hinged seat.

Chairs of X form similar in construction to the folding stools but not collapsible owing to their having backs were also made in the fifteenth century. These, too, were sometimes draped with damasks or silks.

Apart from the stool, the most common types of seat were benches and settles made to take four or more people. The bench or form standing on slab ends has already been mentioned. Some seats of that type were fixed to the wall panelling. Though the terms 'bench' and 'settle' seem to have been interchangeable in the Gothic period, the latter is now normally used for a bench with arms, with which most of the built-in seats were provided. The free-standing settles were often given very high backs as a protection from draughts and many were provided with a foot-rest to raise the feet from a cold floor. Some were fitted with a canopy not unlike that found on contemporary choir stalls.

Beds were the most valuable item of furnishing. It was customary for Royalty to give audience, and ladies to receive visitors, from their beds and they were given an imposing appearance by means of costly and elaborate hangings draped from a canopy that hung from the ceiling. The wooden framework was considered of no importance and does not figure in contemporary inventories but there is frequent mention of rich velvets, silks and satins and tapestry and even cloth of gold. The bedstead itself was a wooden frame with a network of ropes on which lay a mattress filled with straw, wool or, occasionally, swansdown. At the head of the bed, hanging from the canopy or tester, was a draped textile, known as a 'celure'; bedposts and carved wooden headboards were not introduced until after 1500. A truckle bed, fitted with small wheels, which could be slid under the main bed, was sometimes supplied for use by a servant. The room containing the bed would be used as a living-room in the daytime, the hangings at the foot of the bed being gathered up into bag-like shapes at each corner so that the bed could be used as an additional seat.

TABLES

Most tables consisted of long planks of oak or elm resting on trestles shaped like an 'A' or an inverted 'V'. A rarer type had central trestles in the form of shaped pedestals (Fig. 1); two well-known examples of the kind, dating from the late fifteenth century,

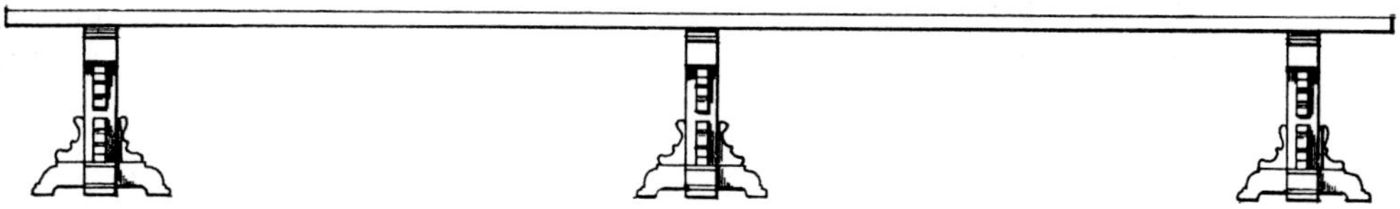

FIG. 1. Trestle table with central pedestals

are at Penshurst, Kent. After a meal these tables would normally be dismantled and stowed away. Less usual was the fixed or 'dormant' table with stout legs linked by a continuous stretcher at floor level that was sometimes used as a dining-table on the dais. Plate 3 illustrates a dormant table of a form that was typical for the fifteenth century, except for the draw-top, which is an unusually early appearance of this feature (see next chapter). These dining-tables could be up to twenty-five feet long but were generally rather narrow; in most cases the diners, particularly those at the high table, sat at only one side. Many contemporary illustrations show the table covered with a linen cloth reaching almost to the floor.

Another type of table seen in manuscripts and paintings has a round or polygonal top on a central support. This type, used for various occupations such as reading and sewing, as well as for meals, was probably confined to a small number of wealthy dwellings.

A special table called a counter- or rent-table, at which the lord of the manor would sit to receive rent, was in use in the fifteenth and sixteenth centuries. It had a large rectangular compartment, raised on four square legs, with a hinged or sliding lid that was sometimes marked out with divisions for making calculations (Plate 4).

CASE FURNITURE

By far the most important and widespread item of furniture in medieval times was the chest. Besides serving the obvious purpose of storage, it could also be used as a seat, a table and even, on occasion, a bed. Chests were used in churches, too, for storing vestments, jewels and archives, and as collecting boxes, when they would be fitted with three strong locks and a slot for money; but many chests that have been preserved in churches were domestic examples, originally put there for safe keeping.

The terms 'chest' and 'coffer' seem to have been interchangeable in medieval times although to-day the word coffer usually implies a rather small chest.

The earliest and most primitive type of chest consisted of a hollowed-out tree-trunk, which gave rise to the term 'trunk'; it was strengthened by bands of iron and a slice of tree-trunk provided a lid.

Slightly less primitive, and made by a carpenter, was a chest that consisted of five broad, stout boards, nailed together with iron nails and strengthened with iron bands, having a sixth board for the lid. Plate 5 shows a chest of Anglo-Scottish (Border) origin, dating from the late fifteenth or early sixteenth century, which is constructed in this way. The shallow carving depicts in the middle a representation of the Fall and at either end a roundel of Gothic tear-drop tracery. The end boards usually extended below the level of the rest of the chest, raising it from the damp of the floor, but sometimes internal stiles at the corners served that purpose.

Framed or joined chests, made by a joiner, date from the thirteenth century onwards; they continued to be constructed in this way right into the seventeenth century, although they became far less common after about 1500. Broad stiles or end supports, extending below the body of the chest, raised it off the ground and a single board was tenoned into them at front and back. No glue was used in the construction, the joints being secured with dowel pegs. The ends were sometimes strengthened with cross-bars. The lid, which was reinforced with rails underneath, was attached by means of a pin-hinge: it consisted of a horizontal wooden pin which passed through a flange at each end of the lid, its ends being slotted into the back stiles of the chest and secured by means of a small metal plate. This type of hinge fell out of use after about 1300, being replaced by iron strap hinges. Inside the chests a small compartment or 'till' was fixed at the top at one end; money or other valuables kept there were easily accessible and the small lid could be used to hold the main lid open.

The most common type of decoration was chip-carving, where shallow incisions in the form of roundels, sometimes inspired by rose-windows, were decorated with geometrical patterns on the front of the chest. A thirteenth century oak chest of such a type is seen in Plate 6 (the lock is a later addition). Sometimes the only ornament was simple grooves carved on the edges of the stiles and front board. Occasionally painted leather or canvas was glued on the chests, and painted scenes or heraldic decoration in oil or tempera were sometimes applied direct to the wood. Carved ornament in the form of tracery based on windows, arcades, buttresses and other architectural forms was often used after the end of the thirteenth century. At about the same time, ironwork in the form of scrolls covering the surface of the chest was introduced and it was sometimes applied over velvet or other decorative material.

Elaborately carved reliefs of figure subjects might appear on chests of the late fourteenth and the fifteenth centuries. Frequently these took the form of knights jousting, giving rise to the name 'tilting chest', but scenes illustrating Bible stories are also known. A popular subject was St. George and the Dragon though most of the chests carved in this way originated in Flanders and there is, in fact, some doubt as to whether any of them were made in this country. The so-called 'spruce' or 'Pruse' coffers, probably made of pine, were imported from Prussia (Prusse) through Danzig. In the second half of the fifteenth century tracery was periodically applied to the surface instead of being carved in the solid wood.

Handles of iron were fitted at the ends of many chests through which a rope might be threaded, enabling them to be slung on a pole and transported easily to accompany the owner on his travels. From the fifteenth century onwards there were also smaller chests designed specifically for travelling and known as 'trussing coffers'. These were normally covered with *cuir bouilli*, which was decorated with an incised design, painted and gilded (Plate 8).

The new method of panelled construction, introduced from the Continent shortly before 1500, was sometimes used for chests, though often only for the front in the first half of the sixteenth century, the rest being constructed by the older methods. Linenfold carving was a very popular form of decoration for such panelling and Renaissance profile heads in roundels or lozenges were also used occasionally. A chest bearing rather crudely carved heads and the inscription *Fere God T. Love God* is illustrated in Plate 7.

Closely related to the chest was the hutch, introduced in the latter part of the fifteenth century, which was used for the storage of clothes or food. It had a chest-like shape, generally with one or more doors at the front, and was raised on four square legs to table height. The example shown in Plate 9, ornamented with openwork panels at the front and linenfold at each end, opens at the top.

In the Middle Ages the term 'cupboard' meant literally a board or boards for the display of cups and plate. A receptacle resembling our present-day cupboard, and used for the storage of food, or, in ecclesiastical examples, vestments, etc., was called an 'ambry' or 'aumbry'; the name presumably derives from one of the uses of such a cupboard – that is, keeping food left over from a meal to be given as alms to the poor. The most common type had a door with iron hinges, the panels being pierced with tracery for ventilation, and was raised from the floor on the corner stiles. The name was also used for similar receptacles let into the wall. 'Close cupboards' and cupboards fitted with ambries are mentioned in medieval inventories and they can be seen in contemporary illustrations with covers draped over the top, on which the plate was displayed. Probably of similar form, although descriptions in contemporary inventories are rather vague, was the livery cupboard – from which food was delivered or *livré*. In this, an allowance of food and drink was put out for the use of members of the household in their rooms at night.

Two types of desk were in use during the fifteenth century. The larger type, somewhat resembling a lectern, stood on the floor and had a sloping top for writing or reading; storage space for books and writing materials was provided in the lower part, which would probably be carved with architectural motifs similar to those used on chests. The smaller, portable type, that was used standing on a table, was also fitted with a sloping lid. Below this there would be an arrangement of drawers and compartments. A fine example, now in the Victoria and Albert Museum, seems to have been made for Henry VIII and bears his royal arms on the underside of a flap below the lid. The inside, which is covered with leather, is brightly decorated in paint and gilding with Renaissance heads and figures – probably the work of a foreign artist working for the King. It dates from about 1525.

II

LATE TUDOR AND EARLY STUART
(including the Commonwealth period)

During the time of Henry VIII's encouragement of Italian craftsmen, many Renaissance forms and ideas had been introduced into the prevailing Gothic style. After the craftsmen had returned to Italy, however, the use of Renaissance decoration was only stimulated in this country by indirect means through the many Flemish and German skilled immigrants, as well as through Flemish and German pattern books. Theirs was a style evolved by engravers and goldsmiths that was a very mannered and distorted version of the original.

The Elizabethan period in particular was a time of exploration, expansion of overseas trade and a great increase in the country's wealth giving rise to a new propertied class. Many old houses were renovated and enlarged and a great many new ones built and, as there was no longer the same need for fortification in this more settled age, they could be more expansively laid out. The all-purpose Great Hall was now replaced by the Great Chamber and numerous private rooms were provided as well as a Long Gallery and Dining Parlour; these developments naturally led to an increase in the amount of furniture required. The spirit of adventurousness and self-confidence of the Elizabethan age are well expressed in the exuberant, if somewhat crude, style of its furniture and other decorative arts.

In the first part of the seventeenth century there is no distinct change of style but rather a certain refinement in many of the forms used as well as a greater stylisation. There were no significant developments in the short Cromwellian period though the official discouragement of the arts and disapproval of elaborate ornament led to a further simplification of form and a reduction in decoration; this has, however, been overstressed and some quite extensively decorated pieces of furniture dating from this time are known.

Oak was still by far the most commonly used wood, although other native woods such as ash, elm, beech, birch and fruitwoods were also employed in furniture-making. Chestnut and deal were less common; so was walnut, which was especially prized.

Inlay became common as a form of decoration, being introduced through Flanders and Germany from Italy. It consists of the use of small pieces of different kinds of wood laid into shaped recesses in the solid wood to form patterns or, occasionally, pictorial representations. Holly, bog oak, box, sycamore, ebony and the fruitwoods were particularly used for this type of decoration, which was often geometrical, with lozenges or chequered patterns, or else based on plant forms. It was sometimes further embellished with ivory or bone and mother-of-pearl.

FIG. 2. Egg-and-dart moulding

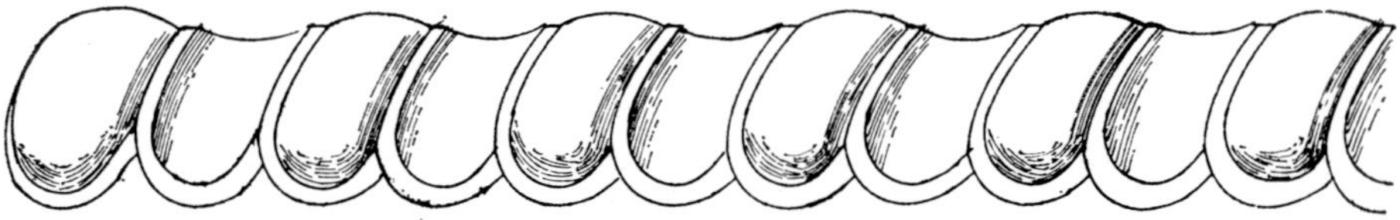

FIG. 3. Gadrooning

Carving was profuse and included fruit and flower forms, acanthus leaves, grotesque masks, egg-and-dart (Fig. 2), gadrooning (Fig. 3), guilloche and fluting, all of Classical derivation. In addition, strapwork, a low relief form of carving (occasionally used in openwork form), resembling the curving of leather straps, was introduced from Flanders and widely employed, specially in the early seventeenth century. Of the pattern books from which these motifs were taken the most influential, *Architectura*, was published in 1577 by Johannes Vredemann de Vries, a Flemish artist and designer. Paint was still used on some furniture but plain surfaces, waxed and oiled, increased in popularity.

A common form in the Elizabethan period was the so-called cup-and-cover, a bulbous support derived from a distortion of the Classical column, at first used mainly for table legs (Plate 21). A deep groove encircling it gave the appearance of a cup with a cover and both parts were generally enriched with carving, especially gadrooning (or nulling), on the upper part and acanthus leaves on the lower. Because of its great girth it was usually made up of several vertical sections of wood. An Ionic capital surmounting it was the only more or less correctly interpreted feature of the Classical column. Heraldic beasts were also adopted occasionally as supports in the Elizabethan and Jacobean periods, particularly for tables and court cupboards. Another motif derived from architecture is the arch form frequently used on case furniture and the head-boards of beds.

Applied ornament in the form of split balusters, lozenges and facetted jewels became fashionable about 1600, various kinds of wood, either glued or pinned, being used, as well as semi-precious stones. At about the same time an arcading of lunettes was used for ornamenting friezes of tables and case furniture, and the cup-and-cover became more refined, its use being extended to seat furniture. Towards the middle of the century it tended to be replaced by bobbin-turning, which found favour in the Cromwellian period because of its comparative simplicity. At the close of the period twist-turning was introduced though it was not widely used until after the Restoration.

The use of mortise and tenon joints, secured with wooden pins, and of panelled construction was, by now, general but glue was seldom used for joints.

Mounts were still made of wrought-iron but often with more refined, Renaissance-influenced designs, having chamfered edges. Frequently they were given an elaborate outline such as the typical 'cock's-head' hinge (Fig. 4) or the back-plate to a lock in the

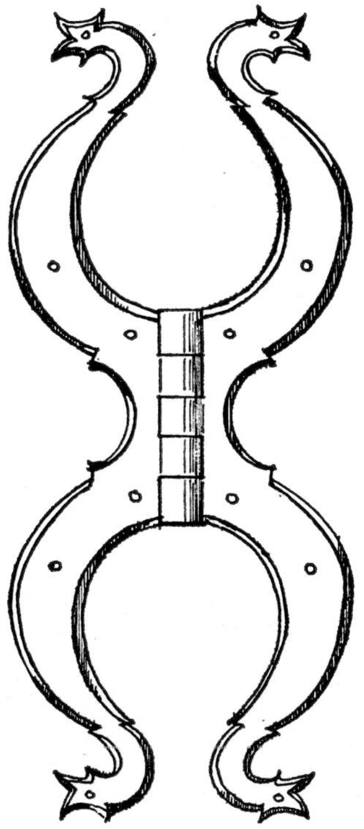

FIG. 4. Cock's-head hinge

form of an escutcheon. The 'H' hinge, with two vertical plates interlocking at the central barrel, was also introduced in the Elizabethan period.

Bills exist for furniture supplied by members of the Grene family to Queen Elizabeth throughout her reign. John Grene was the royal coffermaker from 1553 until his death in 1566; his son, Thomas, supplied Queen Elizabeth from 1566 to 1600, the year of his death, when his son, John II, succeeded to the position which he held until he died in 1608. The furniture, which became increasingly sumptuous, included coffers, chairs, stools, desks and screens, richly adorned with velvets, silks, lace, fringes, and fabrics wrought with gold and silver. (See R. W. Symonds, 'New Light on Tudor Furniture II – Queen Elizabeth's Coffer-Makers, John and Thomas Grene', *Country Life*, Vol. XCIII, June 11, 1943, p. 1054.)

SEATS AND BEDS

By the end of the sixteenth century the oak joint stool, with four baluster legs linked by outside stretchers and a wooden top, had generally replaced the slab-ended stool (Plate 11). The legs, which were sometimes fluted, were really the equivalent of the cup-and-cover form used on other contemporary furniture in a much less bulbous guise; they were often slightly splayed to give greater stability. The seat-rail was commonly given a serpentine or arcaded lower edge. A loose cushion would normally be used with these stools, though upholstered furniture began to come into use about the middle of the sixteenth century. Few upholstered stools have survived, but they did become fairly common, presumably because of their light construction, in beech, sometimes painted and gilded; the legs were generally of columnar form, and upholstery would be of silk or velvet, trimmed with a fringe. Some folding stools, with X-frames, were still made. Benches or forms were of similar construction to the joint stools.

Chairs now became a much more common form of seating and a number of new types appeared. The panelled sides were omitted from chairs of box type in Elizabeth's reign and by 1600 the boxing-in of the lower part had also been discontinued, to be replaced by straight legs linked by stretchers.

Another light type of armchair became widely used for parlours and bedrooms about the middle of the sixteenth century, although early examples had appeared in the 1530s. This chair, introduced from France, to which the name *caquetoire* has recently become attached, was characterised by a tall narrow back panel, outward-curving arms and seat and straight, square legs linked by stretchers almost at floor level (Plate 12). The back panel was generally carved in low relief with a profile head amidst foliage or similar ornament of Renaissance derivation. In the early examples the legs and arm supports would be without decoration but in the early seventeenth century it became customary for the front legs and arm supports to be turned and fluted or incised with rings. A scrolled cresting sometimes surmounted the backs of later examples.

The so-called *caquetoire* seems to have influenced the design of the typical panelled-back chair of the first half of the seventeenth century, which is, however, of a heavier type. The back is broader and, in addition to a scrolled cresting on the top, it often has a double scrolled bracket near the top of each upright (Plate 13). The arms generally curve gently down from the back, curling over in a rudimentary scroll at the front. A popular motif for the back was a round-headed arch, rising from short, truncated columns; the remaining decoration might consist of scrolls, guilloche, plant forms and strapwork. In some examples the ornament is entirely executed in low relief carving, but inlay was also frequently used on the backs and seat-rails of the finer examples, designs of flowering plants being particularly favoured.

Chairs using the ancient X-frame construction were made throughout the second half of the sixteenth and early seventeenth centuries; they were normally covered entirely with velvet or silk fixed with brass-headed nails, the backs fitted with padded upholstery and the seats consisting of loose cushions resting on webbing strung from the side rails. An additional loose cushion was sometimes supplied at the back and the sumptuous appearance further enhanced by fringes of gold or silver thread attached to the back, arms and seat-rail (Plates 14 and 18). A matching footstool was sometimes provided, too.

Towards the end of the sixteenth century there appeared a collapsible folding chair, based on an earlier Italian type (Plate 15), which was essentially a modification of the X-form. The parts of the chair was fastened together by means of pins or bars of wood. Typical decoration of arches carved with guilloche, enclosing lozenges, can be seen on the back. The seat is of panelled construction and would have had a loose cushion.

The houses of the wealthy were already beginning to be furnished with a considerable number of upholstered seats by the end of the sixteenth century. A type that became popular in the early years of the seventeenth century was the low-backed 'farthingale chair' – a term adopted in the nineteenth century – made without arms to allow for the ample farthingale skirts fashionable at the time. (Chairs without arms were known as 'backstools', a term that persisted until the eighteenth century.) Many farthingale chairs had straight, square legs, though legs of columnar form were also common, and the stretchers were attached near the base. The seats were upholstered with velvet, silk or turkey-work (an English imitation of Turkey carpets) fixed with brass-headed nails, and the padded, rectangular back, raised well above the seat-rail, would be similarly covered. Some were also made with wooden arms but in these the proportions were broader. Walnut was occasionally used for the framework; more often this would be of a cheaper wood, such as beech, entirely covered with fabric or else painted and gilded. Much of the gilding and painted decoration can still be seen on the armchair illustrated in Plate 16.

The most common type of chair during the Cromwellian period was basically similar to the farthingale chair, with ball- or knob-turning on legs and arm supports. The front stretcher was generally also turned and raised well above floor level. Leather upholstery, sometimes tooled or embossed and painted, was used for the panels of the seat and back, being fixed with brass-headed nails.

In Yorkshire and Derbyshire a distinctive type of chair was evolved at this time that continued to be made in the following decades. Possibly influenced by imported Italian and Portuguese examples, these chairs, made of oak, had backs of carved and cusped arcading and, in many cases, small balusters. The wooden seat was dished to take a cushion.

A number of turned or 'thrown' chairs were made throughout this period. Based on the traditional triangular stool of the Middle Ages, they had three legs, which extended above the seat-rail, where they were linked by a number of lengths of bobbin-turned wood so as to form a back and arm-rests.

The chair-table, an item of furniture that had been known since the late Middle Ages, became fairly common in the early and mid-seventeenth century. Basically the form was similar to that of a contemporary oak armchair but the back consisted of a large board, pivotted on wooden pins to the backs of the arms, so that it could swing over to rest on them, making a table top (Plate 23). The board was often decorated in a similar manner to the backs of ordinary chairs.

A type of sofa that was rather like an upholstered settle with hinged flanks appeared in the second half of the sixteenth century. The earliest surviving example, at Knole, Kent, is of beech, with back, seat and ends upholstered in crimson velvet, trimmed with a fringe and fastened with brass-headed nails. The legs are entirely hidden by a valance of velvet. The ends are held in position by iron ratchets and can be let down to convert the settee into a day-bed (Plate 20).

The day-bed as such, though probably introduced during the reign of Henry VIII, did not become common until well into the seventeenth century. It had fixed panelled ends, which sloped outwards, and a valance of fine textiles all round, concealing the legs; it was supplied with an upholstered mattress or cushions.

The wooden frame of the bedstead, hitherto not valued greatly except as a framework to support the bedding and the costly and sumptuous hangings, became an important feature of the bed in the second half of the sixteenth century, so that by the end of the century elaborately carved bedsteads were not only the prerogative of the very wealthy. At the same time a certain number of beds of lighter construction, in which the framework was concealed, were apparently still made. From about the middle of the century the typical bed was constructed with the tester supported at the head by an elaborately carved wainscot headboard, often painted. At the foot the bedposts were in the form of enormously bulbous, mannered columns, incorporating a version of the cup-and-cover form and headed with Ionic capitals. These footposts, which were carried to their furthest extreme of elaboration in the early seventeenth century – after which they became more restrained – were elaborately carved with strapwork, acanthus leaves, fluting, gadrooning and other ornament. They generally stood on square plinths which were quite separate from the bedstead itself. The headboard was generally fitted with a shelf just above the level of the top of the pillows, on which a rush-light might be stood; above this it was characteristically decorated with carved, round-headed arches resting on squat pilasters, the whole enriched with elaborate carving and, sometimes, inlay. The tester would be panelled underneath and similarly decorated (Plate 19). Such beds were assembled with large iron bolts, enabling them to be more easily dismantled. They were hung with various materials, including velvets, silks, embroideries and fine woollen cloths.

During the first half of the seventeenth century the carved bedstead began to go out of fashion, to be replaced by a lighter framework, largely made of beechwood, and concealed by the hangings. A bed of this type at Knole is hung with red satin, enriched with an appliqué pattern of silver tissue, the same material being used on the matching stools and armchair.

TABLES

Trestle tables, though still used, were falling out of favour during the Jacobean period. The leg of cup-and-cover type was the most distinctive feature of the dining-table of the Elizabethan and Jacobean periods. It was covered with flat carved decoration, usually of gadrooning and acanthus leaves, and surmounted by an Ionic capital (Plate 21). Heraldic beasts were also occasionally used as supports for dining-tables. The legs were raised on square blocks, which were linked by stretchers round the outside, with additional cross stretchers on longer tables. This form became modified in some tables in the early seventeenth century, the legs becoming less bulbous and sometimes of columnar form, as used on chairs. Some were fluted, whilst on others the decoration was limited to a few ring mouldings. The frieze might be ornamented with geometrical patterns in an inlay of coloured woods or with low relief carving, gadrooning being especially favoured for the lower edge and fluting later becoming popular. The top might still be made of one large board, but cross-framed construction became common whereby planks were jointed into a cross-piece at each end, giving strength and rigidity. Many of these tables were of the draw-top kind (Plate 21). When the table is closed there are two leaves concealed beneath the top, which is not fixed, but prevented from moving horizontally by two large wooden pins underneath. The leaves can be withdrawn from the ends of the table, rising on raked runners; when they are fully withdrawn the top falls back into position between them, at the same level, forming a table of twice the original length.

The gate-leg table, though it appears to have been known already in the Early Tudor period first became widespread during the early seventeenth century. The earliest types were semi-circular or half-octagonal when closed, in which form they could be used as side-tables against a wall. A 'gate', formed of a leg on short rails, fixed by wooden hinges to the centres of the back frieze and stretcher, was made to swing back so as to support the folding top when open; it was attached with wrought-iron hinges fixed with nails. Sometimes the leg of the gate would be split vertically and one of the fixed legs similarly halved, so as to constitute a round leg when the table was closed. Some games-tables made in this way were fitted with a compartment beneath the top for dice, etc. Early in the seventeenth century a new type was evolved which had a flap and gate-leg on either side of a fixed central section. Such tables were usually oval and the central section stood either on four legs or on a slab at either end, having shaped feet and a linking baseboard (Plate 17). The legs of gate-leg tables were often in the form of columns, though many later examples dating from the Commonwealth period had knob-turning.

CASE FURNITURE

The chest was still an important item of furniture throughout this time in spite of the increasing use of cupboards for storing clothes. Although a number of joined chests continued to be made right into the seventeenth century, particularly by country makers, the majority were of panelled construction. In the Late Tudor period the panels were typically decorated with Renaissance arch motifs, the stiles being carved in low relief or decorated with terminal figures. A particular type of chest become widespread at this time. Generally known as a 'Nonsuch chest', a name that is probably of nineteenth century origin, it was characterised by its decoration of architectural perspectives, inlaid in different coloured woods, showing buildings with fantastic skylines of towers, turrets and minarets, claimed to bear a strong resemblance to Henry VIII's Palace of Nonsuch, near Cheam (Plate 10). The whole front was frequently treated architecturally, the stiles being in the form of pilasters and the panels being carved with other architectural features such as arches and pedimented windows, while elaborate inlaid chequered or geometrical designs were used as borders. The contrasting woods used produced a bold decorative effect. These chests bear a close resemblance to chests made in the North of Germany at this time and many are believed to have been imported from the Baltic; others were probably made by immigrant German craftsmen. Decoration with architectural perspectives, though mainly found on Nonsuch chests, was also used on some other articles of furniture such as desks and beds.

After about 1600 the decoration of chests became less spirited, architectural treatment becoming less common and giving way to overall low relief carving of strapwork and flower and foliage designs. Although most were of oak, some chests were made of elm or walnut and early in the seventeenth century a number were made with cypress wood as it was believed to discourage moths. A small compartment was often constructed inside, at the top, to take toilet accessories. Painted decoration was occasionally used and towards the middle of the century applied decoration in the form of split balusters and facetted, jewel-like shapes became popular often combined with inlay of bone and mother-of-pearl. Others were decorated with painted or inlaid designs of flowering plants.

Chests with drawers are mentioned in inventories of the late sixteenth century. During the first half of the seventeenth century many chests were designed with one or more drawers in the base, so that articles that were frequently needed might be kept there and obtained without disturbing the contents of the main chest. They are generally known as 'mule chests', though the term is probably nineteenth century. These were the forerunners of the chest-of-drawers, which appeared about the middle of the seventeenth century and was still influenced in its form by the chest. Generally there would be two stages, either the upper or the lower containing one deep drawer, the other containing shallower drawers enclosed by doors. A number of such chests-of-drawers made during the Commonwealth period were quite elaborately decorated, an exception to the plainness of most furniture at that time. Fielded panels, projecting forwards with deep, bevelled sides were much used, in combination with inlaid floral arabesques of ivory or bone and mother-of-pearl and applied ornament of split balusters. The drawers, constructed with large dove-tail joints, had a groove on either side, enabling them to slide on bearers fixed inside the carcase. Plate 22 shows a chest-of-drawers of this type, dated 1653, in two stages, both of which have doors enclosing the drawers.

Large cupboards or presses, containing shelves and sometimes fitted with drawers or 'tills', and intended for the storage of clothes or linen, were generally of wainscoting, the panels occasionally being enriched with strapwork carving or Renaissance arch motifs. Sometimes a compartment with pegs for hanging clothes was provided, too.

Various other kinds of cupboard were in common use, the simplest being the court cupboard, the name presumably deriving from the French word meaning short. It is a cupboard in the original sense of the word, being open boards or shelves for cups or plate, without an enclosed compartment. There are three shelves, the bottom one being raised just clear of the floor on block feet and the upper ones typically supported at the front corners by cup-and-cover supports and behind by stiles occasionally embellished with terminal figures; the back is open. In the seventeenth century the bulbous supports became much slimmer and carving was often restricted to ring mouldings. Occasionally, heraldic beasts or grotesque monsters were used for the front supports. In the friezes of the top and middle shelves a drawer was normally fitted, grooved at each side and sliding on bearers; the friezes and drawer fronts were elaborately decorated with inlay or carved ornament, such as gadrooning or egg-and-dart.

Closely akin to the court cupboard is the cupboard or press with an open lower stage and a compartment with a door in the upper part. This closed section was often constructed with splayed sides flanking the central door but some were straight-fronted and recessed a few inches behind the supporting balusters. As with the court cupboard, a drawer was usually contained in each of the friezes. Another type, more common in the seventeenth century, had the lower stage enclosed by doors, with shelves inside. On later examples bulbous pendent bosses sometimes replaced the cup-and-cover or baluster supports of the upper stage. Cupboards intended for the storage of food would be fitted with an openwork screen of turned balusters at the front for ventilation. Some food cupboards were made to hang on the wall.

The cabinet, containing a large number of small drawers for storing papers, collections of shells, jewels and other valuables, generally enclosed by two doors, was intended to rest on a table or stand. A number had been imported from Italy and Germany in the sixteenth century but the earliest examples to be made in this country appear to date from the early seventeenth century. There is a rare example in the Victoria and Albert Museum which is decorated in imitation of Near Eastern (Persian) lacquer with moresque designs in gold on black.

The desk consisted of a box with a sloping lid, hinged at the top with an iron hinge; it was fitted with small drawers and compartments and was also designed to stand on a table. Decoration was of carving or inlay of coloured woods similar to that found on contemporary chests and, towards the middle of the seventeenth century, with bone or mother-of-pearl.

MISCELLANEOUS

Elaborately carved, painted and gilded picture frames were becoming common in the first half of the seventeenth century. In the second quarter of the century a popular form of veneer was of tortoiseshell and ebony, or ebonised softwood. The ebony was frequently carved with wave mouldings, and frames entirely decorated in this manner were particularly popular in the mid-seventeenth century. A similar type of frame appears to have been usual for the mirrors of glass or metal that were just beginning to be used as decorative objects to hang on a wall.

III

THE RESTORATION

Charles II and James II

After the austerity of life under the Commonwealth, the inevitable reaction brought a great longing for a richer and more luxurious way of life. So the return of Charles II from exile in 1660 ushered in what Evelyn was to call 'a politer way of living'. He continues with the comment that it 'soon passed to luxury and intolerable expense'. The comparative drabness of life under Cromwell, with the official discouragement of the arts, made the country ready to accept and indeed welcome the elaborate and florid forms and ornament of the Continental Baroque style. Although it is basically alien to the sober English temperament, it was perfectly attuned to the desires of the new age of pleasure-seeking and it was reflected in all the arts.

This style, which was to submerge the more correct Classicism introduced by Inigo Jones, originated in Italy and had been considerably modified and re-interpreted on its way through France, Germany and the Low Countries before it reached England. The Baroque, the taste for which had been engendered in Charles and his Court during their exile in France and the Netherlands, was at first very much a Court style but it was not long before it became generally accepted. In the remoter parts of the country, however, where poor communications always caused a time lag in the penetration of new ideas, furniture continued to be made in the styles of the earlier part of the century throughout this period.

The influence of Holland was the most powerful in the new style, owing to the years spent by the Court in that country and also to its strong commercial ties with England. French influence, too, was considerable, however, stimulated by admiration for the unprecedented splendours of the Court of Louis XIV. Large numbers of Dutch and other immigrant craftsmen poured into the country, bringing with them new ideas and new skills and their numbers were reinforced by a fresh wave of Huguenot refugees fleeing from France after the Revocation of the Edict of Nantes in 1685.

Oak, formerly the most commonly used wood in the making of furniture, was now replaced in popularity by walnut, a wood that had been known in England since the reign of Elizabeth I but had been little used for this purpose. Walnut was used both solid and as a veneer on a carcase of oak or pine. Occasionally, as is the case in some of the rooms at Ham House, an unfashionable wood, such as pine or oak, would be grained in an attempt to give it the appearance of walnut. Two varieties of walnut were produced in England from plantations established in the southern counties, *Juglans regia* (of European origin) and *Juglans nigra*, the black walnut, which was considered superior and came from the eastern states of America. It was necessary to import a great deal as well. Apart from its purely fashionable appeal, walnut had the advantages of being easy to work for carving, having an attractive grain and taking a fine polish.

Many other new woods were introduced at the time such as kingwood (then known as Prince's wood), ebony and amboyna, many of them from the East and West Indies. These, together with such home-grown woods as laburnum, sycamore, holly, bog oak and the fruitwoods, were much used in the new technique of marquetry. This decoration consists of designs made from small pieces of veneer of different coloured woods; it differs from inlay in that it is not set into the carcase but into a ground veneer that covers the whole surface. It is also a much finer and more skilled technique. The type used at this time, known as floral marquetry, consisted of designs of tulips, roses, pinks and other flowers, sometimes in vases, and frequently included birds and butterflies. The designs were generally carried out in light-coloured woods on a dark background like ebony. Ivory was often used for certain flowers and, when stained green, for leaves. Shading was also common, achieved by dipping the pieces of wood into a tray of hot sand, the darkness of shading depending on how far they penetrated the sand. John Evelyn writes in his *Sylva*, 1664, 'When they would imitate the naturall turning of leaves in their curious compartiments and bordures of flower works, they effect it by dipping the pieces so far into hot sand as they would have the shadow'. Briefly, the method was to draw the design on a piece of paper which would be pasted on top of several layers of different coloured veneers that were themselves glued together with sheets of paper interposed between them to enable them to be separated again. The design was then cut out with a fine frame-saw and the various layers of wood separated. Pieces from different layers were then selected for their colour and fitted together like a jig-saw puzzle into the ground veneer. A sheet of paper was glued onto this panel, which was then transferred to the piece of furniture, to which it would be glued. When it had completely dried the paper was scraped off and the surface smoothed ready for polishing. Floral marquetry was widely used on tables, cabinets, clock cases and mirror frames (Plates 31, 33 and 42). There was very little difference between the Dutch and the English work; it did not take the native English craftsmen long to equal the achievements of the immigrants and by the end of Charles II's reign they sometimes even surpassed the Dutch in the quality of their work.

The designs were usually reserved in panels, often oval or of curving geometrical shapes, and enclosed within narrow strips of wood known as cross-banding, in which the grain runs across at right-angles to the length. Sometimes banding was formed of two grains laid at an angle like a herring-bone and this was known as feather-banding. Banding was also used as a decorative frame on doors and drawers. On the stiles and rails surrounding drawers a half-round moulding or bead was applied. Another type of linear ornament, frequently used in conjunction with banding, and called stringing, consisted of very thin strips of wood (usually about 1/16th inch wide), square in section, that were laid into the surface veneer. Stringing was generally of holly, boxwood, sycamore or ebony; but occasionally a type known as porcupine quill was used, which was carried out in small strips of ivory and ebony.

Another popular form of veneer was known as oysterwork, owing to its appearance (Plate 36). It was made from thin slices cut through the smaller branches of trees (usually walnut or laburnum), so as to produce circular or oval shapes marked with the annual growth rings of the tree. These were fitted together and applied as a veneer, often being used to surround the panels of floral marquetry. When the pieces were cut into geometrical shapes before being fitted together the resulting pattern was known as parquetry.

Twist-turning became widely used, particularly for the legs of chairs, tables and stands, a form closely akin to the twisted columns of Baroque architecture.

The love of naturalistic ornament seen in the form of floral marquetry also found expression in the florid, three-dimensional carving of the school of Grinling Gibbons (1648–1720). This highly naturalistic carving was generally executed in limewood, pearwood or some other close-grained soft wood, enabling deep undercutting and minute detail to be carried out. The motifs included swags of flowers, fruit and vegetables, birds and even human beings. Also commonly featured were peapods and ears of corn, but, contrary to popular belief, their presence is no proof of the master's hand as a great many other craftsmen worked in the style and employed the same motifs. This highly skilled carving is found on the frames of pictures (Plate 45) and mirrors, on tables, wall panelling and screens, as well as in tableaux and other decorative *tours de force*. Examples can be seen in many country houses, one of the most notable being at Petworth, where Gibbons carved exceptionally fine decorations for the panelling and picture frames of one of the State Rooms.

The use of gilding on a gesso ground became popular at this time. The wood was first roughly carved in low relief and several coats of a paste of parchment size and chalk were then applied. This surface, when hard, was finely re-carved and overlaid with gold leaf. Raised parts of the design were often burnished, whilst the ground might be given a more interesting texture by the addition of sand before gilding; it was very often decorated with circular punch marks, too, which in seventeenth century work were never allowed to overlap.

The Far East exercised an enormous fascination and its products were highly prized both for their associational value and for the contribution they made to the sumptuousness of interiors. Lacquer wares had been imported from the East since the time of Elizabeth I, mainly by the East India Company, which had been founded in 1599; but after the Restoration there was an enormously increased trade in what the West rather vaguely knew as 'India' wares. Two main types of Oriental lacquer were imported, of which the more popular was that which had a raised and gilded design on a highly polished black ground (Plate 35), the designs consisting mostly of watery landscapes with trees, temples and figures. Some idea of the mirror-like surface of this lacquer can still be obtained from parts that have not been exposed to light and dirt, such as the insides of lacquer cabinets. The second type, incised or Coromandel lacquer, also known at that time as Bantam work, after the Dutch trading post in the Malay Peninsula, was generally imported in the form of panels or folding screens. It consisted of many layers of lacquer, made from fine clay, gums and fibrous vegetable matter, built up to a thickness of anything up to a quarter of an inch, into which the design would be cut, the incisions being painted in various colours. The screens, decorated in this way on each side, were often retained as furnishings in their own right, but they were also frequently sawn through their thickness, the panels of lacquer from each side being used as veneers on cabinets, tables, chests and mirror frames. Even whole rooms were sometimes decorated in this way, two examples having been at Hampton Court Palace and at Chatsworth. These pieces of lacquer were used so as to give a colourful appearance but with little regard to the correct matching of adjacent pieces, so that 'bad joins' in a landscape are frequent. The practice was commented on by Stalker and Parker in their *Treatise* (see below), where they speak of men 'angling for Dolphins in a Wood, or pursuing the Stag, and Chasing the Boar in the middle of the Ocean'.

So great was the demand for Oriental lacquer that it could not be satisfied by imports and began to be widely imitated in England and other European countries. The term 'japanning', used somewhat indiscriminately in the seventeenth century for any type of lacquer, whether Oriental or imitation, is nowadays reserved for the European substitutes, whilst the name 'lacquer' is used only for the genuine Oriental product. Not only was japanning carried out on a commercial basis by cabinetmakers but it became a fashionable accomplishment and pastime as well, particularly for young ladies, who would practice their skill on any piece of furniture that presented a suitable surface. In 1688 John Stalker and George Parker published *A Treatise of Japanning and Varnishing*, containing twenty-four engraved plates of rather naïve interpretations of Oriental designs, together with detailed instructions (Fig. 5). This book proved to be very influential and much of the japanning that survives today is based on designs from it. The commercial work was generally of a higher standard than the amateur products but neither could equal the quality of Oriental lacquer in design or technique. Not only were the

FIG. 5. John Stalker and George Parker. Designs for japanning the drawers of a cabinet. Plate 19 of *A Treatise of Japanning*, 1688

proper ingredients unobtainable in the West, being substituted by size, whitening and gum-lac varnish, but the making of the Oriental product was a very slow process, injurious to health, and relying on the use of cheap labour. The raised parts of the design in japanning were built up with whitening, gum arabic and fine sawdust, polished and gilt with metal dust, brass often being used rather than gold. Where japanning has cracked the white composition can frequently be seen underneath. It also tends to form minute cracks all over the surface. In an attempt to satisfy the demand for lacquer furniture, designs were sent to China for copying and lacquering though this was not a satisfactory solution as the Oriental cabinetwork was of poor quality. In order to secure the double advantage of Oriental lacquer on superior European cabinetmaking, there are recorded instances of furniture having been made in the West and sent to the East for lacquering but this must have been an inconvenient and costly method.

Stalker and Parker also gave instructions for gilding in their *Treatise*, describing the two methods, oil and water gilding. The former was cheaper and more durable but water gilding was of better quality and capable of being burnished. John Poictevin, or Paudevine, was an upholsterer and gilder who worked for Charles II.

Yet another way of increasing the splendour of furniture was by the application of sheets of silver to the wooden framework and even by making some pieces of solid silver. There is still a set of furniture at Knole which is covered with repoussé sheet silver and both there and at Ham House there are examples of furniture embellished with mounts of embossed silver (Plate 36). There are also several pieces of silver furniture in the collection of Her Majesty the Queen.

Brass mounts came into use at this time, particularly for japanned cabinets, where they were based on Oriental prototypes, though of inferior quality. For drawers the brass drop-handle was introduced. The earliest type was generally strap-like and suspended from a flower-like backplate; the subsequent type, shaped rather like a drop of water, generally had a circular back-plate. Hand-filed metal screws with slotted heads also came into use, mainly for fixing hinges, together with brass pins.

Castors of a rudimentary type consisting of wooden wheels on fixed wooden axles were brought into use for such things as baby cages and servants' beds.

SEATS AND BEDS

Even after the Restoration chairs were still considered as seats of honour, less important guests frequently having to sit on stools. They did, however, quickly become more generally used, often being made in sets with armchairs and stools *en suite*. In spite of the new fashion for walnut, oak and beech were still widely used, especially where the chair was to be painted or gilded. In the early years of Charles II's reign chairs of a transitional type were common, retaining the form of the typical Commonwealth chair with leather back and seat panels, fastened with brass-headed nails, but with the addition of a scrolled front stretcher, a feature widely used throughout the period. The chair that was to become typical from about 1665 onwards, however, had a rather high back, with panels of cane in the back and seat; it was introduced from Holland and was found all over Northern Europe. The legs, uprights of the back, arm supports and stretchers were usually twist-turned, with rectangular sections at the joints, which were of mortise and tenon type (Plate 24). The square blocks at the tops of the legs would normally be covered by a fringe on upholstered chairs. On armchairs, the arms generally curved both downwards and outwards, terminating in a scroll. The back uprights were surmounted by an acorn finial and tenoned between them would be a top-rail carved with scrolls and foliage, sometimes incorporating a crown supported by a pair of amorini. This motif, though appropriate in the Restoration period, was actually of Continental origin and had even been used in England before this time. The cane panel of the back was generally oblong on English chairs (often oval in Dutch examples); at first the cane was rather coarse but in later examples the mesh is finer. In later chairs the carving too is often more elaborate, with greater use of openwork carving and with low relief carving of flowers, leaves and scrolls round the seat-rail. The twist-turning of front legs and arm supports tended to give way to a double curve, now sometimes called a Flemish scroll, and carved lions or other beasts were periodically used to terminate the arms. The armchair illustrated in Plate 25 is a particularly fine specimen of a chair of the latter part of Charles II's reign, in which some of these features can be seen. Another modification towards the end of the period was the use of balusters instead of twist-turned members for the uprights of the back. A flat cushion would normally be used on these cane chairs and the front legs often project slightly above the seat-rail so as to hold it in position.

Chairs of similar shape but with upholstered backs and seats were also made, the coverings being of wool needlework on canvas or, in the finest examples, of velvet or silk damask, imported from Italy. Loose covers, attached with metal fasteners, were occasionally used and fringes and tassels adorned the seat-rails and the backs. Stuffing would generally be of horsehair, contained in a case of canvas or ticking and supported on webbing. The arms of upholstered chairs were sometimes padded and often the woodwork was painted and gilded. The completely upholstered winged armchair appeared at this time; there was also a special version of it that had a ratchet at either side, enabling the angle of the back to be adjusted. There is a pair of these at Ham House, described in the 1679 inventory of the house as 'two sleeping chayres carv'd and guilt frames covered with crimson and gould stuff with gould fringe' (Colour Plate A). The front feet are carved as hippocamps or sea-horses. The Royal Wardrobe Accounts show that John Paudevine supplied 'sleeping chairs' to Charles II in 1675 and 1677 respectively. Also at Ham is a set of six chairs and six armchairs, in which the wooden framework is carved with dolphins, gilded and enriched with red paint (Plate 26). These have the low backs sometimes found in early Charles II chairs; they are covered with their original upholstery of satin tissue of red and gold. At the same house the taste for Oriental decoration is reflected in a set of japanned chairs in which an attempt has been made to imitate Chinese form; they are described in the 1683 inventory as 'back stooles with cane bottoms japanned', the term 'backstool' still being usual for a chair without arms (Plate 29).

Stools followed a similar pattern of development, generally forming part of a suite with them. They were usually rectangular, sometimes one of the longer sides being more decoratively treated than the other, indicating that they were designed to stand against a wall, whilst in other examples decorative features, such as scrolled stretchers, are the same on both sides (Plate 28). Some long stools were made, usually having six legs. Sometimes a webbing or cane seat with a loose squab cushion would replace fixed upholstery. This was the case with a low stool, of the type known in France as a *carreau*, that was in many cases supplied with two squabs. Such stools were not footstools but were used – sometimes in pairs – as an additional form of seating, especially in an important bedroom (Plate 27).

Day-beds were of similar design to long stools but with the addition of a sloping head-rest. This was most frequently adjustable by means of a chain or ratchet in the earlier specimens but later examples mostly had fixed ends. Cane seats and head-rests were the commonest, though in time narrow splats often replaced the cane panels of the head-rests; completely upholstered day-beds were introduced before the end of the reign, too. Scrolled stretchers linked the three (sometimes four) legs on each side.

Beds became very high, with a carved wooden cornice surmounting the tester, the height often further increased by a vase-shaped finial at each corner, containing ostrich feathers. Costly velvets and silk damasks woven with silver or gold threads were used to adorn these impressive symbols of luxury; the carved head-boards, cornices and finials were covered with the same materials. A bed at Knole, Kent, dating from Charles II's reign is shown in Plate 40. Plate 34 illustrates a foot, of carved and gilded wood, from a bed of about 1675. Low bedsteads on wheels that could be used by servants were often pushed under larger beds when not in use. They were known as truckle beds.

TABLES

Oval, or occasionally round, gate-leg tables became the usual form of dining-table after the Restoration, meals now being served in a special room, rather than the Great Hall. It was customary to use a number of these tables for the meal. They were generally made of oak or walnut, although yew, cedar and fruitwoods were also used, and they had two gate-legs fashioned with twist-turning. The hinges were of wood and the tops fixed with oak pins. Some dining-rooms were furnished with a pair of sideboards as well, which were in fact side-tables, possibly fitted with marble tops, and used for serving.

Side-tables were an important item of furnishing, often designed *en suite* with a wall-mirror and a pair of candlestands to form a composite unit of wall decoration. They were generally of walnut, with twist-turned legs, united by a flat serpentine stretcher with an oval section in the centre, on which a vase might be placed. The legs, which were supported on ball or bun feet, sometimes had a vase-shaped or straight section at the base (Plate 31). A drawer would be fitted in the frieze and the flat surfaces were decorated with marquetry or occasionally with inset panels of incised lacquer. Some of these side-tables were ebonised or partly gilded and japanning was sometimes used, in combination with inset panels of incised lacquer. There are examples of them, together with matching wall-mirrors and candlestands, that were completely covered with sheets of embossed silver and even solid silver was occasionally used. Embossed and chased silver mounts were applied to this kind of furniture in addition.

In the latter part of Charles II's reign, legs in the form of an S-scroll, generally with a break in the middle, became fashionable for side-tables. Plate 30 illustrates a table with legs of this type which is decorated with incised japanning. Sometimes these S-scrolls incorporate cherubs or other human figures, or complete caryatids form the corner supports; naturalistic carving by Grinling Gibbons or his followers is periodically incorporated. An unusual table of ebonised wood, part of the contents of Ham House, with S-scroll legs carved with auricular ornament, has a top made of cane. The reason for this somewhat impractical material being used for a table top may be that it was designed to match a set of cane chairs and a pair of candlestands that were in the same room, but the 1699 inventory of Kensington Palace also mentions three cabinets as being on 'blacke cained frames'.

The table illustrated in Plate 32 is a typical Charles II side-table except for the straight, columnar, rather than twist-turned legs. This shape of leg is dictated by the use of scagliola, with which the top, frieze and stretchers of the table are also decorated. The comparative crudity of the design suggests that it is an early example of scagliola made in England, rather than imported from Italy. Its close similarity to a fireplace surround at Ham House on which the reversed cipher of the Duke and Duchess of Lauderdale appears strengthens the contention that it is of native origin.

It is at this time that a number of tables for specialised activities first make their appearance, designed for such purposes as tea-drinking, writing and needlework. An early reference to such a specific piece appears in the 1679 inventory of Ham House, where 'One Cedar tea table' is mentioned. Such tables were often japanned or decorated with Oriental lacquer which was deemed appropriate for the serving of a drink originating in China. There is an early writing table at Kensington Palace, dating from about 1685, in the form of a typical side-table, with S-scroll legs, but with the addition of a compartmented superstructure at the back. Cards were generally played on small tables covered with velvet or with a table carpet; the 1679 inventory of Ham House lists 'One green velvet Carpet fringed with Gould' and 'One Crimson velvet Carpet fringed with gold' with the annotation 'for playing at Cards'. According to inventories of the period billiard tables appear to have been quite common in large country houses. Tables specially designed for the playing of chess and backgammon were also made, sometimes with a reversible board let into the top and a space for the counters and chessmen beneath it.

CASE FURNITURE

In cabinets and other case furniture the carcase woods were generally oak or pine or a combination of the two; the drawers were usually made of oak or, in the finer pieces, of walnut. Each drawer would be separated from the one below by a dustboard on which it rested, and which was slotted into each side of the carcase. The bottom of the drawer was rebated into the sides and fixed with nails; the grain of the bottom board ran from front to back, rather than across, irrespective of the shape of the drawer although there were occasional exceptions to this rule in the case of very small ones inside cabinets. On the front the grain ran vertically, with a join in the middle, the veneer being selected so that the two sides matched. The sides were fixed to the back and front with fine dovetail joints, smaller and so more numerous than formerly.

The cabinet became extremely popular at this time, being valued not only for the storage space afforded by its many small drawers, where papers and other small objects could be kept, but for its decorative appearance. In addition to the lacquer cabinets imported from China and Japan (Plate 35), many English cabinets were japanned or decorated with panels of incised lacquer and they were also admirably suited for elaborate decoration with floral marquetry or with parquetry in carefully selected woods, such as walnut, laburnum or kingwood.

Marquetry cabinets were generally closed with two large doors at the front, although a hinged writing flap was occasionally fitted. Inside would be a central compartment, generally with a small door, surrounded by a number of little drawers (Plate 33). Above the outer doors a concealed drawer extending the whole width of the front was generally fitted, made to appear as a convex frieze below the cornice. Further concealed drawers or compartments were often fitted inside the central compartment or even between the other drawers and the sides of the cabinet. The stands for cabinets generally had twist-turned legs linked by flat stretchers, with a drawer (or two) in the frieze, being similarly designed, in fact, to contemporary side-tables, though usually having three or four legs at the front. Occasionally a chest-of-drawers base is found instead of the more typical stand. The floral marquetry decoration is generally in oval reserves, often on a ground of oysterwork.

Plate 36 shows a small and rather unusual writing-cabinet at Ham House, which is decorated with a most attractive veneer of oysterwork and cross-banding in kingwood, enriched with embossed silver mounts. This and another of similar form, decorated with burr walnut and ebony, are listed in the seventeenth century inventories of the house as 'scriptors'. The writing flap closing the front lets down on a hinged metal strut at either side but an alternative sometimes used was a pair of wooden slides or lopers that could be drawn out of the top of the stand to support the flap. A particularly striking use is made of kingwood in the interior of the cabinet illustrated in Plate 52, where the pale yellowish-brown outer grain has also been used. A writing-cabinet of cedar, built into the library of Ham House, is shown in Plate 37.

Oriental cabinets and their Western imitations were usually of similar form but without the surmounting frieze and cornice. All corners were generally protected with brass mounts, the doors held by up to six decorative brass hinges and embellished with large, ornamented keyhole escutcheons. The low plinths used to support these cabinets in the Orient were obviously unsuited to the Western way of life and stands, of pine, elaborately carved and gilded or silvered, were made for them in England. They were intended to complement the cabinets themselves and were lavishly embellished with the naturalistic detail so beloved of the era (Plate 35).

Chests were still in common use for the storage of clothes, linen, blankets and so on, some of the later ones being placed on stands. Plate 38 shows a chest veneered with walnut, having a simple decoration in cross-banding and fitted with carrying handles of gilded wrought iron. It was from the chest with a drawer added at the bottom that the chest-of-drawers had evolved in the middle of the century and after the Restoration it became more widely used in the wealthier houses. Some stood directly on ball or bun feet; others were raised on stands with turned legs, which were also very often fitted with a drawer. Particularly during the early years of the new reign decoration of fielded panels and split balusters continued to be used but the more fashionable pieces were adorned with oval reserves of floral marquetry on the top and drawer fronts.

An entirely new piece of furniture that appeared at this time was the glass-fronted bookcase. Samuel Pepys had twelve of them made in oak in 1666 (now in the Pepys Library, Magdalene College, Cambridge). The bookcase illustrated in Plate 41 came from Dyrham Park, Gloucestershire, and is one of a number made to a similar design, perhaps all by the same maker. The glass panes, which are used in both stages, are held by moulded bars and the shelves can be fixed at various levels. The carved ornament, in which the acanthus leaf appears prominently, is similar to that found on much contemporary wall panelling.

Boxes, made to contain jewels and toilet or needlework requisites, generally followed the larger articles of furniture in the manner of their decoration, with frequent use of floral marquetry and oysterwork, but stumpwork (padded embroidery) and cut paper work were also used for their embellishment. Japanning was popular, particularly for the casket in the form of a small cabinet, with two doors concealing drawers. A good example of japanning can be seen in the close-stool illustrated in Plate 39, which is in the form of a small chest, on ball feet. The brass corner mounts used on lacquer cabinets have here been imitated with carved and gilded wood. (The handle is later.) Such close-stools were fitted with pewter or pottery pans and were placed in the bed-chamber or an adjoining closet.

MISCELLANEOUS

Mirrors became an increasingly important item of furnishing after the Restoration. Large numbers were still imported from abroad, particularly from Venice, but a number of glassworks were established in England at this time, the most important being the Vauxhall Glassworks, set up in 1663 by the Duke of Buckingham. Occasionally whole rooms were panelled with glass but this expensive product was mostly used in the form of wall-mirrors, to be hung between windows or over a side-table flanked with matching candlestands. The 'silvering' consisted of an amalgam of tin and mercury and the glass was given a bevelled edge, cut by hand. It was set in a broad, markedly convex frame, with a moulding round the edge, generally surmounted by a cresting fixed to the top (this cresting has disappeared from many surviving looking-glasses). The decoration of the frames took many forms including floral marquetry, incised lacquer, japanning, ebony, tortoiseshell, stumpwork, strawwork, beadwork and gilded repoussé metal or embossed silver. Plate 42 shows a particularly fine example, at Ham House, decorated with floral marquetry, in which ivory has been used for some of the flowers. Frames of similar shape and proportions were also made in softwood, carved with naturalistic decoration in the Grinling Gibbons manner; these were sometimes gilded or silvered (Plate 43). Toilet glasses to stand on tables, fitted with a hinged supporting flap at the back, were also in use.

Some picture frames were ornamented with naturalistic carving similar to that used for looking-glasses (Plate 45) bur far more common were those composed of flat scrolls, a type of carving known as auricular owing to its resemblance to the fleshy part of the ear (Plate 47). Carved in limewood or other soft wood, picture frames were gilded or simply stained. Where they constituted part of the fixed decoration of a room as in the case of an overdoor or other inset painting they were generally framed with a bolection moulding, often being partially gilded.

The clock underwent a marked change in appearance, largely owing to mechanical improvements. With the introduction into this country of the pendulum just before Charles II's Restoration, its subsequent improvement, and the development of the anchor escapement, which greatly increased the accuracy of clocks, the long-case clock soon became a common and highly decorative feature of fashionable interiors. The most typical decoration was of panels of floral marquetry on a ground of walnut or oyster-work veneer, the hood being embellished with twisted columns at the corners (Plate 51). Many long-case clocks had a circular or oval window in the door, fitted with clear or bottle glass, through which the pendulum could be seen. Brass mounts were sometimes applied in the form of capitals and bases to the twisted columns or as keyhole escutcheons. The flat cornice surmounting the clock was often replaced on later specimens by a broken scroll pediment. Table or bracket clocks were also made in large numbers, their wooden cases often being surmounted by a highly decorative brass or silver 'basket top' (Plate 48). There was generally a glass panel in the back, allowing the works of these spring-driven clocks to be seen. Ebony veneer or ebonising were also popular for both bracket and long-case clocks.

An unusual item of furnishing is illustrated in Plate 49. This japanned book-rest from Ham House, which bears the coronet and cypher of the Countess of Dysart, is *en suite* with a set of chairs made in a simulated Chinese manner (Plate 29) and is recorded in the seventeenth century inventories of the house.

Candlestands were an important feature of the period, being made in pairs *en suite* with a side-table and wall-mirror. Tripod bases of scrolling form and octagonal tops were particularly common. Stands were also made specially for the porcelain tulip pots that had become very popular (Plate 50).

Pairs of globes on stands, one terrestrial and one celestial, often formed part of the furnishings of libraries. In the one illustrated in Plate 46, dating from the third quarter of the seventeenth century, the stand has straight, columnar supports.

The Oriental lacquer screens that were imported in such large numbers were not all cut up and used as a veneer; many were retained for their original purpose. Normally decorated on both sides with incised lacquer, they were sometimes up to ten feet high and had as many as twelve folds. The tripod pole-screen, used for shielding a lady's face from the fire, was uncommon but there is an early example, with an iron frame mounted with silver finials, at Ham House.

Chimney-boards, made to fill the opening of the fireplace when there was no fire, were also sometimes used. They consisted of a wooden frame, covered with panels of tapestry, embossed leather or painted paper.

IV

WILLIAM AND MARY

The style of the period that approximated to the reign of William III (1688–1702) and Mary (1688–1694), though in many ways a continuation of that of Charles II, has enough characteristics of its own, nevertheless, to justify its being treated separately. If there are no pronounced changes, there are modifications and distinctive developments peculiar to the closing years of the seventeenth century, a number of which had already appeared before the end of Charles II's reign.

The full impact of the Baroque style had been felt in England in the Restoration period. Under William and Mary much design was still florid but already there were some signs of the greater discipline and restraint that were to become such marked features of the subsequent Queen Anne style. The period is, in fact, transitional between the extreme ostentation of the Restoration and the elegant simplicity of the early eighteenth century.

Many craftsmen came over from Holland with William and Mary and a considerable number of Dutch craftsmen were employed on the interiors and the furnishings of the new state apartments at Hampton Court and Kensington Palace. French influence was also considerable as some of the immigrants, such as the designer Daniel Marot (1663–1752), a pupil of Pierre Le Pautre, were of French origin. In addition, the effects of refugees coming to this country after the Revocation of the Edict of Nantes in 1685 were still being felt, and a number of Huguenot craftsmen continued to reach this country during the last decade of the century. Despite political antagonism to France there was no reaction against French culture and the splendours of the Court of Louis XIV still exercised a strong fascination. The court style of Louis XIV was used particularly by Daniel Marot, who had entered the service of William of Orange after fleeing to Holland and followed him to England, where he worked from 1694 to 1697 and again in 1698; he probably designed some of the interiors at Hampton Court. The publication of a large number of his engraved designs also served to make the style well-known and were widely influential (Plates 56 and 59). Most of the royal furniture was in this elaborately carved and gilded style, which makes use of the characteristic straight leg with a gadrooned swelling near the top, a very free interpretation of a column and capital. This court style was translated into simpler terms for walnut furniture, the elaborately carved leg being replaced by a turned leg with a swelling like an inverted cup near the top. Scroll legs were still used but twist-turning went out of fashion.

Floral marquetry began to be superseded by a finer type with arabesque and delicate leaf forms, carried out in only two woods and known as seaweed, or endive, marquetry (Plates 61 and 62). Walnut was generally used, in combination with a lighter wood, such as box or holly, and the designs were frequently set in reserves, framed by stringing. Occasionally floral marquetry was used in combination with this newer type on the same piece of furniture. Seaweed marquetry is really a translation into wood of the technique of metal and tortoiseshell marquetry as practised by André Charles Boulle in France. Apparently the only cabinetmaker in England to use marquetry of brass or pewter and tortoiseshell was Gerreit Jensen, also known as Garret Johnson, cabinet-maker to the Crown. His furniture, which shows strong French influence, was also on occasion decorated with seaweed marquetry and japanning.

The influence of the Louis XIV style can be seen in the elaborately carved and gilded furniture which Jean Pelletier (active c. 1690–1710) supplied to the Crown, too. The English joiner and chairmaker, Thomas Roberts, made seat furniture and firescreens of fine quality for the royal palaces. Grinling Gibbons and his followers were still important, particularly in the embellishment of panelled rooms; the panels were by this time very large. Rooms were taller than formerly and furniture tended consequently to increase in height, the vertical emphasis being particularly marked in beds, chairs and wall-mirrors.

There was an increasingly important home production of silks, velvets, brocades and damasks for bed hangings and upholstery, whereas formerly such materials had had to be imported from France and Italy.

SEATS AND BEDS

Chairs of the type that were fashionable in the latter part of Charles II's reign continued to be made in the 1690s but in the more up-to-date examples many innovations were introduced. Balusters, that had already tended to replace twist-turning for the uprights of the back in the late 1680s, now became almost universal. Backs became higher and narrower and the seats smaller, giving a greater elegance, though the construction was less sound. Whereas formerly the top-rail had been tenoned between the uprights of the back, it was now generally fixed to the tops of the balusters with dowel pins (a feature that was to be characteristic of English chairs throughout the eighteenth century, while the French retained the older method of construction); the legs were similarly attached to the seat-rail. The top-rail itself assumed a distinctive arched shape, composed of carved scrolls, which was frequently repeated in the form of the front stretcher (Plates 54 and 55). Occasionally a small apron or pendant carving embellished the seat-rail. Although scroll-shaped front legs continued to be made throughout the period, a distinctive straight leg of turned wood became fashionable about 1690: it had a swelling near the top shaped like an upturned cup and often gadrooned, below which the turned leg tapered towards the base. This kind of leg derived from the Louis XIV type, sometimes used on English furniture, which was square in section and elaborately carved and gilded. Bun feet were usual, either round or octagonal, and often gadrooned but occasionally the Spanish scroll foot, which turned under, was substituted. When the crested front stretcher was used with this type of leg it was joined to it only just above the feet or tenoned into the side stretchers. More frequently, however, they were linked by serpentine, X-shaped stretchers, surmounted by a turned finial in the middle. At about the turn of the century a leg of double curving form, known as the cabriole, was used on a few chairs though this significant development was not widely adopted until the early eighteenth century and will be discussed in the next chapter. Arms were similar to those of Charles II chairs, scrolling outwards and downwards and being supported on scrolls or short balusters.

Stained beech was widely used as a substitute for the more expensive walnut and gilding was often introduced on the finer specimens. Cane, which was now of a much finer mesh, was still used for chair-backs, though narrow uprights or splats of carved scrollwork were sometimes used instead. Cane was even less favoured for seats, where it was largely supplanted by upholstery of needlework or Genoa velvet, materials which were also sometimes used for the backs. Tasselled fringes were often used round seat-rails and on upholstered chair-backs. Some upholstered seats were made to drop into the seat frame.

On completely upholstered chairs there was generally an arching of the top, paralleling the crested top-rail of wooden chairs. Upholstered winged armchairs, with outward-scrolling arms, are also characteristic of the period and were generally supplied with squab cushions.

Sofas were of similar pattern to upholstered chairs, some being designed with double chair backs. Most of them were very sumptuous pieces of furniture with high backs, rich upholstery and comfortable squab cushions (Plate 53) but some simpler ones of double chair form had cane seats and backs.

Stools were still an important item, particularly in the royal palaces, and, like sofas, they followed the general development of the chair. Made of walnut or stained beech and covered with velvet, damask or needlework, they were mostly rectangular. Plate 57 shows a round stool with a separate squab cushion, in which the inverted cup shape of the leg is a very noticeable feature. Both scroll and straight legs were used for stools, in conjunction with either arched or serpentine, X-shaped stretchers. Long stools of bench proportions were also made.

The upholstered day-bed with a fixed end had been introduced during the latter part of Charles II's reign and this type continued to be made, incorporating the contemporary fashions in legs and stretchers. Sometimes the fixed end was given a scrolled top and occasionally a carved cresting was used. A squab seat was usual and a bolster was often provided. Colour Plate B shows a particularly fine example, made for the Duke of Leeds in about 1695. The square section legs, of Louis XIV type, are linked by curving X-shaped stretchers.

Beds were among the items of furniture that noticeably increased in height in this period to accord with the higher rooms, becoming, if anything, even more elaborate and splendid than those of the Restoration period. The influence of Marot is seen in the finest of these beds, such as that illustrated in Plate 56, designed for the Earl of Melville. The hangings are of Chinese white silk and crimson velvet. A new type, known as a half-tester bed, was introduced, in which there were no posts at the foot, that end of the canopy being supported from the ceiling.

TABLES

For tables there was a return to the straight leg, the scroll type dropping out of fashion. In the more elaborate pieces they were generally in the style of Daniel Marot, square in section, with a swelling near the top and elaborately carved and gilded, usually on a gesso ground. This form was particularly used for side-tables, which served rather as splendid pieces of interior decoration than as useful items of furniture. The X-shaped stretchers of such tables, instead of being flat as formerly, now generally curved in a vertical direction and were surmounted at the intersection by a large vase finial. On many of these side-tables a large carved apron embellished the front. The whole table would be elaborately carved, the top generally being ornamented with strapwork patterns on a gesso ground, whilst its edge, the swellings of the legs and the feet were frequently gadrooned.

As in the foregoing period, gate-leg tables were usual for dining, the turned baluster-shaped leg generally replacing the earlier twisted leg.

Gate-legged card- and games-tables were also made, with legs of elongated vase type or with the cup-shaped moulding. Plate 62 illustrates a rectangular table of such a type, the top of which is decorated with seaweed marquetry. The card-table shown in Plate 58 is semi-circular when closed, with gate-legs opening towards the back. The three small drawers in the frieze are a common feature of tables of this type.

Small gate-leg tables were frequently used for writing, being fitted with drawers between the gate-legs. Other writing tables were supplied with a small case of drawers to stand on the top.

CASE FURNITURE

Lacquered and japanned cabinets retained their popularity and stands of carved and gilded or silvered pinewood continued to be made for them. The development of these stands paralleled that of side-tables, the scroll-shaped legs of the Charles II period giving way to the straight leg of Louis XIV type, linked by scrolling X-shaped stretchers with a central finial. The carving was finer and the general appearance more elegant than hitherto. A carved and gilt or silvered cresting was generally made to surmount these cabinets, another instance of an increase in the height of furniture; as it was not fastened to the top it is missing from many cabinets to-day. Plate 59 illustrates a japanned cabinet with a stand and cresting of fine quality carved and silvered pine. In addition to the more usual black, red japanning was sometimes used at this time.

For marquetry cabinets the stand with scroll legs did not immediately go out of fashion but stands with baluster legs or bases with drawers became widely used. Floral marquetry tended to give way to seaweed marquetry, sometimes completely covering the surface within a framework of cross-banding or set in reserves against a background of oysterwork. When floral marquetry was used in combination with seaweed marquetry it was generally finer and more delicate than that of the preceding age. In common with many other kinds of furniture, stands for cabinets usually had bun feet, with or without gadrooning, but a new kind of foot, known as a bracket foot, made its appearance for bases fitted with drawers and other items of furniture without legs.

The collecting of porcelain was very popular at this time, large quantities being displayed on any suitable surface such as shelves over fireplaces and doors and on the tops of cabinets, as well as in glass-fronted cabinets which now began to be made for the purpose. In addition to standing cabinets, hanging corner cupboards were made, with either panelled or glazed fronts and usually surmounted by the fashionable arched cresting. These were a popular subject for amateur japanning.

The bureau with a sloping top or fall-front first appeared at this time, the earliest ones being fitted with a pair of gate-legs at the front, onto which the hinged top opened, forming a writing surface. At the back of this would be a series of small drawers and pigeon-holes. At about the end of the century the type in which the drawers reach almost to the ground was evolved, the writing flap being supported on two wooden slides or lopers. The current trend towards taller furniture perhaps partly accounted for the appearance of the bureau-cabinet: onto the fall-front bureau an upper stage was fitted

B. DAY-BED of gilded wood, upholstered with Genoese cut velvet. Made about 1695 for the 1st Duke of Leeds, whose coronet and cypher surmount the back. Length 5 ft. 2 in. *Temple Newsam House, Leeds.* *See page 55*

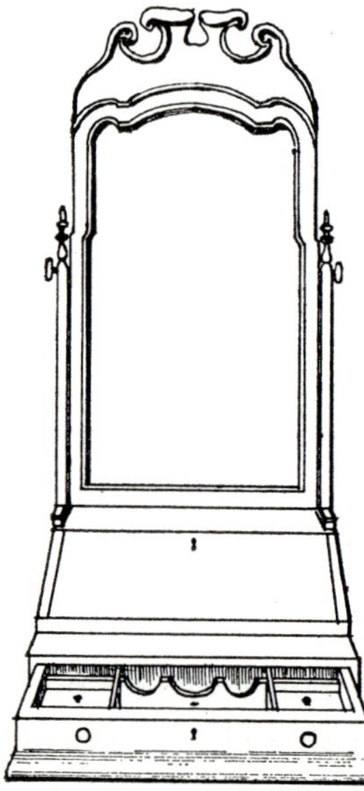

FIG. 6. Dressing-glass, *c.* 1700

considerably taller than formerly, came into fashion. Many of these very splendid stands, which were often designed *en suite* witn a side-table and looking-glass, were richly carved with acanthus and gadrooning. On others the decoration was of seaweed marquetry.

On bracket clocks the architectural treatment, with twisted columns at the corners, became less common and chased brass mounts were frequently used as an embellishment. The 'basket top', with handle, made of chased brass or silver, was a common feature of these clocks and served to emit the sound of the chimes. On long-case clocks the twisted columns on the hood tended to give way to straight columns with brass capitals and bases, while brass finials and domed tops made their appearance. Floral marquetry was still used sometimes but seaweed marquetry became more common (Plate 61).

The wall bracket as a feature in its own right first appeared in the reign of William and Mary. Probably introduced by Huguenot craftsmen, it served to display a piece of porcelain or to support a bracket clock. It was elaborately carved and gilded, incorporating scrolls and other Baroque forms.

Chandeliers of wood, similarly ornamented with elaborate carving and gilded, were another introduction of the end of the seventeenth century.

A new type of firescreen had a framed panel of needlework, velvet or damask, supported between two baluster uprights, standing on legs of scroll form and surmounted by a carved openwork cresting. These screens, which were known as 'cheval' or 'horse' screens, were generally very richly carved and gilded. From time to time the panel was made to slide up, so that its height could be varied.

V

QUEEN ANNE

The opening years of the eighteenth century found the country in a state of increasing prosperity. There was a growing middle class capable of furnishing their homes with a considerable degree of luxury, and items of furniture for specialised purposes such as tea-tables and writing-tables were becoming widely used.

The Queen Anne style is generally considered to be one of the greatest in the history of English furniture. The florid forms of the Baroque are transformed into a characteristically English simplicity and reticence. Attention is concentrated on the creation of harmonious proportions and a pleasing shape, rather than on applied details of decoration, and the selection of wood with a beautiful grain becomes of prime importance. Grains are arranged to form a symmetrical pattern on such things as doors and drawers, whilst other flat surfaces such as table tops are quartered or overlaid with four identical pieces of veneer. Veneers are also used at times on the backs and rails of seat furniture in this period. Subtle serpentine curves (later to be called by Hogarth 'the line of beauty') were used, not as scrolling adornments applied to basically straight forms, as formerly, but as part of the structure: in the hoop back and the cabriole leg, for instance (Plate 64). The latter with its serpentine curve is the most striking single feature of the new style. Although it had made its appearance before the close of William III's reign it was not until Anne was on the throne that it completely ousted the straight or scroll leg and attained its fully-developed form, which was to continue in use, with only minor modifications, into the second half of the century.

Walnut remained the most popular wood throughout Anne's reign, the beauty of the wood itself, and perhaps a cross-banded border, being considered to render additional decoration superfluous. The plain, unadorned surface, often consisting of a burr veneer, is the most characteristic of the period (Plate 63). Marquetry and japanning did not entirely fall out of use, however, nor did gilding and gesso, though they were seldom used. Decorative side-tables, candlestands and mirrors were sometimes gilded, such as those made by Gerreit Jensen for Queen Anne's drawing-room at St. James's Palace.

A double half-round moulding was frequently adopted for the stiles and rails framing the fronts of drawers. On other pieces, a quarter-round moulding, projecting from the drawer front over the surrounding rails and stiles, was employed. Dovetails were now commonly stopped short of the veneered surface at the front of the drawer on better furniture; this is known as lap-dovetailing. A strip of grooved wood, known as a draw slip, was used in the construction of drawers, on which the bottom board rested at each side.

The loop handle was introduced but the drop handle also continued in use. Each end of the loop handle passed into a brass knob that formed the head of a screw, passing through the drawer front and secured with a nut on the inside. Backing the handle was a shaped back-plate with chamfered edges, sometimes ornamented with engraved lines. A variation on this design in which the whole of the centre part was cut out appeared about 1710. Keyhole escutcheons were of a similar form. Boxwood castors with metal axles were introduced, too, allowing a lateral movement.

In the eighteenth century the difference between furniture made in London and in the provinces became more pronounced. The main reason for this was that in country districts one craftsman had to do everything, whereas the large market of London made specialisation possible, and thus enabled a higher standard to be attained. This tendency was intensified by the migration of many of the best craftsmen to London. Moreover, a great deal of country furniture was made by estate carpenters who were simply employed for all work in wood and were not specifically chairmakers or cabinetworkers.

John Gumley was a cabinetmaker who set up a glassworks in 1705 at Lambeth, and sold mirrors and some other items of furniture from his premises in the Strand. In 1714 he went into partnership with James Moore, who specialised in gesso furniture. Gumley's name appears on mirrors with coloured glass borders and scrolled crestings at both Hampton Court and Chatsworth. Thomas Roberts continued to supply the Royal palaces, mainly with seat furniture, as well as working at Chatsworth.

SEATS AND BEDS

The cabriole leg, a feature that apparently orginated in China, came to be used on all fashionable furniture. The earliest type terminated in a hoof or scroll foot (hence the name, derived from 'capriole', meaning goat's leg) and was often connected to the seat-rail by a square block, such as was commonly used on late seventeenth century chairs, where it would normally be covered by the fringe. The early cabriole legs were linked by stretchers, the recessed front ones sometimes retaining something of the arched form of those of the previous reign. The overall proportions of the back resembled those of the William and Mary chair but consisted of curving uprights merging into the shaped top-rail and a vase-shaped central splat with pierced carving of Oriental inspiration. A set of chairs of this type was supplied to Hampton Court in 1717 by Richard Roberts, who was probably the son of Thomas Roberts.

From these early examples the typical Queen Anne chair evolved. The top-rail, secured to the uprights with dowels, had rounded corners, making a continuous curve and forming the characteristic hoop back. The stiles and rails might be either square or round in section. The back was also given a very slight serpentine curve to fit the back of the sitter, creating what is called a spoon back. The vase-shaped splat, occasionally decorated with marquetry, was jointed into a shoe-piece at its base, that was joined to the seat-rail. The curved lines dominating the back were now sometimes introduced into the seat-rail, which became curved at the front and waisted towards the back.

The back legs were made out of the same piece of wood as the uprights of the back, despite the considerable curvature, which meant that a great deal of wood was wasted in their shaping. The knees of the front legs broaden into a kind of bracket where they join the seat-rail, into which they project, each section of the latter being tenoned into them. This strong construction allowed stretchers to be eliminated, thus creating a more elegant design. In provincial examples or in armchairs, however, stretchers were often still used (Plate 64). The front legs were in some cases attached to the seat-rail with a hip-joint, in which the curve of the knee was carried up into the corner, coming to a point, sometimes terminating in a tiny scroll. Sometimes the knee was carved with a scallop shell or palmette motif. The simplest type of leg was left completely plain and terminated in a club foot or a pad foot, which had a disc of wood underneath. Occasionally the legs were made square in section, having an angular termination, known as a spatulate foot (Plate 68). Another type of square leg was given a definite break in the curve and usually had a strongly Oriental flavour in the shaping of the square foot. A less common type was the trifid foot, divided into three parts. The ball-and-claw foot, an ancient Oriental form that had occurred in isolated instances in the late sixteenth century and in the Restoration period, did not come into common use until about 1710, and the club foot retained its popularity as an alternative throughout the first half of the eighteenth century. (An early use of the ball-and-claw form can be seen in stands and stools of the Charles II period in the Green Closet at Ham House.) In order to save wood, the feet used with the cabriole leg were frequently built up with slivers of wood at the sides, rather than made of one single piece, and these often became broken off (Plate 65).

Seats, made of horsehair supported on a webbing base, and upholstered in needlework, velvet or tapestry, were either stuffed over or of the drop-in type, consisting of a covered wooden framework filled with stuffing. Some of these chairs were japanned and on finer, and particularly later, examples the seat-rails, splats and uprights were veneered with burr walnut. Arms, when present on chairs of this type, were of the scroll-over kind. The support rose in a concave curve from the side of the seat-rail (not the front corner, as formerly), breaking forward again in a convex curve and levelling out for the arm-rest. The join between the vertical and horizontal parts of the arms, secured with a dowel peg, can be clearly seen on the armchair in Plate 64.

Chairs of similar form but with upholstered backs were also made, these backs being square or arched. Winged armchairs differed little from those of the late seventeenth century, apart for the substitution of the cabriole, for the straight leg. The wings were often made continuous with the arms that then scrolled outwards at the front. They were generally fitted with upholstered seats on a webbing base, on which a thick squab cushion would be placed for greater comfort (Plate 65).

Sofas, made to go with a suite of chairs, were of similar form. The sofa of double-chair type had two linked hoop-backs, wooden arms, six cabriole legs and an upholstered seat. The completely upholstered kind usually had a low, straight, square back, scrolling arms and six or eight cabriole legs, many of the early examples being made with stretchers. The seats normally had squab cushions.

Stools were still an important item of furniture, oblong ones being the most favoured, though round and oval ones were also made. They were fitted with either drop-in or stuffed-over seats and cabriole legs similar to those used on chairs.

Day-beds were generally completely covered in velvet or damask but sometimes the end support was modelled on the hoop-back chair. Stretchers were often included in their design to strengthen the cabriole legs.

Rich velvets and damasks were used for the hangings of the finest beds and they were also glued to the simple moulded cornice that commonly surrounded the tester. The carved headboard and the finials that frequently surmounted the bed were covered with the same materials. Fringes and tassels were less used on beds now, as was the case with seat furniture, a braided edge being preferred (Plate 66).

TABLES

With tables, as with chairs, the straight leg was replaced by the cabriole. Occasional exceptions to this general rule, as well as to the usual simplicity of most Queen Anne furniture, were the elaborately carved and gilded side-tables still made periodically for the more sumptuous rooms and often continuing in the style of the previous reign. Table tops in general were now fixed with screws which passed at an oblique angle through the underframing and into the top.

Card-tables, which became widely used, were made with a square top having rounded, projecting corners, from which the cabriole legs emerged, below the frieze. The rounded corners were dished to hold candlesticks, and wells or oval recesses were let into the surface of the top, to hold counters or money. Baize or needlework was used as a covering material. As with chairs, the club or pad foot was usual on the earliest examples, the ball-and-claw type being seldom seen before about 1710. Many of these card-tables were made so that one of the back legs could swing from a wooden hinge, centrally placed, through an angle of ninety degrees, so as to support the opened flap. This meant that the table was slightly unstable when open, as one of the corners was left unsupported.

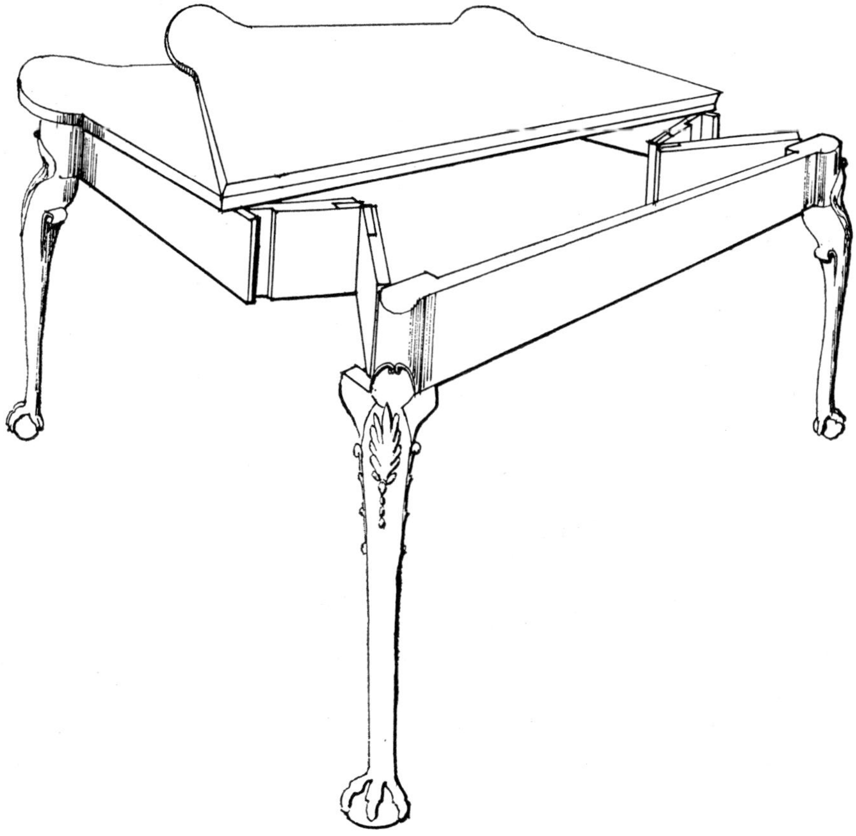

FIG. 7. Card-table with 'concertina' construction. Early 18th century.

That disadvantage was overcome in another type that was introduced (though both kinds continued to be made) which had what is called 'concertina sides'. When the table flap was closed the back legs could be drawn forwards and the sides of the frieze, hinged in three places, folded inwards like a concertina (Fig. 7). These folding sides were held rigid when the table was open by means of a sliding tray underneath. The legs were generally of solid walnut with a veneer used on the frieze and top.

For dining-tables the oval or round top was still popular but cabriole legs became generally adopted.

Small tables, either with three small drawers in the frieze and cabriole legs or with pedestals of drawers and a central recess below a frieze drawer, were apparently used both as writing and dressing tables. A brushing slide, a flat shelf that could be pulled out, was often included in the design of such pieces, which were known as 'Union Suites'.

CASE FURNITURE

Most items of case furniture were very plain, decoration being in general confined to cross- or feather-banding on doors and drawers; great use was made of large flat surfaces for the display of finely grained veneers, as in the cabinet on a stand illustrated in Plate 68.

Japanning was still used, particularly for the bureau-cabinet. This item of furniture, which had been introduced at the end of the seventeenth century, achieved during the reign of Queen Anne the wide popularity it was to retain throughout the eighteenth century. The lower stage generally stood on bracket feet and had the standard arrangement of long drawers with a sloping fall-front above, which could be let down onto lopers to form a writing surface; small drawers and pigeon-holes were fitted at the back. The two doors of the upper stage would be fitted with panels of wood or bevelled glass; the panels had arched tops, the same shape frequently being repeated in the cornice above and at either side. Inside the doors a central compartment surrounded by small drawers and a space for books above was the usual arrangement, secret drawers sometimes being incorporated in the design. The bureau-cabinet illustrated in Plate 67 has a cresting of carved and silvered pine; the bun feet are a somewhat old-fashioned feature by this time.

Bureaux alone, without a surmounting cabinet, continued to be made; some had cabriole legs, whilst others stood on bracket feet and had drawers in the base.

Chests-of-drawers, like bureaux, generally stood on bracket feet but another type was supported on a stand with cabriole legs, several small drawers being incorporated in the stand. The veneered drawer fronts were usually divided from each other by a half-round bead on the stiles and rails. Sometimes a folded top was fitted which, when opened, rested on a pair of lopers and formed a writing surface (Plate 63). The name 'bachelor's chest', though not a contemporary term, is to-day commonly used for such pieces. The chest-on-chest, or tallboy, had a lower stage containing the usual arrangement of drawers, surmounted by a multiple moulding, within which rested a slightly smaller upper section, similarly fitted with drawers and topped by a cornice.

MISCELLANEOUS

Some candlestands, supported on tripod scrolls and elaborately carved and gilded, remained, like the more ornate side-tables, little changed from those of the end of the previous century. The simpler kind were supported on a base of three short cabriole legs.

Many mirrors retained the tall proportions that had become fashionable in the last years of the seventeenth century and were surmounted by an elaborately carved and gilded cresting. Mirrors of greater width than height, generally divided into three parts, were designed for surmounting chimneypieces and given an arched cresting or serpentine top. Frames of glass were still made but wooden ones became more common; these might be of gilded wood or gesso, carved in low relief, of plain walnut or japanned. The cresting was generally solid, with an irregular outline, and carved in low relief. The glass in pier-glasses and other tall mirrors was usually still in two parts.

The dressing-glass on a stand, made to rest on a table, began to be more generally used. The glass, set in a plain moulded walnut or japanned frame, usually with an arched or serpentine cresting, was suspended on swivels between two uprights which were fixed to the base. This most often contained one long drawer fitted with compartments for toilet requisites, and above it there was often a sloping fall-front which opened to reveal small drawers and compartments arranged like a miniature bureau. Many of these bases were given an irregular serpentine front and they were supported on bun or bracket feet. Plate 69 shows a dressing-glass fitted with its own stand, which incorporates a brushing slide. The legs are of unusual shape, inspired by Oriental forms.

Burr walnut veneer was much favoured for long-case clocks but seaweed marquetry and japanning were also used. The dial was frequently given an arched top, which might contain the second-hand dial or an indicator for the phases of the moon. The cornice above usually repeated the arched shape and the whole was surmounted by a dome top with carved and gilded finials or brass balls, usually three in number.

VI

EARLY GEORGIAN

1715 to 1745

Furniture continued to be made in a similar style after the death of Queen Anne in 1714. However, there was a tendency for it to become heavier and more elaborately decorated, mainly with carving. There was also a strong influence on furniture design in general from the Palladian movement. Basically an architectural movement but also developing its own furniture, this was fostered by the Whigs who came to power with George I's accession to the throne. There was a reaction against the Baroque school, partly due to its associations with the Tory party, and its effects were particularly important in the field of furniture during the 1730s and 1740s. Led by William Kent, under the patronage of Richard Boyle, third Earl of Burlington, the reaction against the Baroque took the form of a return to what was considered to be the pure and correct version of Classicism, as practised by the sixteenth century Italian architect, Andrea Palladio, and originally introduced to this country in about 1620 by Inigo Jones. The Palladian architects of the early eighteenth century designed the interiors of their houses with tabernacle frames, with doorcases and chimneypieces embellished with columns and pediments, with deeply coffered ceilings and with other forms derived from the architecture of Roman baths and public buildings, all executed on a monumental scale. For such interiors it was necessary to design furniture of appropriate massiveness and grandeur. William Kent and his fellow Palladian architects did this by creating it in an architectural idiom, frequently embellished, like the walls, with columns, pilasters and pediments (Plates 75 and 84). Whilst such designs were possible for case furniture, they were not so readily adaptable to other types, such as chairs. For seat furniture, for which Kent could find no Classical prototypes, he drew his inspiration either from French sources, like the designs of Jean Le Pautre and Daniel Marot, or from the Italian furniture that he had seen in the houses built by Palladio himself. Since this was Baroque in character anyway, the return to a strictly pure Classicism was to a great extent an illusion as far as furniture was concerned. It was ornate and much decorated with gilding and gesso and sometimes with white paint that gave the massive forms the appearance of having been carved out of stone. Although designed for a comparatively small number of large Palladian mansions, it had a very marked influence on contemporary English furniture in general as can be seen in the use of architectural forms and motifs, increasing heaviness of design and greater elaboration of the decoration.

For the majority of furniture, walnut continued to be the most widely used wood until the mid-1720s, when mahogany began to overtake it in popularity, partly due to the desire for elaborate carving, for which mahogany, a hard wood, was far more suitable than walnut. It had the additional advantages of being less liable to attack by woodworm, and far less likely to warp or split, of taking a high polish and of being obtainable in larger pieces. Moreover, greater supplies of mahogany became available with the removal in 1721 of a tax on timber imported from the West Indies and other British colonies. Unlike walnut, mahogany was seldom veneered, the solid wood mostly being used, though occasionally mahogany veneer was applied to a pine carcase. The kind in commonest use at this time, known as Spanish mahogany, was of a dark, reddish colour and came from Cuba, Jamaica, Puerto Rico and San Domingo. Rosewood was sometimes used as a decorative veneer in small quantities, together with other woods. Drawers were generally made of oak though mahogany was also used.

The late 1730s saw the appearance of the first of the pattern books that were to become such an important influence on English furniture design during the rest of the century. In 1739 William Jones published the *Gentlemen's and Builders' Companion*, a book of engraved designs for furniture, most of which showed the strong influence of the Palladian architect-designers, although there is an early appearance of Rococo forms in some of the designs based on the work of the Frenchman, Nicholas Pineau. In the following year Batty and Thomas Langley produced the first of several pattern books, *The City and Country Builder's and Workman's Treasury of Designs*, a publication intended for the guidance of builders and furniture makers that included twenty-five designs for furniture, relying heavily on the work of the Frenchmen, Berain, Marot and Pineau, for inspiration. A number of furniture designs by Kent himself appeared in 1744 in the publication of the Palladian architect-designer, John Vardy, *Some Designs of Mr. Inigo Jones and Mr. Kent*. Henry Flitcroft (1697–1769) was another architect of the same school who designed furniture for his interiors.

The leading cabinetmakers during the reign of George I (1714–25) were the partners, John Gumley (d. 1729) and James Moore (d.1726), who were cabinetmakers to the Crown until the latter's death. Gumley, who had been producing mirrors in his Lambeth glassworks since 1705, handled this aspect of the output, whilst Moore specialised in the gesso work. After Moore's death Gumley went into partnership with his mother as 'Mrs. Elizabeth Gumley and Co.', continuing to supply furniture to the Royal Household until 1729, when royal disfavour was incurred. A cabinetmaker who came to importance at the beginning of George II's reign was Benjamin Goodison

(d. 1767), who supplied the Royal Family from 1727 until 1767. His work was mostly in the Kentian manner. Also in the front rank of cabinetmakers during the reign of George II was Giles Grendey who had a considerable export trade, much of his furniture being decorated with japanning. Many of his mahogany pieces are recognisable by the characteristic shaping of the panels. An unusual form of decoration, possibly due to his training in Germany, was practised by the cabinetmaker, John Channon. It was the use of an inlay of strips of brass, frequently combined with elaborate brass mounts, on furniture of high quality (Plate 86). G. Coxed and T. Woster of St. Paul's Churchyard, London, flourished from about 1710 to 1736, the year of Woster's death.

SEATS AND BEDS

Hoop-backed chairs continued to be made, particularly during the reign of George I, that were basically similar to those produced in the time of Queen Anne but, especially after about 1720, they were usually of sturdier proportions with lower backs and more elaborate carving. The vase-shaped splat was frequently linked to the uprights of the back and given a more elaborate outline, with scrolls. The seats, now broader, were given an apron, often in the form of a shell or, later, of elaborate foliage. The hipped joint at the knee became a common feature, in conjunction with wide brackets, and a lion mask or, occasionally, a human mask was a popular alternative to the shell carving on the knee; towards the end of the period the cabochon, a jewel-like carving, was sometimes used on the knee. The paw foot (Plate 73) was introduced at this time, being particularly appropriate for use with the lion mask, but the claw and ball retained its popularity and even the simple club or pad foot was not entirely superceded. The deeper and crisper type of carving necessitated by the lion mask and paw foot were made possible by the use of mahogany. The arms of chairs became more diverse, the scrolled-over type giving way to arm rests terminating in lions', eagles', or even snakes' heads (Plate 72). Under the influence of the Palladian movement partial gilding was applied to the carving of this kind of chair from time to time.

Chairs specifically designed for Palladian interiors were usually partly or completely gilded, often on a gesso ground with low relief carving (Fig. 8). Most were profusely embellished with carving, many of the most favoured motifs being drawn from architecture. They included the Vitruvian scroll, the Greek key motif, the guilloche, acanthus leaves and large shells; decorations resembling fish scales or in the form of overlapping coins were popular, particularly on the legs. These details were large and the chairs themselves were, in fact, Baroque in spirit, despite the avowed intention of the Palladian designers to reject this style. They generally had upholstered seats and backs, the latter being surmounted by a carved cresting. Italian cut velvet with a bold

FIG. 8. William Kent. Design for an armchair. Plate 43 of *Some Designs of Mr. Inigo Jones and Mr. William Kent*, 1744, by John Vardy

design of flowers and leaves was the most common kind of upholstery used or, alternatively, a native product of the same type, produced at Spitalfields. On some Kentian chairs there was a re-introduction of the old-fashioned X-form for the front legs (Plate 72); a simplification of this type of design can be seen in the set of chairs and sofas designed in the 1730s for Ham House (Plate 71).

The pronounced influence from the Palladian movement on furniture design in general led to greater variety as well as to an increase in ornament. Chairs with upholstered seats and backs became common, designed both with square (Plate 73) and with rounded outlines. The broad seats and backs now becoming widespread were suited to the voluminous skirts of the period and the concave, backward-sweeping arm supports were also appropriate for the fashion. Winged armchairs with squab seats, though still made, were by now far less common.

There was an increase in the number of chairs designed for specific purposes. One such type was that generally known as a writing chair, which had a leg at the front, one at the back and one at either side, with the back of the chair and the arms curving round in a semi-circle. Another kind of chair designed specifically for writing or reading was that often mistakenly termed a 'cock-fighting chair' to-day. It was designed so that a man might sit astride, facing towards the back, with his elbows resting on the arm-rests which formed a continuous arc with the back. Hinged to the top-rail was a sloping book-rest that could be let down when not in use. The arm-rests each contained a hinged compartment or tray for writing-materials and a bracket for a candlestick was also incorporated. In the front of the seat-rail there was usually a drawer. These chairs would be upholstered in leather like most chairs designed for use in a library. Leather upholstery was sometimes held in place by small discs of leather, fixed to silk tassels, spaced out at regular intervals on the back and seat.

A chair was specially designed to stand in the entrance halls and corridors of Palladian houses. Formal in appearance, hall chairs were made of oak or mahogany, without upholstery, the seat normally being dished or saddle-shaped, and arms sometimes being fitted. They were particularly suitable for architectural treatment and often displayed the arms or crest of the family in paint or carving on the back. Plate 74 shows a type of hall chair in common use which was based on an Italian Renaissance shape.

Another kind of all-wooden chair, of much humbler origin, which became widely used was the Windsor chair. It was usually made with a saddle-shaped seat of elm, with legs and back spindles of beech (for which reason the industry was centred in the beech-woods around High Wycombe, Buckinghamshire) and the encircling bow of ash or yew. The various parts of the chair were dowelled together. As well as being used in inns and simple interiors, the Windsor chair was popular for use in summerhouses when it was often painted.

Stools followed a similar line of development to chairs and could be of various shapes, including the occasional long or double stool, designed to seat two or more persons. The cabriole legs terminated in claw and ball, paw, or club feet and were embellished with shell or lion mask ornament. Both stuffed-over and drop-in seats were fitted and seat-rails were frequently given an apron and carved with a Vitruvian scroll or Greek key motif, particularly those designed for formal Palladian interiors.

Sofas of double chair-back form continued to be made and even some with triple chair-backs (Plate 76), though these were seldom made until the stronger mahogany, more suitable for their construction, came into use. As with chairs, the splats of the hoop backs became more decorative and the shell motif, found on seat-rails and knees, was often incorporated in the cresting and at the point where the hoops of the back joined. Upholstered sofas mostly had fairly low, straight backs with padded, outward-scrolling arms or, occasionally, wooden scrolled-over arms.

In addition to the chairs, stools and sofas, which formed a suite of furniture for a drawing-room, a wide seat just broad enough to seat two people is sometimes found. They are often known as 'love-seats', though the term is probably of nineteenth century origin; like the seventeenth century 'farthingale chair' they were probably made to accommodate the new voluminous skirts ladies were now wearing. They were of similar form to sofas and in some cases provided with wings; some were also made with hoop backs. The 'love-seat' shown in Plate 77 retains the simple pad foot, more often associated with the Queen Anne period.

Day-beds with hoop backs were still made, as well as examples having upholstered scrolled-over end supports, which were sometimes fitted at each end of the day-bed. The cabriole legs and seat-rails are treated similarly to those of chairs and sofas, sometimes with the addition of stretchers. Day-beds that could be unfolded from chairs or sofas were also occasionally made.

Very ornate beds, of four-poster or half-tester type, continued to be produced, their testers and headboards covered with rich velvets and damasks and their hangings of the same materials. A particularly splendid example was designed by Kent for Houghton Hall in about 1730, incorporating an enormous shell motif on the headboard and hung with green velvet embroidered with gold. Plate 75 shows a mahogany bed with tester upheld by Corinthian columns. Much plainer beds with less elaborate testers and hangings were made for simpler interiors.

TABLES

Card-tables remained an important item of furniture, as they had been in the opening years of the century. Their form was little changed, though there was often an increase in the amount of decoration. This was particularly the case on mahogany tables, where quite deeply carved lion masks were frequently used to decorate the knees, combined with paw feet and either a naturalistic carving of an animal's leg or with acanthus carving. Walnut tables continued to be made after the first quarter of the century in spite of the general preference for mahogany. On some card-tables the very striking laburnum wood was used as a veneer, giving a striped effect, with the light, yellowish, inner wood alternating with the deeper brown wood from the outer part of the trunk. Slight additional decorative features sometimes appeared, such as a gadrooning along the lower edge of the frieze, the inclusion of a shell or other minute apron and even a serpentine or irregular outline given to the top and frieze. Instead of the plain green baize, petit- or gros-point needlework might be used for the top. The recesses for counters and candlesticks were usually of the standard type but in some later examples of the period square compartments for candlesticks were introduced as a variation on the more usual round ones (Plate 82). Another innovation was the fitting of an additional leaf, or even two leaves, for chess or backgammon or for writing; these multiple leaves were fixed with knuckle joints, so that they would always be level. Occasionally card-tables were lacquered but that was not common.

Tea-tables, which had in fact been in use since the reign of Charles II, now became far more widespread with the increased popularity of tea-drinking. One type was rectangular, with cabriole legs and a detachable tray-top, generally held in position by a slat at each end underneath. Towards the end of the Early Georgian period the tripod tea-table became very popular (Plate 78). It had a central carved shaft supported on three cabriole legs, with a circular or serpentine top, which was occasionally given a raised and carved ornamental edge, widely known to-day as a pie-crust edge, although most tables of the kind had plain tops. The decorative edge could either be an attached moulding or the remaining edge of the top after the centre had been scooped out. A variation of the tripod tea-table was the supper-table, a serving-table with a series of dished compartments to hold plates. These might be constructed with a so-called 'bird-cage', which was a square platform, above which the top was fixed on a hinged support with a releasing catch, so that it could be tilted up to stand against a wall when not in use.

Kettle-stands were a smaller version of the tripod table, used to support a kettle on its silver stand.

The use of such a hard wood as mahogany made it possible to design gate-leg tables with only four legs, two of which would be made to swing out to support a flap at each end. Some larger ones, however, were made with six, or even eight, legs. Wooden hinges were still used in this period. The decoration of the legs followed a similar pattern to that of other furniture with cabriole legs. These gate-leg tables were mostly round or oval and some could be extended by the insertion of a leaf. Pairs of tables with rectangular flaps were also made, which could serve as side-tables when not in use for dining or be joined together to form one large table. One of the advantages of mahogany was that each section of the top could be made of one piece of wood, instead of consisting of jointed panels as they had formerly done.

Side-tables were a very important feature of the Palladian interior. Generally gilded or partially gilded, with tops of marble, porphyry or scagliola, they were diverse in form but characteristically heavy and monumental, with elaborate carving. Though cabriole legs were sometimes used, a heavy scroll type was more usual, or alternatively eagles, wolves, sphinxes or other animal or human forms. The legs commonly stood on a very thick base, matched by a correspondingly heavy frieze. Acanthus leaves, swags of oak leaves, human masks and shells, all large in scale, were used as embellishments linking the various parts of the tables. Motifs of falling coins or fish scales often decorated the legs and the Greek key and Vitruvian scroll were popular for the frieze and base. Plate 79 shows a side-table, designed by Matthias Lock, partially gilded and with a marble top; it typifies the monumental quality of such pieces of furniture.

A particular type of side-table, usually designed to stand against a pier between two windows, was supported at the back by the wall itself. Known as a console-table, it was sometimes supported at the front by a scroll; animal forms were also commonly employed for the purpose, one of the most popular being an eagle with outspread wings, standing on a rocky base of painted wood or marble.

C. LONG-CASE CLOCK, japanned in gold and red on a blue ground. The movement by James Markwick of London. About 1725. The elaborately carved finials and brackets are of silvered wood. Height 9 ft. 4 in.
Victoria and Albert Museum
Copyright Fratelli Fabbri, Milan
See page 75

Many side-tables intended for less monumental interiors were strongly influenced by the Palladian examples, being made of carved mahogany, without gilding, but incorporating such motifs as the Vitruvian scroll, the Greek key pattern and large masks or shells. Marble or scagliola tops were usual on tables of the type and heavy cabriole legs terminating in paw feet were common (Plate 80). Marble mosaic was an alternative treatment for the tops. Side-tables decorated with gesso, of the type that came into fashion at the end of the seventeenth century, were still made, though usually with cabriole legs.

A small dressing table, on which a hinged toilet-glass would stand, came into widespread use during this period. Supported on four cabriole legs. the dressing table generally had a frieze, shaped to allow for knee space, which contained a shallow drawer in the middle and a deeper one on either side. Most were of walnut or, as time went on, of mahogany, but examples decorated with gesso or japanning are known, too. Another type had two pedestals of drawers with a central kneehole and seems to have been used also for writing.

The writing table, or library desk, with pedestals containing cupboards or drawers flanking a central kneehole, first became common in the 1720s and was to retain its popularity right through the century. A particularly fine example of mahogany, with carved and gilded enrichments, designed by William Kent for Chiswick House is illustrated in Plate 83. The elaborately carved stiles were a characteristic feature of these pedestal desks, lion-headed terminals being particularly favoured. On some of the later examples the top drawer pulls out on supporting stiles, having a writing surface inside which slides back to reveal compartments below. Some library desks were intended to stand against a wall and were fitted with a cupboard at the back of the kneehole but most were of open pedestal form and designed to stand in the middle of the room, being decorated on all sides. Where lion-masks were featured they were mostly fitted with brass rings in their mouths, that could serve as handles; other handles were of circular or loop form.

CASE FURNITURE

Cabinets designed for Palladian interiors were in general strongly architectural in form. Some were inspired by the Palladian window, having an arched central opening flanked by lower, square-topped windows, and enriched with columns or pilasters and a heavy entablature. The latter often contained secret drawers and the top was usually surmounted by a broken pediment with a central plinth for a bust or escutcheon. A cabinet of the type can be seen in Plate 84. It could be used as either a bookcase or a china cabinet and the shelves could be set at varying levels, resting on fixed slats at the sides. The lower stage had additional storage space behind wooden doors.

Cabinets in general were strongly influenced by these architectural examples, being frequently adorned with pilasters and broken pediments. Bureau-cabinets, basically similar to those that appeared at the beginning of the century, were now given increasingly diverse decorative treatment. Sometimes a single door, incorporating a mirror flanked by pilasters, was fitted on the upper stage, in place of the pair normally used in earlier examples. Cabinets were particularly suitable for decoration with inlaid brass, combined with brass mounts, as practised by John Channon. The brass inlay took the form of stringing lines round panels and drawers as well as quite elaborate geometrical or arabesque designs. The cabinet illustrated in Plate 86 has the additional decorative feature of tortoiseshell inlay in the cavetto moulding of the curved entablature. The three small plinths at the top were originally fitted with gilded statuettes. Bureau-cabinets, in common with most case furniture, generally stood on bracket feet though other types, such as paw feet, were not unknown. The interiors of the writing section were often very elaborate; architectural features, such as pilasters, often formed the fronts of tall, narrow drawers; other drawers were given excessively serpentine contours or even made in the form of a series of steps leading down from a central opening flanked by pilasters, and hidden drawers were frequently secreted within the interior of the writing section. Bureau-cabinets were also a popular subject for japanning, often of a high standard, as in the case of the bureau-cabinet shown in Plate 85.

A variation on the bureau-cabinet with sloping front was that in which the top drawer of the lower stage let down at the front on metal quadrants to form the writing surface. The bureau as such, without the surmounting cabinet, continued to be made as well (Plate 87).

There was little change in the chest-of-drawers, apart from the practice of attaching a bead to the edges of the drawers, instead of to the rails and stiles between them. Occasionally a little architectural treatment was given, with the inclusion of pilasters in the design, particularly in the chest-on-chest, or tallboy. The tallboy shown in Plate 81 has quarter Corinthian columns at the corners and the unusual feature of ivory talons on the claw-and-ball feet.

There was a revival in the use of the chest for sumptuous interiors when it was often made in the form of a sarcophagus, of soft wood, gilded (Plate 88), or of carved mahogany. Japanned examples on separate stands were also popular.

MISCELLANEOUS

Stands were an important feature of the Palladian interior, being used as supports for candelabra, vases and busts. Some were in the form of a pedestal, tapering towards the base; another popular type was a terminal figure with a human head surmounted by an architectural capital. The pedestals, which stood on a square plinth or small Kentian scrolls, were many of them carved with the fish-scale motif (Plate 93). Simpler candlestands, made of mahogany with a central shaft on a tripod base of cabriole legs, were popular for more modest interiors.

The looking-glass frame became noticeably more architectural in treatment, the tall, narrow shape going out of fashion with a return to the general proportions of those of the Restoration period, though many were now larger. Oval frames, which had been practically unknown before this time, were now used periodically. The carved wood of the frames was in general partially or completely gilded and a pair of candle branches was often attached to the lower corners. Many large pier-glasses in architectural frames were designed in pairs, *en suite* with side-tables, thus forming an important feature of the wall decoration, comparable with the tabernacle frame of stone introduced by the Palladian architects into many of their interiors. The mouldings and motifs used on the frames were frequently repeated in other parts of the room, such as on door and window cases and on cornices. The pier-glass with gilded wood frame illustrated in Plate 89, one of a pair at Ham House, Surrey, shows the outset corners and broken scroll pediment that are typical of these pieces. In Plate 90 there is a rather simpler, though still architectural, frame of painted wood. An egg-and-dart moulding is a noticeable feature in both examples.

A similar trend is seen in picture frames, which were also gilded, but their design tends to be slightly more restrained.

Wall-brackets were widely used in architectural interiors for the display of bronze or marble busts or for vases and were mostly in the form of a heavy, gilded scroll.

Chandeliers were given the additional adornments used on other types of Kentian furniture, such as masks or eagles, or were decorated with fish-scale ornament. This can be seen in the chandelier of gilded wood illustrated in Plate 91. A not dissimilar treatment, particularly in the use of acanthus leaves, has been given to the brass one shown in Plate 92.

Cheval screens were given gilded frames and fitted with sliding panels. The tripod pole-screen became widely used, having a stand similar to that of circular tea-tables, with a central turned shaft supported on cabriole legs terminating in claw-and-ball feet.

The design of clock cases underwent little change but there was a marked fashion for their decoration with japanning, on a ground of red, green, blue, black or yellow, with the details in gold and other colours. A fine example, japanned on a blue ground, made about 1725 by James Markwick of London, is illustrated in Colour Plate C. The bracket clock shown in Plate 94 by Windmills of London, is unusual in being decorated with panels of mirror glass, with columns of clear glass at each corner.

With the growing importance of libraries, movable steps on castors were introduced during the period. The library steps of oak shown in Plate 70 have a platform with a book-rest and a hinged collapsible seat. The large castors are of the usual type, formed of leather discs. Another ingenious invention was a wooden armchair, hinged at the front of the seat-rail, that could be converted into library steps by pulling the chair-back forwards until the top of it rested on the floor; it disclosed four steps that had been hidden below the seat (Fig. 9).

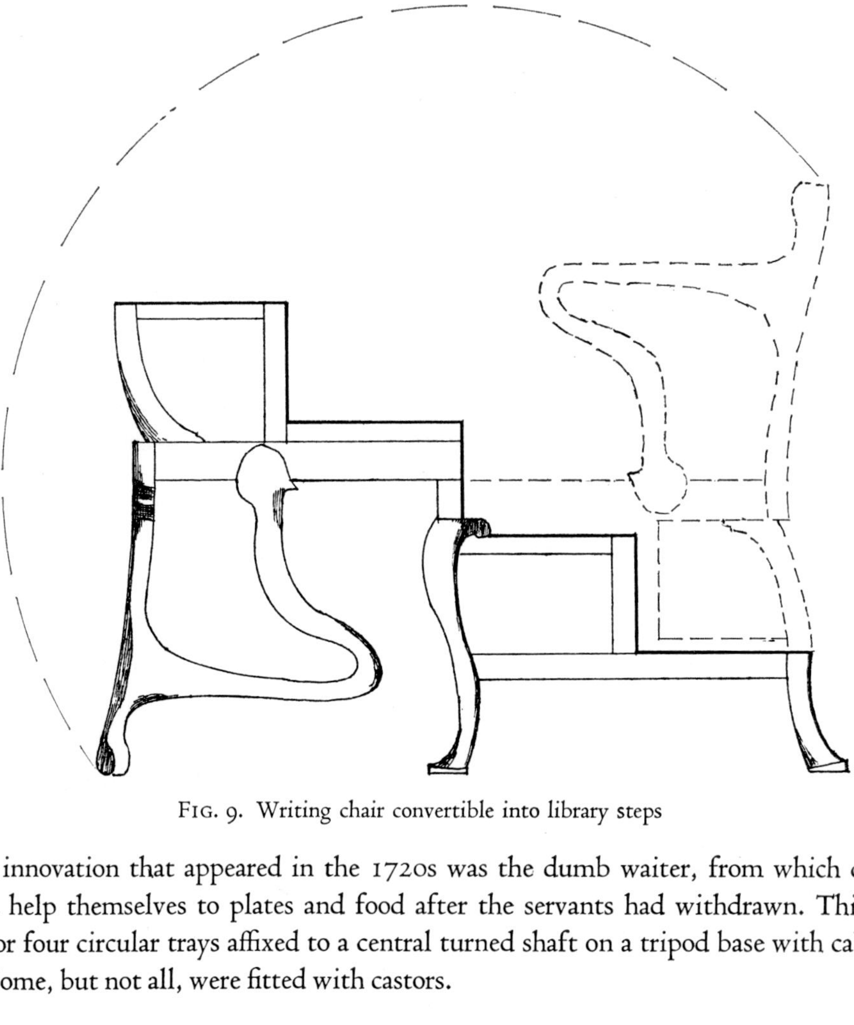

FIG. 9. Writing chair convertible into library steps

An innovation that appeared in the 1720s was the dumb waiter, from which diners would help themselves to plates and food after the servants had withdrawn. This had three or four circular trays affixed to a central turned shaft on a tripod base with cabriole legs. Some, but not all, were fitted with castors.

VII

THE MID-EIGHTEENTH CENTURY ROCOCO STYLES

The Rococo style had begun to evolve in France around 1700, as a lighter, more delicate and playful development of the Baroque. In England, partly owing to the strong bias towards Classical forms encouraged by the Palladian movement, and partly to its lack of appeal to the more sober English temperament, its effects did not begin to appear on furniture until the 1740s, and even then it met with violent hostility from many contemporary critics. A distinctively English version of the style was evolved, which was far more restrained than Continental equivalents. In such things as mirrors, candlestands and console-tables, however, where the structural requirements were less limiting than in seat and case furniture, it reached its closest approximation to French models and its most extreme form.

The new linear style was in marked contrast to the heaviness of the preceding Palladian movement, being characterised by lightness of both form and ornament. This was achieved in the former largely by the disguise of the structural shape with broken curves and scrolls and by the elimination (sometimes complete) of straight lines (Plate 96). A deliberate asymmetry was often sought, though it was usually confined to ornamental details. Ornament consisted of crisp carving of delicate, flamelike shapes, 'C' and 'S' scrolls, tattered shells and other small-scale motifs, for which the still popular mahogany was ideally suited. Walnut was occasionally used, however, even at this time. Marquetry was out of favour until about 1760 but gilding was often used on the more extravagantly carved pieces. The Rococo style seldom extended to the interior architecture in this country and even then it was on a far less extensive and less polished scale than on the Continent.

Alongside the pure Rococo style or 'French Taste', as it was called, and frequently mixed with it, was the so-called 'Chinese Taste' in which Chinoiserie motifs, drawn from real or imaginary Chinese sources, were incorporated in the design, including temples, pagoda roofs, Chinese fret, icicles, cranes, dragons and figures of Chinamen (Plates 99, 104 and 112). The revived interest in the Far East extended to wallpapers and textiles imported from China which were also imitated in this country. It was particularly fashionable to have a bedroom decorated entirely in the Chinese Taste.

Another aspect of the mid-century Rococo style, peculiar to England, where it assumed considerable importance, was the 'Gothic Taste'. Furniture made in this style bore no more than a superficial relationship to furniture of the Middle Ages, being in form and construction the same as any other mid-eighteenth century furniture. It was distinguished by the incorporation of motifs taken from medieval architecture, such as pointed arches, cusps, pinnacles and crockets (Plates 95, 103 and 109). The Gothic revival extended to whole interiors and, indeed, exteriors. In fact, its development was largely due to the gothicising by Horace Walpole of his 'little plaything house' at Strawberry Hill, Middlesex, which he began in 1747 to enlarge and alter in accordance with his romantic leanings.

Developments in ornamental details included a new type of loop handle: the large back-plate was replaced by two small circular or star-shaped plates, to which the ends of the loop handle were secured. Many handles and keyhole escutcheons were treated in a Rococo manner, with much use of chased brass in asymmetrical designs. Under French influence there was an increased use of ormolu mounts, too, particularly on the corners and feet of commodes in the French Taste (Plate 106). The evidence of English brass-founders catalogues shows that by now finely chased ormolu mounts were produced in considerable numbers here.

The practice of making the baseboards of drawers with the grain running from front to back was abandoned and on wide drawers they were fitted with the grain running lengthways.

Leather castors came into general use about 1740. They consisted of several discs of leather on an axle, held between two prongs of brass attached to a swivelling metal plate that was fixed to the wooden leg.

The best-known cabinetmaker of the period, Thomas Chippendale (1718–1779), although he was indeed head of one of the leading firms of cabinetmakers, owes his subsequent fame to his pattern book *The Gentleman and Cabinet-Maker's Director*. It was first published in 1754, with 160 plates, and cost £2. 8s. There was a second edition in the following year and a revised and enlarged edition was published in 1762. The book, which contained designs in the pure Rococo style, the Chinese Taste and the Gothic Taste, was bought by other cabinetmakers and by wealthy subscribers who would order pieces to be made from Chippendale's designs by local craftsmen, sometimes in a simplified form. This has led in the past to a greatly exaggerated assessment of Chippendale's output, as most pieces of furniture made to his designs (Plates 102 and 107) did not, in fact, come from his workshops. Nevertheless, he can be given credit for having evolved a specifically English version of the style, which is now generally known by his name.

Although he popularised the style, he was not responsible for introducing it to this country. It was pioneered by a carver and designer named Matthias (or Matthew) Lock (fl. 1740–69) who also, together with his collaborator Henry Copland, provided a number of the designs published in Chippendale's *Director*. Lock introduced Rococo designs into the pattern books that he published from 1740 onwards. These included *A New Drawing Book of Ornaments, Shields, Compartments, Masks, etc.*, published about 1740, *Six Sconces*, 1744, *Six Tables*, 1746, *A Book of Ornaments* and *A New Book of Ornaments*, 1752. If his designs were in the delicate manner characteristic of the Rococo style, his executed work is noticeably heavier (Plate 110); it may be due to the fact that his training had been in the more weighty manner of former times.

The designer and cabinetmaker who carried the Rococo style to its furthest extreme here was Thomas Johnson (*fl.* 1755–66). Many of his designs were quite bizarre and incapable of execution without considerable simplification. He was, however, a highly skilled craftsman, who produced work of the highest quality (Plate 111). In 1755 he published *Twelve Girandoles* and in 1758 *One Hundred and Fifty New Designs*, in monthly instalments, which consisted of such items as candlestands, candelabra, side-tables, lanterns and frames, all of them pieces that lent themselves to fanciful treatment.

A leading cabinetmaking partnership of the period was that of William Vile (d. 1767) and John Cobb (d. 1778). Vile, the senior partner, is now known to have been the leading cabinetmaker of the period, although his name had until quite recently been overshadowed by that of the better-known Chippendale. He worked for the Prince of Wales and, after the latter's accession as George III in 1760, continued to supply furniture for the Royal Family. His obscurity until recently was no doubt due to the fact that he did not publish any of his designs, but his identified works are all of the highest quality (Plate 108). His work is in complete contrast to that of Thomas Johnson, most of it being in the somewhat old-fashioned Palladian, and therefore architectural, style, the Rococo influence being restricted to applied decoration on flat planes. Also in contrast to that of Johnson, his output was almost entirely of case furniture. (In the eighteenth century it was usual for all except a few large firms to specialise.) He had a highly individual style, particularly favouring the use of pendent swags of foliage and flowers, circular or oval wreaths embellished with clasping acanthus leaves and the low relief decoration known as card-cut fret. By the time of Vile's death the Rococo style was giving way to the Neo-Classical (see next chapter) and Cobb's identified pieces, produced after Vile's death, are all characterised by ornament of Neo-Classical type (Plate 124).

John Bradburn, an employee of Vile and Cobb, was a first rate carver who, from 1764 until his death in 1777, was in business on his own account and supplied some furniture to the Royal Family.

William Ince and John Mayhew, who were partners in one of the most important cabinetmaking and upholstering businesses, published the *Universal System of Household Furniture* that came out in instalments between 1759 and 1762. An influential book, it contained designs in the Chippendale manner and included Gothic and Chinese forms as well as pure Rococo.

Robert Manwaring, cabinetmaker and chairmaker, produced several publications, including *The Chair-Maker's Guide* in 1769. Among other publications, Sir William Chambers (1726–96) produced *Designs for Chinese Buildings, Furniture, Dresses, etc.* in 1757; William and John Halfpenny included a few designs for chairs in the Chinese style in *New Designs for Chinese Temples,* published in 1750. William Hallett (1707–81) was another important cabinetmaker of the time.

Pierre Langlois (b. 1738), a Frenchman who took up residence in London in the 1750s, produced in the following decade a number of very fine pieces of furniture for wealthy clients, which were embellished with ormolu mounts and mostly decorated with floral marquetry in the French manner (Plate 106). In fact, the introduction of gilt bronze mounts and the revived fashion for floral marquetry as practised in Paris seem to have been almost entirely due to Langlois.*

John Linnell (d. 1796) of Berkeley Square was a leading designer, carver and cabinetmaker who worked with his father William Linnell (d. 1763), although most of his work was executed some years later, in the Neo-Classical style. A collection of his drawings in the Victoria and Albert Museum shows a number of Rococo designs and he is believed to have supplied suites of seat furniture in this style for the Duke of Northumberland and for Robert Child of Osterley Park, Middlesex (Plate 115).

SEATS AND BEDS

Owing to their structural requirements, chairs and other seat furniture were not subject to such extremes of Rococo design as less functional items. There was an increase in the number of different types of chair designs in the middle of the century and a marked tendency to lighter construction (Fig. 10). The rounded back became little used and a new type of openwork wooden back appeared in which the uprights turned out slightly to meet the top-rail, shaped like a 'Cupid's bow', often at an acute angle. The solid, vase-shaped splat gave way to openwork, carved in an infinite number of ways; it was sometimes made of plywood. The heavy ball-and-claw or paw feet were largely abandoned in favour of the more delicate French scroll foot. A dolphin termination was occasionally used and this form is illustrated in the *Director.* A delicate foliage or flamelike carving was applied to the backs and legs of chairs and often as an undulating apron round the

* A. Coleridge, 'Pierre Langlois, His Oeuvre and Some Recent Discoveries', *Gazette des Beaux Arts,* September 1967.

FIG. 10. Thomas Chippendale. Drawing of three chairs for Plate 14 of *The Gentleman and Cabinet-Maker's Director*, 3rd edition, 1762

seat-rail. The cabochon, an oval carving resembling a polished gem, was used particularly to decorate the knees of chair legs.

Chinese and Gothic motifs were frequently introduced, straight legs with block feet being usual for chairs with these characteristics. With chairs in the Chinese Taste a pagoda roof motif was commonly the central feature of the top-rail and it was also introduced into the openwork carving of the back, which would be based on Chinese fret or railings. The flat surfaces of the seat-rail, the back and the straight legs would be carved with shallow card-cut fret of similar character. Chairs in the Gothic Taste were generally of the same form as other chairs of the period, apart from the straight, square leg favoured for this particular style, but the openwork back would incorporate pointed arches, quatrefoils and other features from Gothic architecture, similar sources being used for the card-cut fret decoration on the legs. An alternative to the straight, square leg was that in the form of cluster columns; closely similar ones, presumably intended to represent bundles of bamboo, were sometimes used with the Chinese Taste. A certain number of chairs were made in a more whole-heartedly Gothic style with the back itself taking the shape of a pointed arch. The Windsor chair illustrated in Plate 95 has this feature and much use has been made of the pointed arch motif in the detailing; surprisingly, the front legs have been given a cabriole form.

A popular form of openwork-back chair evolved by Chippendale was what he called the 'Ribband-back', in which the splat was elaborately carved to resemble ribbons. A sofa of the type is shown in Plate 100 and the characteristic delicate carving of scrolls and flamelike forms can be clearly seen on the back and legs. These fashionable designs were often simplified by provincial makers, who fitted their chairs with plain square legs, linked by stretchers.

The completely upholstered armchair was frequently given a finely carved frame to the back and seat-rail of curving outline. Chippendale published a number of designs for what he called 'French Chairs', in most of which this undulation of the outlines was carried to the point where straight lines were entirely eliminated, the back being given a cartouche shape. The armchair illustrated in Plate 96 has these characteristics and it also shows the use of the French scroll foot. The gilded one illustrated in Plate 97, from the drawing-room at Osterley Park, is of similar shape but has rather more restrained lines. In many of these armchairs the raising of the back on short supports to give a gap above the seat increased the appearance of lightness in the design. The term 'Burjair' (from the French *Bergère*) was adopted at the time to refer to a much heavier armchair with wings, thick upholstery and a deep seat, usually supplied with a bolster cushion. Plate 98 illustrates an armchair of this type, dating from the mid-eighteenth century, having completely plain, undecorated legs and rails that make no concessions to the newly emerging Rococo style.

Sofas of double or triple open chair-back type were made in all versions of the current style (Plates 99 and 100). Stretchers were often used for greater strength, particularly with the straight legs used for the Chinese or Gothic Tastes. Upholstered sofas similarly followed the designs of the chairs they were made to match. The back was fairly low and undulating and the arms, of scroll type, continued the same line. Sometimes a wooden surround with Rococo carving ran round the back, while the seat-rail was given a delicately carved serpentine edge, so that subtle curves were continued round the whole piece of furniture. The upholstery might be fastened with brass-headed nails or a padded drop-in seat might be fitted. A bolster cushion was commonly provided at each end.

Stools became less widely used and Chippendale does not illustrate any in the *Director*, although his firm is known to have supplied them to various wealthy clients. They appear to have been little favoured by the middle classes. Those that were made formed part of a suite with chairs and sofas, as hitherto, and were designed in a conforming style. A stool designed to stand in front of a large easy chair was, however, illustrated by Chippendale in two versions, the two pieces together combining to form what was known as a *Péché Mortel*.

Various types of convertible seat furniture were now made, such as the double-chair-back sofa with a seat that unfolds to make a couch. A piece of furniture of this type, having a ribband-back, forms part of a suite at Nostell Priory, Yorkshire.

Couches with elaborately carved canopies, sometimes removable, and with hangings, were designed to stand in alcoves. The *chaise longue* appeared, too, being illustrated by Ince and Mayhew in their *Universal System*.

The Rococo style was seen to advantage in the elaborate testers surmounting beds of the mid-eighteenth century. These testers were occasionally of mahogany but more usually of carved pine, gilded or left bare or covered with silk, velvet or brocade which was attached with glue. A considerable number were designed in the Chinese Taste, which was appropriate for the very fashionable 'Chinese Bedroom' of the period; in general appearance they were not unlike the Chinoiserie garden temples illustrated by William Halfpenny in his *New Designs for Chinese Temples*. A particularly fine example of a bed in the Chinese Taste was that made for the Chinese Bedroom at Badminton, Wiltshire, now in the Victoria and Albert Museum. This bed, formerly thought to have been made by Chippendale, but now believed to have come from the firm of John Linnell's father, William,* has a pagoda roof, surmounted by dragons, a motif used on Chinese buildings to ward off evil spirits.

Chippendale illustrates one design for a bed in the Gothic Taste.

TABLES

In side-tables, especially console-tables, the Rococo style was often carried to extravagant lengths, frequently coming near to French prototypes. Thomas and Batty Langley illustrate several examples in their *Treasury of Designs*, published in 1740, that are almost direct copies after Nicholas Pineau. Owing to the fact that the back of a console-table is supported by the wall, the front supports can be fashioned in a delicate and fanciful manner with little regard to practical considerations. Frequently asymmetrical, the supports were formed of 'C' and 'S' scrolls with delicate foliage and shell-like carvings and, unlike their French prototypes, they often incorporated forms taken from wild life and the chase (Plate 101). They were almost invariably gilded and were fitted with marble tops, Chippendale describing them as 'frames for marble slabs'.

In contrast to console-tables, many side-tables with four legs were of carved mahogany, but on these too a marble top was usual. The legs were generally of cabriole form, terminating in scroll feet, except where the table was designed in the Chinese or Gothic Taste, in which case they would be straight and possibly, like the frieze, embellished with appropriate fret decoration. Openwork fret brackets linking the legs to the frieze were usual with the Chinese Taste (Plate 102). Intermediate or transitional examples are also to be found, in which paw feet or other old-fashioned motifs are mixed with Rococo features.

Card-tables altered very little in form, though the tops were sometimes given a serpentine outline. The legs became more graceful, French scroll feet being the most

* Helena Hayward, 'Some Furniture Designs of John Linnell in the Victoria and Albert Museum', *Furniture History*, The Journal of the Furniture History Society, Vol. V, 1969, p. 83.

common termination; the legs and frieze were decorated with delicate scrolls and flamelike foliage in low relief. The edge of the top was frequently embellished with a Rococo moulding, particularly with ribbon and rosette carving. Straight legs were occasionally used, decorated with Chinese or Gothic card-cut fret.

Tea-tables of various types became widespread, guests being served with tea at individual tables in many houses. The tripod table, with a central shaft supported on a base of three cabriole legs, acquired the fashionable French scroll foot and light Rococo carving. An excellent example of this type, possessing a square top with pie-crust edge, can be seen in Plate 105. An interesting feature is the hollowing out of the shaft, dividing it into three naturalistically carved parts – a typically Rococo breaking-up of structural members. As an alternative to the carved edge, a wooden gallery was often fitted to the table top, having an open fret or, sometimes, small spindles. Rectangular tea-tables standing on four legs and having detachable tray-tops were also given the fashionable slender proportions and fitted with galleries to the top. Where they were in the Chinese or Gothic Taste their straight legs were generally linked by cross stretchers.

To cater for the custom of taking breakfast in the bedroom, the breakfast-table was evolved, designs for it appearing in the *Director*. This was a small straight-legged table having two flaps and a small drawer in the frieze; below it was a shelf, enclosed by open fretwork with a pair of doors, recessed for the knees, at one side. Stretchers were sometimes provided to strengthen the rather slender legs; castors were normally fitted. The one illustrated in Plate 107 corresponds with Plate XXXIII in the *Director*, 1st edition, 1754.

Of similar proportions, though without the fretwork and shelf, was the Pembroke table that first appeared about the middle of the century. Like the breakfast-table, it had straight legs, usually linked by stretchers, and the top, of various shapes, was sometimes given a serpentine outline. The two flaps, when opened, were supported on hinged wooden fly brackets.

The dressing-table underwent considerable development at this time. One type, illustrated by Chippendale in the *Director*, where he calls it a 'buroe dressing table', had two pedestals of drawers with a kneehole recess containing a cupboard. As the name implies, it served for both dressing and writing. The top drawer had a baize-covered writing slide that could be pushed back to reveal a number of small compartments for cosmetics and toilet articles and a hinged mirror which also served as a book-rest. These rather heavy pieces were sometimes given a serpentine plan and undulating bracket feet, and were ornamented with card-cut fret or similar fashionable decoration. From the early eighteenth century dressing-table on which a separate toilet-glass would be placed, there was evolved a mid-century piece of furniture, illustrated in the *Director*, which incorporated a swivelled glass between a pair of tall cupboards on a table base with drawers. Smaller and lighter ones, having toilet fittings in the top drawer or below hinged flaps at the top, continued to be made.

The library table with two pedestals of drawers and a central recess was by now well-established and many of these pieces continued to be made, a considerable number being illustrated in the contemporary pattern books. Some were made in pairs to stand back to back with a leaf between. The Rococo style generally affected them merely in the form of the carved ornament applied to them. Chippendale showed one example of what he called a 'Gothic Writing Table' (*Director*, 1st edition, 1754, Plate LII). Occasionally they were made serpentine in plan or embellished with Rococo ormolu mounts, but stiles were generally in the form of the traditional console, and often headed with a lion mask. A library table of traditional type, attributed to William Vile, is shown in Plate 108. It is very characteristic of his work, showing a strong Palladian influence, the only appearance of Rococo feeling being in some of the ornamental details – notably the wreaths clasped with Rococo acanthus leaves, a feature frequently used by Vile.

CASE FURNITURE

The china cabinet had become of considerable importance as an item of furnishing. Some were made in the form of hanging cabinets but the majority stood on cabriole or straight legs or on a base with cupboards and were of break-front form, with glazed doors. In this period much lighter bars, of astragal moulding, replaced the heavier glazing bars formerly in use. The complicated designs given to these bars, with the use of many curved sections, necessitated their being rebated at the back to take the panes of glass, which would then be fixed with putty. Sometimes very intricately carved sections would be glued onto the front of the glass. Many china cabinets were designed in the Chinese Taste and in these the glazing bars would be inspired by Chinese fretwork, similar sources being drawn on for the ornamentation of the woodwork. A pagoda roof, complete with imitation bells, was often fitted to these cabinets. A design for such a piece, Plate CXXXIV from Chippendale's *Director*, 3rd edition, 1762, is illustrated in Figure 11. The cabinet shown in Plate 104, made to house a smaller Chinese cabinet, is fitted with a superstructure in the form of a complete Chinese temple. The cabinet in Plate 103, on the other hand, shows an extravagant use of Gothic features, including surmounting ogee arches with finials.

Closely resembling china cabinets, though generally a little heavier in proportions, were bookcases, which were generally of break-front form, having a lower stage with cupboards. The earlier architectural tradition was not altogether abandoned but it tended to be treated in a much lighter way; where a broken pediment was used, for

FIG. 11. Thomas Chippendale. Design for a 'China Case'. Plate 134 of *The Gentleman and Cabinet-Maker's Director*, 3rd edition, 1762

example, it might be lightened with an infilling of openwork fret. All forms of the Rococo were drawn upon for the carved ornament and the shaping of the glazing bars.

Another type of cabinet made in the mid-eighteenth century was fitted with shallow trays that had recesses to take collections of coins or medals. Both hanging and standing versions were made.

Oriental lacquer cabinets were generally fitted with stands having straight legs and japanned decoration. The cross stretchers were often made to rise in serpentine curves to a central finial or vase shape.

The now well-established bureau-cabinet, possessing an upper stage with doors, surmounted by a pediment, and a lower stage with sloping front, did not go out of fashion but was given lighter decorative treatment, both openwork and card-cut fret frequently being used. The doors of some were glazed, in a similar manner to those of china cabinets. As with most case furniture of the period, the feet were generally of bracket type, with serpentine outlines. The writing surface was usually made to let down on two metal quadrants and in many examples it closed to a vertical position, being fitted with two handles to appear like another drawer. The shapes and proportions of bureau-cabinets were more varied than formerly; in one made by William Vile for Queen Charlotte in 1761 a bombé shape was chosen for the lower part.

From the middle years of the century the term 'chest-of-drawers' was largely superseded for fashionable furniture by the word 'commode', a French term that had arisen earlier in the century. Some designers, such as Chippendale and Ince and Mayhew, used the name 'commode chest-of-drawers', presumably wishing to be fashionable whilst still ensuring that potential purchasers should understand their meaning. There is no hard-and-fast distinction between the two but 'chest-of-drawers' is generally applied to a plainer piece with little or no French influence, intended for a bedroom; the word 'commode' implies a more elaborate piece of furniture, somewhat in the French manner, whose drawers are often concealed behind a pair of doors (a feature that is, however, more often found in English than in French commodes). The commode could be designed for a bedroom or a drawing room.

Most chests-of-drawers were given a fashionable serpentine outline, though this was sometimes restricted to the front. Frequently an almost bombé effect was given by the addition to the front corner stiles of a flattened console. This feature, the shaped bracket feet and often an apron, were decorated with Rococo carving. Sometimes short legs of undulating bracket form were fitted, in which case there would be three, instead of the more usual four, drawers. Occasionally the top drawer was equipped with small boxes and compartments for toilet requisites.

The commode, being more closely based on French models, mostly stood on elegant curving legs, carved with Rococo ornament, which continued the subtle curves of the front stiles. Occasionally ormolu mounts in the French manner were applied to the feet and the upper parts of the stiles, but more often these embellishments were translated into carved wood on English commodes. Unlike their French counterparts, the English ones were normally fitted with wooden, rather than marble, tops. The top drawers of some were equipped with toilet fittings, pieces of the type being designated 'dressing commodes' by Chippendale. Some, especially those intended for use in one of the 'Chinese bedrooms', would be japanned or have panels of Oriental lacquer incorporated in them, within a japanned framework.

About 1765, when the Rococo style was beginning to go out of fashion, there began a revival of the use of marquetry on commodes, in imitation of that seen on contemporary French furniture. Mostly of floral marquetry, it was subtler and more delicate than the Late Stuart type, generally concealing far less of the background and, where it was contained within a framework, the latter was of an irregular Rococo type. The commodes on which this type of decoration was used were usually very strongly in the French manner and often enriched with ormolu mounts. A particularly fine example of such a commode, attributed to Pierre Langlois, is illustrated in Plate 106. The elaborate ormolu mounts are believed to be of English make. The top is of marble.

The chest-on-chest or tallboy continued to be made, generally with a lower stage of four drawers, on which stood a slightly narrower upper stage of four or more drawers. The decoration followed that used on the simpler types of chests-of-drawers.

Cupboards of various kinds, mainly of the clothes-press or wardrobe type, were widely illustrated in pattern books of the time. The version called by Chippendale a 'commode clothes-press' consisted of an upper stage with doors, standing on a base in the form of a commode. The cupboard part was fitted with shallow drawers or sliding trays for clothes. A bombé form was sometimes used for the lower part or a serpentine outline might be given to the whole piece of furniture. A Rococo bracket foot was generally used on this type of furniture, sometimes being given a wildly contorted outline – though more conservative makers, such as Vile and Grendey, tended to favour the paw foot.

The night-table or pot-cupboard appeared about now, superseding the close-stool. It consisted of a small cupboard, standing on straight legs, with a door at the front and usually a gallery round the top. Some examples were decorated with Chinese or Gothic motifs. Another new item of furniture, not unlike it in appearance and also for use in the bedroom, was the wash-stand, or 'Bason Stand', as it is called in the *Director*. It generally had a hinged top, below which were recesses for a basin and soap dishes, with cupboard and drawer spaces underneath. In another type, a circular framework for a bowl and, below this a triangular platform with drawers and soap container, were upheld by three supports, the whole resting on a tripod base.

D. GIRANDOLE of gilded wood. One of a pair made for the Saloon at Temple Newsam about 1760, possibly by Matthias Lock. This exuberantly Rococo design, incorporating a stag, a hound and bulrushes, is 6 ft. 10 in. high. *Temple Newsam House, Leeds.* *See page 90*

MISCELLANEOUS

There were several types of candlestand designed in this period. Some, of polished mahogany, consisted of an open, tripod framework made up of slender serpentine sections and scrolls, supporting a top with a fretted gallery. Others, usually gilded, were in the form of a solid pedestal, enriched with delicate carving and standing on elegantly scrolling feet. The example illustrated in Plate 111 is based on a design by Thomas Johnson. Among the Rococo scrolls and broken outlines appear a pair of elongated Classical columns. This apparently unrelated feature was commonly incorporated in the most extravagantly Rococo English designs, particularly on mirrors and girandoles, where, as in this instance, it constituted the only feature with straight lines; it may perhaps have been felt that it supplied a need for stability in otherwise rather frivolous designs.

In the design of mirror frames full reign could be given to Rococo fantasy and straight or regular lines were frequently entirely absent (Plate 113). In the earlier designs the frame is still fairly 'solid', although carved with delicate Rococo forms, but it soon disintegrated into a loose openwork surround. The glass was often divided into a large central plate, surrounded by a number of irregularly shaped small ones, the wooden divisions being carved with Rococo scrolls and foliage. It was not normally bevelled owing to the irregular shapes. Little temples, storks and Chinese figures were frequently used in these designs, amongst other Chinoiserie motifs. Gothic forms were not often favoured although the mirror illustrated in Plate 109 shows the use of this style. Animals from the English countryside and figures from the chase were often introduced into these designs, unlike their Continental counterparts. Such creatures can be seen in the looking-glass illustrated in Plate 110, where hounds and a stork appear at the bottom and the head of a hare at the top of the glass. Designed and made by Matthias Lock, together with a side-table and a pair of candlestands, for the Tapestry Room at Hinton House, Somerset, it shows clearly the rather heavy quality given to Rococo forms by this maker. A much lighter and more typical treatment can be seen in the mirror, one of a pair, illustrated in Plate 112. Less elaborate frames, of mahogany, with carved and gilded applied ornament were quite common, too.

In some mirrors designed to go over fireplaces, where they were known as chimney-glasses, the width exceeded the height. In many chimneyglasses the carved ornament of the frame continued down into the chimneypiece itself, a further example of the disguising of structure and outline.

Wall-lights, for which the French term *girandole* became generally adopted, often incorporated one or more plates of looking-glass in their design, which served to reflect the candlelight. Mostly made in pairs, they tended to be asymmetrical in design, with two or more twisting, naturalistic candle branches, irregularly placed. An exceptionally fine example, one of a pair, is illustrated in Colour Plate D. Their gilded designs were, if anything, even more extravagant than those of contemporary mirrors. Like these, they often incorporated a single attenuated Classical column in their design.

The development of the looking-glass frame was closely paralleled by that of the picture frame. Though the requirements of the picture naturally necessitated a virtually straight inner edge to the frame, extremely elaborate and delicate Rococo carving, sometimes in openwork form, surrounded it.

Richly carved and gilded brackets were an important feature of the mid-eighteenth century interior. They were usually designed in pairs and carved with French Rococo and Chinoiserie motifs, often being of asymmetrical form. Used to support porcelain, candelabra, clocks or busts, they were illustrated in all the leading pattern books. A few were made of mahogany, most of them adorned with an openwork fret.

The tripod pole-screen became increasingly light, the formerly universal vase-shaped base of the shaft often being carved into an openwork form, and the very delicate, upward-turning French scroll foot generally replacing earlier types. The frame of the panel was commonly given an irregular outline of Rococo scrolls and flamelike leaf forms. Tripod pole-screens were likely to be of polished mahogany but cheval screens were often of gilded wood, their outlines richly carved, with perhaps an asymmetrical rocaille feature surmounting the top. The panels of both types of screen were mostly of needlework in tent- or cross-stitch though Chinese paper was also used. The screen shown in Plate 114, probably made about 1740, even if still based on the Queen Anne style, illustrates the use of such paper. For the larger, folding screens painted leather was sometimes used as an alternative to needlework.

Chandeliers of glass, as well as the more common brass or gilded wood, became fashionable about the middle of the century, though few early ones have survived. Strings of drop-shaped pendants were incorporated in their otherwise rather simple design.

Lanterns were made both for hanging from the ceiling and for wall-mounting. They were used mainly for halls, staircases and passages. Made of brass, carved mahogany or carved and gilded softwood, they were variously shaped and ornamented with all types of Rococo decoration. They were illustrated in the pattern books of the leading designers.

The hanging wall clock became popular in the mid-eighteenth century, whilst the long-case clock, less amenable to Rococo treatment, declined in popularity. One type of hanging clock with a large dial, has wrongly been called an 'Act of Parliament clock'; this name should properly be reserved for a plain version of the same type which was designed to hang in public places after the tax imposed on clocks by Pitt in 1797. Many of the hanging and bracket clocks were in the traditional form of the table clock with the addition of fashionable Rococo ornament in gilded brass or wood. Some hanging clocks, however, known as cartel clocks, were given elaborately carved and gilded openwork frames, resembling and complementing those of contemporary girandoles. Fret decoration was widely used on the more traditionally-shaped mahogany cases and the inclusion of a Chinese motif, such as a pagoda roof, or of a Gothic form, such as a pointed arch, was common. The smaller number of long-case clocks made at the time were also adorned with such fashionable features, and fret carving was particularly favoured for the ornamenting of their hoods.

VIII

NEO-CLASSICISM I

The Grand Manner of the Architect-Designers

The term 'Neo-Classicism' is generally understood to refer to the new interpretation of Classical forms in the decorative arts that first made its appearance in English furniture just before 1760 and was to affect design for the rest of the eighteenth century. This return to Classical forms was in part a reaction against the Rococo, which had never been so whole-heartedly accepted in this country as on the Continent. It was also strongly influenced by the growing interest in Antiquities and the study of Classical remains which had been stimulated by new discoveries in the second quarter of the century, particularly at Pompeii and Herculaneum. Information about such finds was spread by publications like Robert Wood's *Ruins of Palmyra*, of 1753, and *The Antiquities of Athens*, by James Stuart and Nicholas Revett, published in 1762.

The new form of Classicism differed from the Palladian version in that it was based on a greater knowledge of Classical decoration than had earlier existed, the discoveries of recent years having been largely of Roman domestic interiors, as opposed to the baths and other public buildings that most of the earlier excavations had revealed. The stucco arabesques and painted scenes of the walls and ceilings of Roman houses were now adapted by the leading eighteenth century English architects and designers for the houses of the wealthy. Their activities, like those of the Palladian designers before them, embraced the designing of furniture and fittings as well as architecture. Neo-Classical furniture in its strictest interpretation was designed for a limited number of great houses and for a specific place in their interiors. (The popularisation and dilution of Neo-Classical forms by designers such as Hepplewhite will be dealt with in the next chapter.) Although it was based in its early stages on a more literal interpretation of Classical forms, a much lighter treatment soon became apparent, particularly in the work of Robert Adam, where Classical features were used with a Rococo delicacy.

There has been much discussion as to whether the new style originated in France or in England. It depends to a great extent on how the term is defined, i.e. when an entirely new interpretation of Classical forms can be said to have begun, in contrast to a mere revival of an earlier style. What is certain, however, is that parallel but distinct Neo-Classical movements sprang up in the two countries, each having some influence on the other.

Neo-Classicism saw a return to the straight or regular line, that made for a simplification of form; the serpentine line disappeared almost entirely except in a few pieces of transitional type. Decoration was more restrained and strictly subordinate to form; it was typically of low relief or applied carving and marquetry decoration came back into fashion. Light-coloured woods, such as satinwood and harewood were much used and rosewood was also popular, though mahogany was still favoured, especially for library and dining-room furniture. Painted decoration became fashionable, at first in the form of small Classical scenes in roundels or panels and later as all-over decoration, when it was generally known as japanning, irrespective of whether or not it was in imitation of Oriental lacquer. There was an extensive use of gilding, too. The most popular motifs, all drawn from Roman sources, were the anthemion, the ram's head or skull, the patera, either round or oval, strings of husks or bell-flowers, griffins, winged sphinxes and urns, combined with other motifs that had been used in earlier revivals of Classicism. These motifs, together with the painted or marquetry roundels of Classical figures, were often echoed in similar features in the decoration of the walls, doorcases or chimneypieces. Decorative marbles and marble mosaics (the latter probably fashioned by Italian craftsmen) were widely used for table tops. Sometimes the marble was inlaid with composition, this technique being known as Bossi work, after the name of an Italian who specialised in this work in Dublin.

Brass mounts in the form of rams' heads, paterae, swags, etc., were extensively employed, many of the finest supplied by Matthew Boulton, the leading designer of decorative metal objects in England at the time. Some were gilded to brighten their appearance and prevent tarnishing, whilst others were lacquered. A new type of handle was introduced that took the form of a ring having a circular patera for a back-plate. Loop handles, attached at each end to a small round or shaped back-plate were still used. Door-plates stamped out of sheet brass were introduced in the last quarter of the century. Castors made entirely of brass now became generally used on heavier chairs and certain other items of furniture.

The leading figure in Neo-Classicism in this country was Robert Adam (1728–92), the second of four sons of the Scottish architect, William Adam. Having spent the years 1754 to 1758 in Italy, studying Classical architecture, he returned to design or re-model and furnish a large number of town and country houses in England and Scotland during a working life of thirty-odd years. The widely-held belief that he designed everything in his interiors down to the smallest detail is an exaggeration; although he normally designed fixed items, such as pier-glasses and side-tables (Plates 121, 131 and 133) (as well as grates, carpets, etc.), in many cases he left the design of some things, and particularly chairs, to others, even if these would almost invariably be in a conforming style. Adam was not a craftsman and did not have a cabinetmaking business himself but many of the leading artists and craftsmen of the day were employed at the houses where he was working, though not necessarily under his direct control. These included Thomas Chippendale (some of whose finest work was in the Neo-Classical style, such as the furniture he supplied for Harewood House, Yorkshire, in 1772–75 (Colour Plate E)), John Linnell, designer and cabinetmaker, who supplied much of the furniture for Osterley Park, Middlesex (Plate 115), Joseph Rose, the plasterer, and the painters Antonio Zucchi and Angelica Kauffmann.

Adam's style, at first fairly sturdy, and frequently showing Palladian influence, progressed into a lighter and more delicate interpretation, with the absorption after about 1775 of influences from the Louis XVI form of Classicism. It finally became excessively refined and rather feminine in much of the work of his later years.

By about 1770 the style had been adopted by all leading architects and designers. However, the amount of furniture designed by them was comparatively small. One of them, James 'Athenian' Stuart, had, in fact, preceded Adam in the new style with his designs for Lord Curzon at Kedleston, Derbyshire, dating from 1757 or 1758, and it appears that some of Adam's early designs are based on Stuart's work. James Paine, James Wyatt, Thomas Leverton and Henry Holland were among other architects who designed furniture for the houses where they were working. Holland employed a number of French craftsmen, notably a certain François Hervé, and strong French influence can be seen in much of the furniture he supplied in the late 1780s and early 1790s, as at Althorp, Northamptonshire, and Carlton House, London.

Among the leading cabinetmakers who supplied the Crown were William Gates and the firm of France and Beckwith. Furniture of high quality was also being produced by William Hallett and Samuel Norman, and John Cobb (d. 1788) continued to make fine furniture after the death of his partner, William Vile, in 1767. All had their workshops in the St. Martin's Lane area.

SEATS AND BEDS

Perhaps the most noticeable feature of the new style as far as seat furniture was concerned was the universal adoption of the straight leg. In fact, there was no known Classical precedent for chairs and stools and some of the first of the new designs show tentative attempts to find an appropriate form. In Stuart's sofas and chairs for Spencer House, St. James's, for example, he relied heavily on Kentian forms for inspiration, and used naturalistic legs with paw feet. However, various forms of the straight leg quickly became the rule, either square in section or, from about 1770, of baluster form, both types being frequently fluted and terminating in spade or block feet. The junction of the leg and seat-rail was commonly decorated with a patera. Seats were generally straight-edged or rounded at the back but sometimes a slightly serpentine form was given to the front. Where the seat-rail was visible, as, for example, with a drop-in seat, fluting was usually used (Fig. 12).

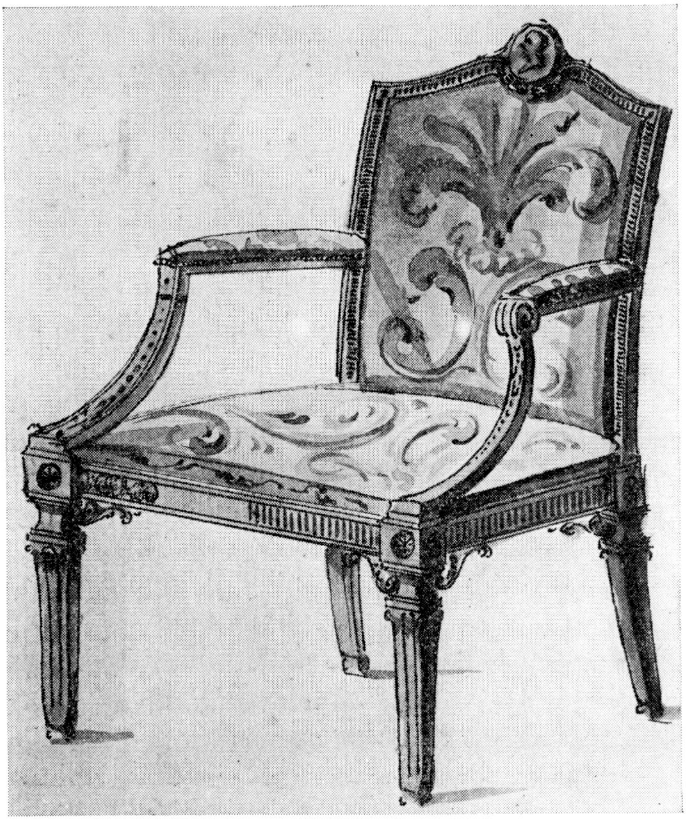

FIG. 12. John Linnell. Design for an armchair, *c.* 1775

Chair-backs were of various shapes, most of them based on the square or the hoop, but a cartouche-shape was still sometimes used. About 1775 the oval back, a French form, was adopted by Adam. The lyre-back, so-called because this ancient musical instrument provided the shape for the splat, was evolved by Adam but also used by other designers, notably Chippendale and Linnell (Plate 115). The arms of upholstered chairs were in general fitted with small pads, covered with upholstery to match the seat and back (Plates 116 to 118). The arm supports usually rise in a concave curve from the corners above the front legs but some, particularly in early designs, are jointed at the sides of the seat-rail (Plate 116). Upholstery, mostly fastened with brass-headed nails, tended to be of silk damask or tapestry but for dining or library chairs leather was used. Cane was also occasionally used for seats, which would then be provided with squab cushions covered in leather or silk. Chairs were generally made of mahogany or of gilded beech, with a seat-rail of oak. Later in the period painted chairs became fashionable.

Some ten years before the end of the eighteenth century some chairs strongly influenced by the style of one of the leading French chairmakers, Georges Jacob, were supplied to Carlton House, among other places, which was being furnished by Henry Holland. Holland himself may have been responsible for the design of some of them but the majority were probably designed by François Hervé, working under his supervision. They all had rectangular backs, many with uprights in the form of colonettes, and the top-rail was jointed *between* the uprights in the French manner, instead of fitting on top. In some cases the back legs were vertical, according to the French custom, rather than set at an angle in the usual English way.

Hall chairs were generally of mahogany or painted wood, their solid backs being carved or painted with Neo-Classical ornament. Various types of straight leg were employed and the square or shaped seat was dished (Plate 127).

As with his early chairs, Adam's first essays in the design of sofas show inspiration drawn from both the Palladian and the Rococo styles. Indeed, although the straight Neo-Classical leg soon became universal, the serpentine line, of Rococo origin, was frequently retained in the backs of settees. The ends were usually completely upholstered and outward-scrolling, and a bolster cushion would be provided at each end. The serpentine seat-rail found on some of the earlier examples was widely superseded by the straight type, with fluting or other fashionable ornament. A variation on the sofa was the 'confidante', introduced from France, in which a chair-like section, sometimes detachable and usable on its own, was attached to each end (Plate 120).

Formal arrangements were still the rule at this time, chairs and sofas being arranged round the walls. As they were not intended to be seen from behind, the decoration was not continued round the back. Stools, which had until the middle of the century formed an important item of furnishing in the more sumptuous interiors, now became much less common, with the exception of the window seat, a long, upholstered stool, which usually had scrolled ends similar to those on settees. Stools of similar type were also occasionally designed to be placed along the walls; they might be of mahogany or of painted or gilded wood, in conformity with the rest of the suite. There was a revival of the stool with X-shaped legs for hall seats, made of mahogany and having a dipped or saddle-shaped seat.

The elaborate beds designed for these sumptuous interiors gave great scope for Neo-Classical treatment. The irregular scrolling testers formerly in fashion were replaced by more restrained, architecturally-based designs, in which the bed-posts were more closely based on Classical columns, though many of these beds were by no means simple in

E. LIBRARY TABLE in the Neo-Classical style. Rosewood veneer with marquetry decoration in various woods and ormolu mounts. Attributed to Thomas Chippendale. This outstanding example of eighteenth-century craftsmanship was made about 1770 for Harewood House, Yorkshire. Length 6 ft. 10 in. *Temple Newsam House, Leeds.* *See pages 94, 98 and 100*

character. A well-known example is the extremely ornate bed designed by Adam for the State Bedchamber at Osterley Park in 1776. Most of the features, notably the bedposts and the cornice, are freely adapted from Classical architecture. Adam also designed slightly less ornate beds for Castle Howard and for the Taffeta Bedroom at Osterley; both are of satinwood, inlaid with green-stained wood and have gilded decoration with cherubs surmounting the cornice (Plate 119).

TABLES

The side-table played a very important part in the decorative schemes of Adam and the other architect-designers. Together with its surmounting pier-glass, the gilded side-table formed in effect a three-dimensional extension of the wall decoration. Earlier ones were rectangular with straight legs grouped in two pairs at the front and one at each of the back corners. At first the legs were square in section and fairly heavy but about 1767 Adam introduced the turned and carved baluster type (Plate 121). Later, he frequently used a lighter form of the leg with rectangular section. Stretchers were seldom used but below the carved frieze there was often a pendent decoration of swags or husks. Marble tops were usual with these side-tables, sometimes being of mosaic or inlaid with composition. The semi-circular or elliptical side-table was introduced shortly after 1770 (Plate 121). The console-table (supported at the back by the wall) was seldom featured in Neo-Classical interiors.

An important innovation adopted by Adam for the furnishing of dining-rooms was the composition of a sideboard flanked by urns on pedestals (see page 101). The sideboard was of similar form to the side-table but sometimes fitted with a brass rail at the back for supporting plate. Either marble or mahogany were used for the tops of such sideboards.

A dining-table does not seem to have formed a permanent part of the arrangement of the dining-room of the Neo-Classical architect-designers, since the chairs were formally arranged round the walls when not in use, as in the other state rooms. In the inventory of the contents of Osterley Park, taken in 1782, for instance, there is no mention of a dining-table in the Eating Room but several folding tables are listed as having stood in the passage outside, whence they could be fetched when needed. Nor do dining-tables appear among Adam's existing designs. Those of the period that survive are of mahogany, with straight, fluted legs; made to be removed when not in use, they are fitted with a hanged flap at one end and, very often, a leaf, to be inserted between two units. The hinges used on folding and gate-leg tables were, from about 1760, often fixed with lathe-made screws.

Pembroke tables, though they were undoubtedly to be found in great houses of the time, probably never formed an intrinsic part of the furnishing of an interior in the Grand Manner of Neo-Classicism and did not fall within the province of the architect-designer.

Card-tables in true Neo-Classical style are also very rare though there is a pair at Syon House, Middlesex. They were probably made by Pierre Langlois and are gilded, with marquetry tops.

A rare example of a billiard table of Neo-Classical design is at Alnwick Castle, Northumberland. It has an anthemion frieze in marquetry and is mounted with brass swags and paterae, in a manner strongly resembling the library tables at Osterley Park.

Of the library tables designed in the Neo-Classical style the finest is that made for Harewood House, Yorkshire, probably by Chippendale (now at Temple Newsam House, Leeds). Dating from about 1770, it is in the traditional pedestal form and decorated with marquetry, embellished with very fine ormolu mounts of rams' heads, husks, anthemia and paterae (Colour Plate E).

CASE FURNITURE

Satinwood replaced mahogany for case furniture, and marquetry in various woods took the place of the carved decoration formerly used. Some of the marquetry designs, copied from the French, took the form of delicate sprays of flowers spreading over the surface. Mostly, however, the marquetry decoration was entirely Neo-Classical in character, often incorporating roundels with Classical figures, set off with ormolu mounts (Plates 125 and 126).

A change in the construction of drawers that took place was that those of considerable width were now generally fitted with baseboards made in two parts, jointed into a bracing strut across the middle.

There was a tendency for the serpentine line to persist, particularly in commodes, some of which were made in a bombé form with curving legs, whilst the ornament was fully Neo-Classical. These commodes in a transitional style were usually mounted with ormolu at the front corners in the French manner. A particularly fine example of the type, which also shows the use of floral marquetry combined with ribbons and husks and a frieze of anthemion, is illustrated in Plate 124. This commode is believed to have been made by John Cobb, being very similar to one made by him for Corsham Court, Wiltshire, in 1772. The use of doors to enclose the drawers is a common feature of English work, though seldom found in France.

Some commodes in the Neo-Classical style were decorated with panels of Oriental lacquer or were japanned, particularly those designed for bedrooms, where the Rococo taste for Chinoiserie had not yet completely gone out of fashion.

The pair of commodes in the Drawing Room at Osterley Park (Plate 125), for parts of which there are drawings by Adam in the Soane Museum, are in a very different version of the Neo-Classical style; their semi-circular plan, a shape introduced by Adam, became widely adopted by other Neo-Classical designers. The stiles in the form of attenuated pilasters are ornamented with Adam's characteristic delicate arabesques in ormolu and the pendent friezes are also typical of his designs. The fine ormolu mount of a Classical head flanked by griffins is repeated almost exactly in carved and gilded wood in the door-cases of the room, an instance of Adam's frequent use of variations on the same motif in different parts of a room. These two commodes are purely decorative, being hollow and not fitted with either doors or drawers. James Cullen, cabinetmaker and upholsterer of Greek Street, London, commented that commodes and side-tables were 'more intended to furnish & adorn than for real use'.

Cabinets were treated in a similar way to commodes, being decorated with Neo-Classical motifs in marquetry on a satinwood ground and often embellished with ormolu mounts. Glazing bars, where used, were generally of geometrical or curvilinear shape. Plate 123 shows a cabinet designed by Adam for the Duchess of Manchester at Kimbolton Castle in 1771. It is decorative rather than functional, although access to the inside is provided by doors at the ends, and was made to display a series of Florentine early eighteenth century landscapes in coloured marbles (*pietre dure*). Pilasters of marble and ormolu adorn the front. The piece is really an interpretation in Neo-Classical terms of the Italian seventeenth century architectural cabinet.

A number of large wardrobes and cupboards were made in the Neo-Classical style, some of them with japanned Chinoiserie, such as the one in green, decorated with gold and silver landscapes, designed by Chippendale for the Chinese Bedroom at Nostell Priory, Yorkshire.

Chests-of-drawers and chests-on-chests, or tallboys, though decorated with ornament drawn from the contemporary repertoire, were seldom treated in the Grand Manner of Neo-Classicism. They generally stood on rather short, straight legs, often of peg type; they might be straight, bow-fronted or even slightly serpentine and they were fitted with ring handles. The chest-of-drawers illustrated in Plate 129 was designed for the Taffeta Bedroom at Osterley Park, *en suite* with Adam's bed, shown in Plate 119. It is of satinwood, banded with rosewood and inlaid with green-stained wood. A pair of night-tables was designed to form part of the same suite of furniture, as was the normal practice. Such pieces would be fitted with doors or a tambour-front to the upper part, the lower section pulling out on trusses.

Bookcases tended to be built-in in the interiors of the architect-designers, as was the case, for example, with those designed by Adam for Osterley Park, Nostell Priory and Mellerstain. Where they were designed as free-standing pieces of furniture – even if still intended for a particular position in the room – they were usually of the traditional break-front type and often of carved mahogany, though a light Neo-Classical handling replaced the heavier architectural forms of Kent or Vile. As an alternative to decorative glazing bars a brass trelliswork, backed by pleated silk, was occasionally used. Classical vases in carved wood frequently surmounted these bookcases.

Bureaux and bureau-cabinets were seldom designed in the Grand Manner of Neo-Classicism, their function being performed by the library desk and the bookcase. An exception is the fall-front secretaire probably designed by Adam and made by Chippendale for Harewood House, Yorkshire. It is a French form, unusual in England, and is decorated with a Neo-Classical design in various woods on a satinwood ground, incorporating a Classical figure in ivory on an ebony ground. Also made by Chippendale for Harewood is the library table illustrated in Colour Plate E.

MISCELLANEOUS

Pairs of candlestands were an important feature of the Neo-Classical interior, their design usually being based on that of the Roman sacrificial altar or ceremonial tripod. They were in general of gilded or painted wood and the ram's head was a particularly common motif, used to surmount each of the three corners. The exceptionally fine example illustrated in Colour Plate F was designed about 1760 by James Stuart for the Painted Room at Spencer House, London. Plate 130 shows a variation on this type of stand, designed to be fixed to the wall and to support a lamp (Osterley Park). Two sets designed by James Wyatt for Heveningham Hall, Suffolk, have metal candle branches attached; one, in the Etruscan style, supports a Classical vase.

The broken outlines of the mid-eighteenth century looking-glass frame were replaced by a more regular architectural or geometrical treatment (Plate 131). In 1773 a new process of casting glass was introduced from France, whereby much larger sheets of glass could be made for the enormous pier-glasses that practically filled the wall space between windows in fashionable interiors. Chippendale provided a pair for Mersham, Kent, in 1779, each of which he said 'fills the pier in width'. These glasses, which are now at Audley End, Essex, have the narrowest of frames. There is a note in the 1782 inventory of Osterley Park, stating of the chimney-glass (or overmantel mirror) designed for the State Bedroom by Adam, that it was 'the first plate made in England', implying that it was the first of these large sheets of glass made by the newly-introduced process (Plate 132). Pier-glasses were mostly rectangular, of one single sheet of glass, although the broad frame sometimes incorporated further sheets of mirror glass overlaid with Neo-Classical ornament in carved wood. Painted plaques were sometimes introduced into the cresting of pier-glasses and it became quite customary for some of the minute decoration to be carried out in gilded composition, rather than in carved wood. Adam's which the anthemion, rams' heads and husks figure prominently, In chandeliers, strings of beads and glass drops were much used, whilst the central shaft was often given the shape of a Classical vase.

IX

NEO-CLASSICISM II

Hepplewhite and Sheraton

It was not long before the Neo-Classicism of the architect-designers began to be disseminated in a somewhat simplified version among the middle classes. Knowledge about the new style was increased by the inclusion of Neo-Classical designs in pattern books, such as the *New Book of Pier Frames* published by Matthew Lock in 1769 that included some early examples. Throughout the last quarter of the century a very considerable amount of furniture was made in this lighter, less expensive, though still elegant, version of Neo-Classicism. Naturally, although they were intended for less spacious houses, many pieces of furniture of this type found their way into the more sumptuous interiors, particularly into rooms of lesser importance, such as bedrooms.

Furniture of this kind is universally associated with the names of Hepplewhite and Sheraton, although, in fact, very few pieces are likely to have been made by the firm of Hepplewhite and, as far as is known, Sheraton never produced any furniture at all. Even more than is the case with Chippendale, they owed their fame to the design books that bear their names.

George Hepplewhite (d. 1786) was the owner of a small cabinetmaking business in Cripplegate, London, having learnt his trade with the firm of Gillow of Lancaster. After his death the business was carried on by his widow, Alice, under the name of A. Hepplewhite & Co. and it was she who in 1788 published about 300 of his designs in *The Cabinet-Maker and Upholsterer's Guide*, of which a second edition came out in 1789 and a third, with additional designs, in 1794. The avowed aim was 'to unite elegance and utility, and blend the useful with the agreeable'. The designs were not entirely new but rather a reflection of the prevailing taste, as is acknowledged in the introduction to the last edition: 'we designedly followed the latest or most prevailing fashion only, purposely omitting such articles, whose recommendation was mere novelty.' The *Cabinet-Makers' London Book of Prices*, first published in 1788, also included a few designs signed 'Hepplewhite' in the second edition in 1793. Most of the designs in this pattern book were by Thomas Shearer, a cabinetmaker and designer, whose work closely

F. One of a pair of CANDLESTANDS designed for the Painted Room at Spencer House, St. James's, by James Stuart about 1760. Gilded and painted wood. Surmounting ormolu and marble tripod incorporates a perfume-burner. Height 6 ft. 9 in. *In the collection of the Earl Spencer at Althorp, Northamptonshire.* *See page 100*

particularly in Sheraton's designs, and pleated silk behind a brass trelliswork became widely used for door panels.

The general repertoire of Neo-Classical ornament was drawn on but especially favoured were strings of husks, upheld by tied ribbons, Classical urns, paterae and fan shapes. Applied decoration was sometimes made of papier mâché or composition, a practice introduced by Adam himself, such forms as strings of husks being mounted on a wire core. Metal mounts were also mass-produced, door-plates and keyhole-escutcheons being made of sheet metal pressed into moulds and filled with composition at the back. The most common type of handle was the ring, hinged to a patera-shaped back-plate, but loop handles with a small backing disc at either end were also used. Castors made entirely of brass were general after about 1770, as were lathe-made screws with regular threads.

Many large cabinetmaking firms were now in existence. One of the largest and most fashionable was that of George Seddon of Aldersgate Street, London which in 1786 employed about 400 journeymen, including carvers, joiners, gilders, metalworkers and upholsterers. Robert Gillow of Lancaster, who opened a branch in Oxford Street, London, in about 1760, also had a large cabinetmaking business, with a considerable export trade, producing furniture of good quality. Japanned goods of papier mâché were the speciality of a certain Henry Clay of King Street, Covent Garden, who is known to have made, amongst other things, trays, boxes, tea-caddies and, for Osterley Park, a Pembroke table.

SEATS AND BEDS

The commonest types of chair-back in the Hepplewhite style are of oval, heart or shield shape, the latter being particularly associated to-day with his name, although he was not, in fact, the inventor of it. Derived from the Adam type of oval back, which was in turn of French origin, all these forms were raised from the seat-rail on short supports, generally as an extension of the back legs, and embodied a multiple splat or other openwork design. This might take one of a number of forms, composed of curved members, specially popular motifs being Classical urns, swags of drapery, ears of wheat and the Prince of Wales's feathers (Plate 138). One type of oval back that was very popular was completely filled with a large openwork design of stylised honeysuckle (Plate 139). These anthemion-back chairs were not illustrated by Hepplewhite but one appears in the Gillow's records* for 1785. In the 1794 edition of the *Guide* a number of designs were added for square-backed chairs, which had by then become fashionable. In many armchairs the arms curve down to join the seat-rail at the sides, in the manner used in

* In the Westminster Public Library.

the middle of the century, but a type became widely adopted in which the supports swing forwards to the corners, where they join the front legs. Seat-rails were either square or rounded at the back and a bowed or serpentine edge might be given to the front. Legs were almost invariably straight, though occasionally the cabriole was used, as shown on two 'State chairs' in Plate 13 of the first edition of the *Guide*. They were made either square or round in section, plain or fluted, or, in the case of the square type, sometimes panelled. Many chair legs were tapered down to the floor, without feet, a slight splaying out at the bottom being adopted in some later examples, but where feet were included in the design they were generally of tapered block shape, known as a therm or spade foot (Plate 138). Sheraton specially favoured legs with reeding, sometimes spiral, or with cable moulding.

Mahogany was widely used for chairs, embellished with a little low relief carving and sometimes inlaid on the back or seat-rail with lighter woods, mainly in the form of paterae. A few chairs with upholstered backs are illustrated by Hepplewhite, which he somewhat confusingly terms 'Cabriole Chairs', in conformity with his definition in the *Guide*, where he says that 'Chairs with stuffed backs are called cabriole chairs'. (Sheraton defined the cabriole as a 'French easy chair'.) Upholstery was mostly of horsehair, the seats being of stuffed-over type, fastened with brass-headed nails or, sometimes, with braid. Silk was occasionally employed and painted with a Classical scene, Sheraton illustrating a few examples of this type. Hepplewhite states that 'Mahogany chairs should have the seats of horse hair, plain, striped, checquered & c. at pleasure, or cane bottoms with cushions, the cases of which should be covered with the same as the curtains'. The seat-rail was very often left exposed below the upholstery, when it was commonly fluted.

In contrast to Hepplewhite, Sheraton favoured chair-backs of basically square form, which he claimed to be more fashionable, although he also includes one shield-back design in the *Drawing Book* (Fig. 14). His designs show a marked vertical emphasis and use of straight lines rather than curves and often lack the easy fluency of Hepplewhite's work. A common feature of many of them is the raising of the central part of the top-rail, sometimes with the incorporation of a rectangular panel of carving or marquetry. The legs are mostly of baluster type and the seat-rails rounded or shaped at the front on 'Drawing Room chairs' but straight for 'Parlour chairs'. Sheraton also illustrates 'Conversation Chairs' in the *Drawing Book*, which had waisted seats and padded top-rails, the user being enabled to sit facing the back, leaning on the top-rail.

In the introduction to the *Guide*, 1794, Hepplewhite says 'For chairs, a new and very elegant fashion has arisen within these few years, of finishing them with painted or japanned work, which gives a rich and splendid appearance to the minuter parts of the ornaments, which are generally thrown in by the painter. Several of these designs are particularly adapted to this style, which allows a frame-work less massy than is requisite

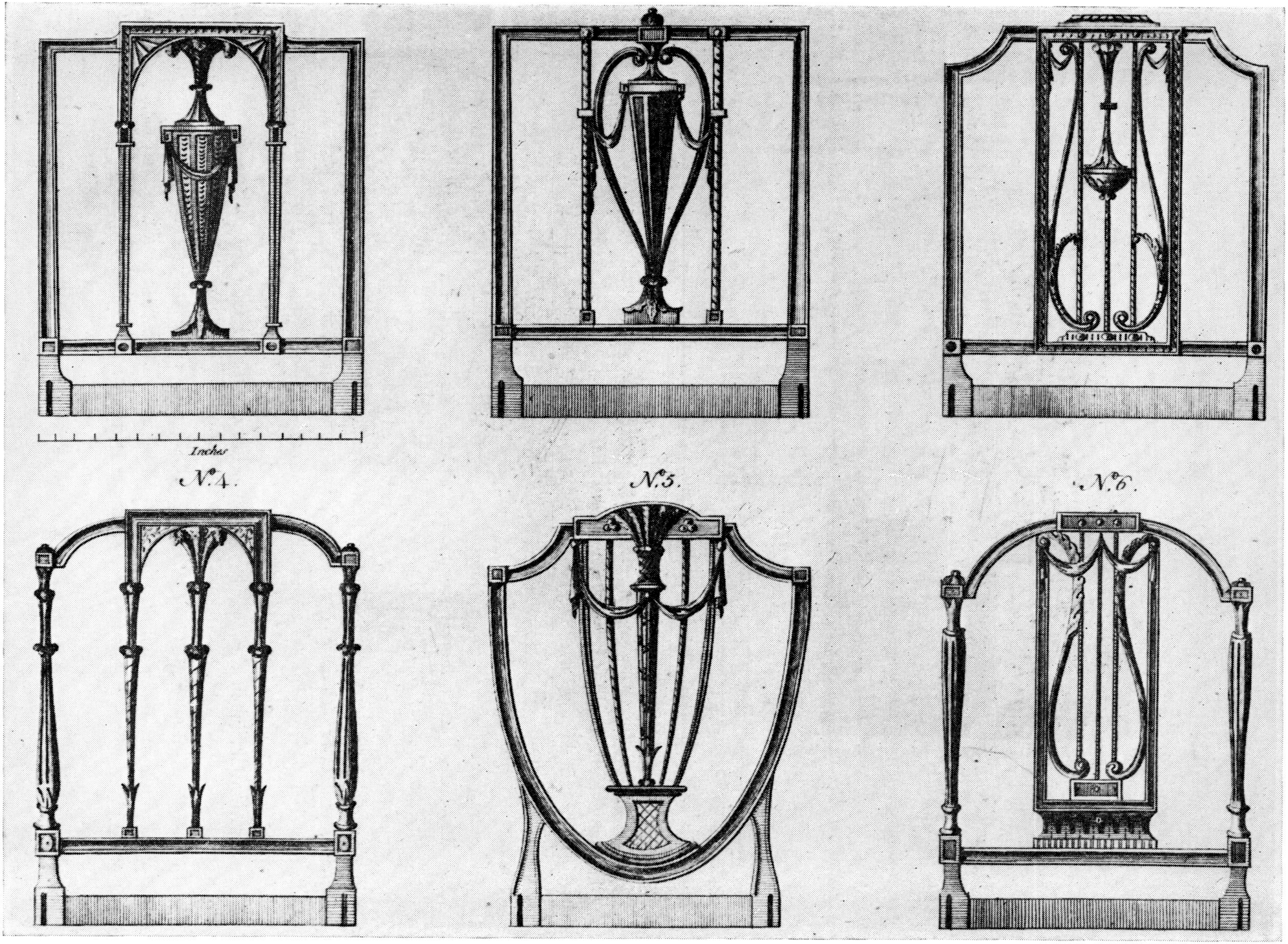

FIG. 14. Thomas Sheraton. Design for six chair backs. Plate 36 of *The Cabinet-Maker and Upholsterer's Drawing-Book*, 1792

for mahogany; and by assorting the prevailing colour to the furniture and light of the room, affords opportunity, by the variety of grounds which may be introduced, to make the whole in harmony, with a pleasing and striking effect to the eye. Japanned chairs should have cane bottoms, with linen or cotton cases over cushions to accord with the general hue of the chair'. Such chairs, cheaper than those of mahogany but of similar design, would usually be made of beechwood. The painting, of Neo-Classical motifs or of flowers, was mostly carried out on a whitish ground but was done on a veneer of satinwood from time to time. A black ground came into fashion in the closing years of the eighteenth century, when either colours or gilding might be used for the ornament.

There are three designs for hall chairs in the *Guide*, the backs being respectively oval, shield-shaped and in the form of a Classical vase with cover.

Sofas were designed with openwork backs, sometimes of multiple chair form, of carved mahogany or painted softwood, or they were completely upholstered. The *Guide* illustrates a 'Bar back Sofa' (Fig. 15), designed in the manner of four shield-back chairs, having a serpentine top-rail that extends round into the arms. The serpentine line survives in many settees of the period but square-backed types were also made, particularly towards the end of the century. These were often given panels of cane in the back, seat and ends and were usually painted (Plate 141); cane seats were fitted to sofas made of satinwood or japanned. Seats were generally deeper than those on Adam-type sofas, giving greater comfort, with less formality. Baluster and square, tapering legs

FIG. 15. George Hepplewhite. Design for a 'bar back sofa'. Plate 26 of *The Cabinet-Maker and Upholsterer's Guide*, 1788

were both used, the former being usual with upholstered settees, although Hepplewhite also illustrates a 'French Sofa' with cabriole legs. In Sheraton's designs the horizontal arms are supported by vertical continuations of the front legs (Plate 141). A rectangular panel was frequently inserted in the middle of the top-rail.

A variation on the settee, known as a 'confidante', had a section like a chair at each end, which was in some cases removable, so that the ends could, as Hepplewhite observed, 'be used as Barjier chairs' (Bergère chair – an upholstered armchair with a deep seat).

The newly-adopted custom of reclining was catered for by another innovation, called a 'duchesse', which consisted of a Bergère chair with a large stool fitted in front of it or of two Bergère chairs with a stool between them, forming a kind of day-bed. The duchesse was sometimes of one piece, the two ends, which would be rounded, linked by the stool section. The term 'duchesse' was also used by Sheraton, rather confusingly, to refer to a kind of bed with a draped canopy.

Stools were of less importance in middle class houses of moderate size than in the formal interiors furnished by the architect-designers but there are a few illustrated in the *Guide*, though none appears in Sheraton's designs. They were mostly of the window seat type, having upholstered, scrolled ends but other kinds were also shown in the *Guide*, with either straight or cabriole legs, as well as a 'Gouty Stool', which had a hinged, adjustable top.

Beds continued to be designed very much in the mid-century, Chippendale, tradition, of carved mahogany but with Neo-Classical ornament. Bed-posts generally had a vase-shaped lower section, commonly carved with leaves, and tapered towards the top – sometimes being fluted, or, after 1790, reeded. Plate 140 illustrates a bed of painted wood made by Thomas Chippendale for David Garrick, the actor, in about 1770. Hepplewhite and Sheraton both show very elaborate designs for canopies, many with a dome incorporated, but, judging by surviving examples, it seems that the executed designs were generally much simplified, and had a straight cornice and valance. A canopy composed of gentle, serpentine curves was known as a 'sweep top'; a 'Venetian' or 'waggon' top was one in which the cornice had an arched section in the middle. Some of these were painted. Sheraton particularly favoured domed beds, among which may be cited an oval or 'Eliptic Bed for a Single Lady' and two 'Field Beds', made to stand with one side to the wall, in which the draped dome is upheld by supports sloping up from the head and foot of the bed. He also shows a forerunner of the modern twin beds, where the two linked beds are described as a 'Summer Bed in two Compartments'. The hangings might be of printed cotton or linen, silk or velvet, the valance sometimes being gathered in festoons.

TABLES

Dining-tables were frequently made in two parts, having either folding flaps or separate leaves for insertion; they stood back against a wall when not in use (Plate 142). They were generally of mahogany, with straight, fluted legs, and the corners of the tops were sometimes rounded or shaped. Towards the end of the century a new type of support became popular that consisted either of a central pedestal to each section of the table, resting on four splayed legs, or, alternatively, four balusters on a platform, also supported by four splayed legs. These legs were usually fluted on the top edge and terminated in brass paw feet with brass castors.

Side-tables of semi-circular form were popular; one with cabriole legs and scroll feet is illustrated in the *Guide*, together with several of irregular outline. Most legs were straight, square in section or of baluster form, the latter type, together with the frieze, often being gilded. Satinwood with an inlay of other woods and painted softwood were both widely used but mahogany seldom. Stretchers were not usual, although Sheraton, whose designs for side-tables are characteristically more elaborate, recommended their use – surmounted by a carved vase or basket of flowers. He particularly favoured baluster legs with reeding or cable moulding and tops of an irregular 'D' shape. Marble was seldom used for table tops in the late eighteenth century; however, Sheraton recommends that the frames should be gilded or painted white with gilded ornament. Sometimes a pane of mirror glass was fastened between the table legs or on the wall behind, continuing the reflecting surface of the pier-glass.

The sideboard evolved at this time from being a decorative table to a piece of furniture that provided storage space in the form of drawers and cupboards, becoming thereby far more practical for smaller rooms. It generally approximated to a rectangular or 'D' shape in plan, sometimes concave in the middle, and was supported on six legs. Hepplewhite's description in the *Guide* gives a good idea of the type of fittings in sideboards at this time: 'the right hand drawer has partitions for nine bottles . . . behind this is a place for cloths or napkins the whole depth of the drawer. The drawer on the left hand has two divisions, the hinder one lined with green cloth to hold plate, & c. under a cover; the front one is lined with lead for the convenience of holding water to wash glasses, & c. . . . there must be a valve-cock or plug at the bottom, to let off the dirty water; and also in the other drawer, to change the water necessary to keep the wine, & c. cool; or they may be made to take out. The long drawer in the middle is adapted for table linen, & c.' Sometimes the flanking urns on stands of the formal Adam composition would be incorporated into the sideboard to form a single piece of furniture. Hepplewhite does not illustrate this type but Sheraton shows one example, described as a 'Side Board with Vase Knife Cases', in which one of the pedestal cupboards is open, showing a spirit burner below a metal rack, used for warming the plates. There are brass rails along the back of the sideboard, against which plates might be rested, and branches for candles. Mahogany was sometimes used for sideboards, in common with other dining-room furniture, the decoration consisting of carving or of inlay, particularly of stringing lines in light-coloured woods such as holly and satinwood.

There was an increasing number of small tables, often designed for specialised activities, with variously shaped tops, and many of them were supported on slender tripod or four-legged 'pillar-and-claw' supports. The tops were often made to tip up into a vertical position when not in use. Pembroke tables were mostly of satinwood, decorated with marquetry or paint (Plate 143). A type of Pembroke table developed in which a nest of drawers, housed with its top flush with the table top, could be raised by means of an ingenious mechanical device, of which Sheraton gives an explanatory diagram. It is known as a 'Harlequin' table, the name having been given, according to Sheraton, 'for no other reason but because in exhibitions of that sort, there is generally a great deal of machinery introduced in the scenery.'

Small work-tables for ladies' needlework were made in various forms. Plate 144 shows one of painted wood with applied ornament of gilded composition. There is a hinged top, giving access to a bag of green silk, with a wooden baseboard. Another type, based on a French model, had a tray, one side of which could be let down on hinges, the whole resting on two end supports and having a shelf below. These were of satinwood or painted wood.

Card-tables were made in various forms, and had square, round, oval or serpentine tops. Some were similar in form to Pembroke tables, whilst others were of gate-leg or 'concertina' type. Although straight legs were usual, a rather restrained, slender type of cabriole leg was sometimes used. Dished recesses for counters and candlesticks were not generally supplied.

Great ingenuity was used in the design of writing-tables, particularly in Sheraton's designs, where a multiplicity of fittings was enclosed within a small piece of furniture. Many were surmounted by a brass gallery. Library tables with the traditional two pedestals were still made though these were often oval or serpentine in plan, and had perhaps drawers in one pedestal and cupboards in the other, with, occasionally, drawers that pulled out at each end. A type of writing-table known as a Carlton House table appeared at this time (Fig. 16), both Hepplewhite and Sheraton having designed versions of it. It consisted of a rectangular table on four legs, with shallow drawers in the frieze, on the top of which was a superstructure of small drawers and cupboards, ranged along the back and sloping down at either side of the writing surface; there was usually a brass gallery along the top and the whole table was often rounded off at the back corners. Another, much smaller, kind of writing-table had two flaps folding inwards to enclose the top, below which were various compartments and fittings; others were closed by means of a sliding cylindrical top or slotted tambour front. Some small tables of this kind were also used for dressing, and were equipped with fittings for toilet requisites. A feature of many writing-tables was a board on an adjustable ratchet, which could be fixed in various positions, and some were designed to be used in a standing position. The ordinary bureau, so popular earlier in the century, fell largely out of fashion. Some small tables, designed particularly for ladies, included a sliding firescreen in their design, and there was even a form of cheval firescreen, which, by being given a depth of a few inches, was made to incorporate shallow drawers and compartments and a writing flap letting down on metal quadrants; this type was illustrated by both Shearer and Sheraton.

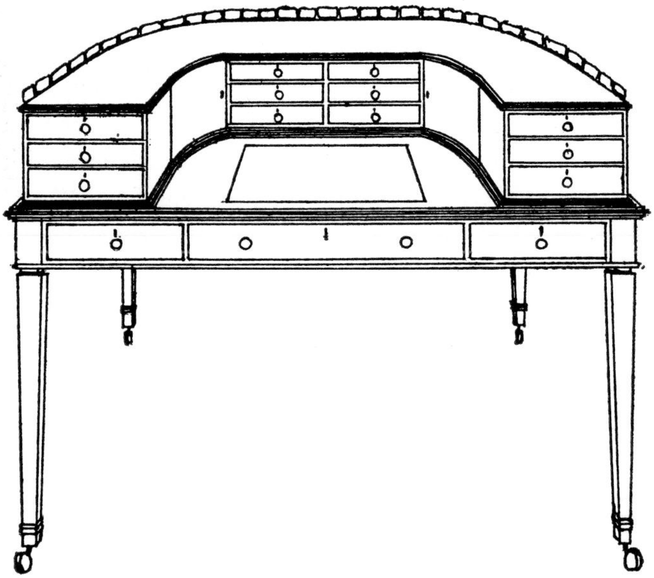

FIG. 16. A Carlton House table. Late 18th century

Dressing-tables were equally varied and elaborate. Most incorporated a swing mirror or looking-glass on a ratchet that folded away when not in use. One, called by Hepplewhite a 'Rudd's Table', had a swivelled mirror, the supports of which were attached to a quadrant, enabling it to be folded down into a drawer when not in use. Sliding boards that could be used as brushing slides or for writing were a common fitting and numerous small compartments for toilet requisites were concealed beneath them. Some dressing-tables incorporated a washstand, whilst others were designed as shaving-tables, with special compartments for a razor, soap, etc. There was great diversity of both form and size, although the tendency was towards compactness, despite the elaborate fittings (Plate 137).

CASE FURNITURE

Bookcases were frequently of mahogany, sometimes with an inlay of a lighter wood, in the form of banding or stringing. Many were in the traditional form established earlier in the century but with more intricate astragal glazing bars and the use of urns and Neo-Classical scrolls on a straight cornice, although the broken-scroll pediment was occasionally still used and was, in fact, illustrated by Sheraton. They were seldom of pronounced architectural form, however, and the lower stage was often considerably higher than formerly. Glazing bars of metal, gilded or painted in a light colour, were recommended by Hepplewhite and his designs for these are mostly of flowing curves. Sheraton illustrates a number of alternative designs for glazed doors, which are characteristically more intricate than Hepplewhite's. Occasionally a small looking-glass occupied a central position in each of the glazed doors. The feet of Hepplewhite's bookcases, like those of most of his case furniture, are mainly of plain bracket type but a common alternative was the French foot, a curving splay form, continuous with the serpentine lower edge of the case. The *Guide* includes three designs for a 'Desk and Bookcase', with a sloping front that lets down on lopers, above drawers and cupboards, and two designs for a 'Secretary and Bookcase', in which the lower stage projects with a flat top and the top drawer front falls down on a quadrant to form the writing surface (Plate 145). On a slightly larger scale is the 'Library Case', of which two break-front and two straight examples are shown. Shearer's designs are of a very similar type. Sheraton's, on the other hand, often show a tendency to over-decoration, together with a marked verticality. He particularly favours oval decorative devices on panels and the use of draperies or door panels framing pleated silk behind a brass trellis. Drawers fitted for writing were included in the designs of many bookcases.

Combined bureau-bookcases as well as bureau-cabinets were given a great diversity of form, some of them being quite low, although in two stages. Mahogany or satinwood or even a combination of the two were used, both inlay and painted decoration being employed, sometimes as an alternative to glazed doors on the upper stages. The cylinder front, in the form of a quadrant panel of wood, which slid into the interior (Plate 146), and the tambour front, composed of slats of wood, glued to linen or canvas to form a flexible shutter, were sometimes used. In some cases the withdrawal of the writing slide or top drawer operates a mechanism that causes the cylinder front to rise. Sheraton gives a diagram showing the construction.

China cabinets, though of similar form to bookcases, tended to be lighter in construction and were more often of satinwood than mahogany.

Wardrobes or clothes presses were generally rather plain but some were painted. The upper stage would have a central cupboard space with shelves, flanked by compartments for hanging clothes, and the lower stage would be fitted with drawers.

Hepplewhite illustrates several types of chests-of-drawers, including two designs for a 'Double Chest of Drawers' or tallboy. The short peg leg was commonly used on this item of furniture but the French foot, combined with a serpentine lower edge, was also employed. Occasionally the drawers were flanked by narrow cupboard sections. Both mahogany and satinwood were used and some examples were painted. Of similar form was the 'Commode Dressing Table', illustrated in the *Guide*, which was fitted with compartments for toilet requisites and an adjustable mirror in the top drawer (Plate 148).

Sheraton says that commodes were intended 'chiefly for ornament, to stand under a glass' but in fact they were usually fitted with drawers or with shelves behind doors in furniture of this style (Plate 149). The latter type would be intended for a drawing-room rather than a bedroom or dressing-room. They were made in various shapes but a semi-circular plan became particularly popular, this type usually being closed with a large central door. Sheraton illustrates one type where a curved central part is flanked by straight sections behind pairs of baluster legs. The tops were nearly always of marquetry or painted. A certain number were made in the French style, but even these were usually fitted with wooden, rather than marble, tops.

Night-tables consisted of small cupboards on straight legs, often fitted with a tambour front and, as Sheraton says in the *Drawing Book*, 'sometimes finished in satinwood and in a style a little elevated above their use.' Towards the end of the century some were designed in the form of bedside steps, Gillow's records for 1794 mentioning a 'Bed Step Night Table' supplied for £1. 19s. 9d., in which the sides and risers were filled with panels of cane.

Washstands were often of rather similar appearance to night-tables, having a top enclosed by hinged flaps and supplied with recesses for a basin and soap. They were also made in the form of corner cupboards, with folding tops, which, when opened, served to protect the walls from splashes (Plate 150). An open-frame type, with three or four supports, and recesses for a basin and soap at the top and for a jug at the base, was generally fitted with a small drawer halfway up.

MISCELLANEOUS

Candlestands might be of openwork construction or have a slender central shaft; the base could be circular or of tripod or four-legged type. Various types of legs were used, including a delicate cabriole, an outward-curving leg with a scroll foot and a 'claw' support, in which the curves of the cabriole were reversed, so that it met the floor at right-angles. Some candlestands were fitted with long scrolling branches of lacquered brass and all were of very light construction. Eight designs for 'Terms for Busts' are illustrated in the *Guide*, all of tapering columnar form. Another kind of stand in popular use had straight, splayed legs supporting a small fixed tray top, edged with a gallery, for standing a silver kettle on, and generally fitted with a small slide, which, as Hepplewhite explains, 'draws out to set the tea-pot on.' Plate 151 illustrates an urn stand of painted beech, of typically slender proportions, in which legs of curved shape have been used.

Plate 152 shows a stand for reading, intended for use in a library, of a type that became popular at this time. Hepplewhite gives examples of two similar 'Reading Desks' in the *Guide*, though they are fitted with the additional refinement of a telescopic extension to the central shaft.

Hanging shelves, intended for displaying porcelain or a few books, were fitted with two or three stages, and had ends of solid or fretwork design. A case containing open shelves and designed to stand against a pier between windows or in a recess, was also made, usually being supplied with a gallery round the top.

Looking-glass frames were designed in a lighter adaptation of the Adam style, much use being made of strings of husks surrounding the main frame. Many of the decorative details were made of lead or of composition on wire, enabling an effect of great delicacy to be achieved. The whole was painted and gilded. Hepplewhite states that square pier-glasses were more fashionable than oval ones and includes only three of the latter, as against eight rectangular ones in the *Guide*, although, in fact, both types were widely made. Wall-lights were similarly richly adorned with very delicate strings of husks and ribbons, mostly of composition which was also used for the applied ornament on picture frames.

Firescreens of both the pole and cheval forms were popular, the former being the more numerous. Some pole-screens were fitted with circular bases, weighted for stability, whilst others had a tripod base, with cabriole legs. Mahogany or satinwood were mostly employed in their construction and painted decoration was sometimes added. Panels were generally oval or shield-shaped, being of painted or gathered silk, needlework or paper with a printed or painted design usually protected with a sheet of glass. They were generally held in position by means of a brass ring with a wedge or screw but Sheraton describes a type in which a pulley with a weighted tassel passes through the hollow shaft, forming a counter-weight to the screen panel. He also claims to have invented a 'lyre-screen', which has a swivelled panel that can be turned to any angle. Describing a popular kind of cheval screen, Hepplewhite says, 'The screen slides in grooves in the inner side of the uprights, and is suspended by the weights, which are shown on the outside; and are connected to the screen by a line which passes over a pulley in the top of the frame.'

Some clock cases continued to be made in the long-established form, the only concession to the taste of the time being the addition of fashionable motifs, and in particular, inlaid paterae or fan-shapes. Sheraton shows two examples of long-case clocks in the *Drawing Book*, however, in which the traditional shape is modified and enriched with a considerable amount of inlaid or painted ornament. A new type of bracket clock, known as a 'balloon clock', appeared, in which the face is enclosed in a rounded case and joined by a waisted section to the base. This shape was even adopted for the hoods of some long-case clocks.

Knife-cases, which were widely used at this time, were of two types. The box type had a serpentine front and a deep lid, sloping downwards towards the front. It was usually of mahogany, sometimes ornamented with stringing lines or a patera in a light-coloured wood, and embellished with silver mounts, including (sometimes) small feet. Inside, the sloping surface was punched with holes just large enough for the insertion of knives, forks and spoons (Plate 154). The other type was shaped like a vase and cover; it was often of a light-coloured wood, such as satinwood, enriched with inlaid or painted decoration. Faceting, or its imitation in inlay, was often used on this type (Plate 153). The lid would be fixed to a central shaft and could be supported in an open position by a spring; the openings for cutlery were arranged concentrically round the shaft. An acorn or similar finial served as a handle at the top of the cover. These knife-cases stood at either end of the sideboard or on flanking pedestals.

X

THE REGENCY

The style known as 'Regency' was current for a much longer period than the years during which the Prince of Wales acted as Regent and is generally considered to have begun in about 1790 and continued until about 1830, when it merged into the Early Victorian style.

In 1796 Henry Holland, the architect and designer, sent his assistant, Thomas Tatham, to study archaeological remains in Rome and three years later Tatham published the first edition of a book entitled *Examples of Ancient Ornamental Architecture.* It provided the inspiration for much of the furniture Holland supplied in the new style about the turn of the century for Carlton House and for Southill Park, Bedfordshire.

Designs in the new Regency style also appear in Sheraton's *Cabinet Dictionary* of 1803 and his uncompleted *Encyclopaedia*, the first part of which appeared in 1805 (see page 105).

After 1800 there developed an intensified search for archaeological accuracy, in which Tatham's book played no small part. In this respect the new style was more uncompromising than the Neo-Classicism of the preceding period. A swing towards heavier designs also became apparent, in strong contrast to the delicate proportions of most late eighteenth-century furniture. New discoveries were still being made at Herculaneum and Pompeii and the early nineteenth-century designers were able to make exact copies of the furniture depicted on Greek vases and on bronzes and reliefs. Where no precedents for certain types of furniture could be found, close copies of forms and motifs from Classical ornament were incorporated into new designs. The leading figure in this antiquarian approach was Thomas Hope (1768–1831), a Classical scholar who had made extensive studies of archaeological remains and who owned a large collection of Greek, Roman and Egyptian antiquities. He was a friend of the French architect and designer Charles Percier; he also had antiquarian interests and published his influential *Receuil de Décorations Intérieurs* in 1812.

Hope designed interiors for his houses at Duchess Street, London, and Deepdene,

Surrey, as settings for his collections. In 1807 he published *Household Furniture and Interior Design*, a book containing designs for furniture based very closely on Greek, Roman and Egyptian originals. Typical of the cold, archaeological approach were the designs after the Greek *klismos* chair (Plate 155), the Roman cross-framed stool and the Egyptian sofa.

This was the first time Egyptian sources had been used in England, even the sphinx as used by the Neo-Classicists having been taken from the Greek version. Motifs in the Egyptian style were particularly popular in the first decade of the century. It was largely due to Napoleon's expedition to Syria and Egypt in 1798–1801, accompanied by the scholar Baron Denon, who in 1802 published a record of his trip through Lower and Upper Egypt, that contained many illustrations of Egyptian ornament. Such a style was used by Thomas Chippendale the Younger for furniture for Stourhead in 1804 and 1805.

The style that most consistently found favour during the Regency period was the Greek style. The buying of the Parthenon sculptures by public subscription in 1816 and the revolt of the Greeks against the Turks in 1821 both served to stimulate interest in Greek art and this was the most favoured style in the latter part of the period.

The Gothic style, however, had never entirely fallen out of fashion since its revival in the mid-eighteenth century, being kept alive particularly in architecture, and motifs from Gothic sources appear in many pieces of Regency furniture (Fig. 18). Also of native origin was the so-called 'Elizabethan' style.

A certain amount of furniture was designed in the Chinese manner. This renewed interest in Oriental forms was stimulated by the inclusion of a Chinese Drawing Room for the Prince of Wales at Carlton House and by the interiors of the Royal Pavilion, Brighton, that had been designed in a rather theatrical Chinese style in 1802 and between 1815 and 1821. These interiors contained a considerable amount of furniture made of bamboo, or beechwood painted to look like bamboo, as well as Chinese lacquer and japanning, with much use being made of embellishing dragons and Chinamen.

There were even isolated instances of a Rococo revival towards the end of the period, as in the set of chairs and sofas made by Gillow's for Tatton Park, Cheshire, but that style did not properly re-appear until a little later (see next chapter).

In 1808 the cabinetmaker and designer George Smith published *A Collection of Designs for Household Furniture and Interior Decoration*, containing 158 Plates in colour, which served to popularise, as well as to debase, the severe, scholarly style introduced by Hope. Although he was not justified in the claims he made as to correctness of detail, his book was very influential. A few Gothic and Chinese designs were included. 1826 saw the publication of Smith's second design book, *The Cabinet Maker's and Upholsterer's Guide, Drawing Book and Repository*, in which he mainly favoured Greek designs but also included Egyptian, Etruscan, Roman, French and Gothic examples. In the same year Peter and Michael Angelo Nicholson brought out a book with many designs in colour entitled *The Practical Cabinet Maker, Upholsterer and Complete Decorator*. A guide to the quickly-changing taste of the early nineteenth century was provided in the issues of *The Repository of the Arts*, published monthly by R. Ackermann between 1809 and 1828, each issue containing an article and coloured illustrations on currently fashionable furnishings.

Particularly in its later phases the Regency style was much influenced by the newly-rich middle classes and lacked the informed leadership of the upper classes that had obtained in the eighteenth century. There was a notable tendency towards weightiness of design, often combined with coarseness of detail, which foreshadowed developments of the Victorian period. In its use of animal supports, particularly on side-tables, as well as in the large scale of much of the ornament, furniture of the late Regency is sometimes reminiscent of the Palladian style.

Satinwood largely fell out of favour and was replaced in popularity by rosewood, which was widely used both in the solid and as a veneer, as well as being imitated by artificial graining on cheaper woods. Mahogany was still popular for dining-room and library furniture; calamander, amboyna and zebrawood were much sought after, though the last-named became rather scarce after about 1815. Plain unbroken surfaces showed off the rich grains of these woods to advantage. French polishing came into favour in the 1820s, giving a hard, glossy surface. By repeated applications of a solution of shellac dissolved in methylated spirits a glossy, protective finish was built up on the veneer. Carving and marquetry were little used, although there was a revival of the Boulle technique of tortoiseshell and brass marquetry generally known as 'Buhlwork'. The best-known maker of this type of furniture was a Frenchman named Louis le Gaigneur, who established a workshop in the Edgware Road in about 1815. Penwork became a popular form of decoration, the background being inked in so as to allow the design to stand out in the natural colour of the wood (Plate 172). Some furniture was lacquered to give the appearance of bronze, and the technique was often employed together with gilding.

An inlay of ebony, or ebonised wood, particularly in stringing lines, was a common form of decoration. Brass inlay also became very popular, in the form of stringing or of designs made up of anthemion, scrolls or floral forms. Two London cabinetmakers who specialised in this form of decoration were George Bullock and Thomas Parker. Brass was also much employed for mounts, particularly for beading, paw feet and the large studs or stars used for enriching seat-rails and friezes. Other ways in which brass was employed were for colonettes and scroll supports to shelves, for galleries and as a trellis, usually backed by pleated silk. Handles in the form of lion masks with brass rings in their mouths were often fitted; knob handles of brass or wood were also common for simpler pieces of furniture.

Classical motifs, such as the lion mask, anthemion, acanthus and acroter continued to be used, tending to be on a larger scale than formerly and having a distinctive early nineteenth-century flavour. The lion-headed monopodium was a striking feature employed as a support on many types of furniture. (Plates 158 and 160.) Terminal figures of both Greek and Egyptian type were used and the Egyptian sphinx was now added to the repertoire of ornament, where formerly only the Greek version had been used. Other Egyptian motifs included the palmette, the lotus and even, occasionally, the crocodile. Heavy paw feet were a popular terminal to both naturalistic and straight legs, whilst peg top feet were often used on case furniture – particularly that influenced by late eighteenth-century French models. Reeding was commoner than fluting, though spiral fluting was sometimes employed. Serpentine fluting, derived from antique sarcophagi, was occasionally used for flat surfaces. Case furniture was often embellished with colonettes or balusters recessed at the corners, in the French manner introduced by Holland. In later, more florid Regency designs the winged paw foot is much used. The Gothic style is represented by the use of arcading, tracery and finials.

From about 1800 drawers were generally constructed with a quarter-round bead attaching the sides to the base on the inside (Plate 169). At about the same time it became the custom for some of the larger firms, such as Gillow's, to stamp their furniture on the front edges of the drawers or the tops of cupboard doors. (During the present century these stamps have occasionally been removed by antique dealers who feared that, with such marks, the pieces would be taken for reproductions.)

In 1828 the first patent was taken out for coiled springs of iron or steel wire for use in upholstery.

Holland's assistant, Thomas Tatham (1763–1818), was for a number of years in partnership with William Marsh, the firm of Marsh and Tatham supplying a considerable amount of furniture for the Prince of Wales at Carlton House and for Southill Park, Bedfordshire. In 1809 he became the senior partner in the firm of Tatham and Bailey. Seddon's and Gillow's continued to flourish throughout the period.

SEATS AND BEDS

In the last decade of the eighteenth century a new kind of chair appeared which had a low back with a horizontal splat. Sheraton illustrated several chairs of the type in the *Cabinet Dictionary*, to the exclusion of earlier types. The uprights of the back scrolled over at the top, being linked by a top-rail of baluster form or sometimes with a painted panel of Classical figures. The arms curved upwards, meeting the uprights just below the junction with the top-rail. The legs were of baluster type, sometimes straight and reeded, but in many cases splayed out at the base. These chairs were usually of beech, painted black and decorated with gilding and other colours, and were fitted with a cane seat and squab cushion. After about 1805 many such light chairs were designed with the inclusion of a rope-moulding forming the top-rail or part of the uprights; they were commonly called Trafalgar chairs.

In the early years of the new century chair design tended to become more closely based on antique types and, in particular, on the Greek *klismos*, as exemplified by Thomas Hope. Plate 155 illustrates a chair based on a design of this type by Hope; it is painted in 'Etruscan' colours, terra-cotta on a black ground, the enormous curved back decorated with a frieze of Classical figures. A freer use of *klismos* form is seen in the mahogany chair with leopardskin seat illustrated in Plate 156; this chair, dating from about 1820, has the large-scale ornament typical of much Regency design executed in high quality carving. A much modified form of the curved back was frequently used during the Regency; it was usually attached to conventional uprights though extending beyond them.

The splayed, or narrow 'sabre' leg of the *klismos* was widely adopted, the front legs being given a concave curve. A continuous undulating line was often formed thereby, running from the front legs into the seat-rail and curving up into the uprights of the back. That was frequently decorated with fluting or a line of brass inlay. In the chair illustrated in Plate 157 this decoration consists of gilded fluting; the chair, which is a modification of the Trafalgar type, also shows the use of rope moulding and is embellished with brass mounts on the back.

The less scholarly approach of George Smith is exemplified in the chair illustrated in Plate 158, which has legs of the widely adopted lion monopodium form; the scrolling over of the back uprights should be noted, formed in this case by backward-facing lions' heads, as well as the use of stars to ornament the seat-rail. The wood is painted to look like bronze and partly gilded.

An important change in the arrangement of rooms that had begun to take place shortly before the end of the eighteenth century in more progressive households was that furniture, and particularly chairs, was informally placed and often grouped round the fireplace instead of being formally arranged round the walls. This had an important effect on the design of chairs, in that they were now frequently decorated at the back, which had not been the case in the previous century. The reversed lions' heads on the chair in Plate 158 conform to the new trend.

An armchair in the Gothic style is shown in Plate 159. It clearly shows the use of architectural forms to embellish a typically Regency shape. Of mahogany with gilded decoration, it was designed in 1823, probably by William Porden, for the Drawing Room of Eaton Hall, Cheshire.

Shortly before 1830 another native English style was drawn upon for chair designs. This was the so-called 'Elizabethan' style, although, in fact, based on the typical Charles

II chair with turned supports and cane panels. Such a chair is illustrated in Gillow's records for 1827, where it is called 'An Oak Antique Arm'd Chair with twisted back and front legs' and priced at £6. 15s. 10d.

The two 'Drawing Room Chairs' illustrated in Fig. 17 are of about the same date, and are taken from Peter and M. A. Nicholson's pattern book, *The Practical Cabinet Maker, Upholsterer and Complete Decorator*. They are typical of many chairs made in the late Regency period, with their rather large ornamental details, the one on the right having a curving top-rail with scrolled ends, derived from the *klismos* type, which became very popular.

FIG. 17. Peter and M. A. Nicholson. Design for two chairs from *The Practical Cabinet Maker, Upholsterer and Complete Decorator*, 1826

A short, stumpy, reeded baluster leg became widely used on seat furniture in the late Regency and legs in the form of a lotus or of cornucopiae also became quite common. A type of wooden arm in common use throughout the period was in the form of a large scroll that curled under, being jointed to the seat-rail at the sides.

Deep buttoning, with the buttons covered in the same material, instead of the formerly-used tassels of silk, became very popular. Brass nails for fastening upholstery went out of fashion, giving place to tacks, hidden under borders of gimp.

Settees of Grecian type, with the somewhat weak support of sabre legs, came into favour. These had outward-scrolling ends and a serpentine back, and were supplied with bolster cushions, but an alternative type, specially intended for reclining, and also adapted from the antique, had only one raised end, the back sloping down to the seat-rail. Sometimes a bolster cushion was fixed at the foot end of these sofas: see the example shown in Plate 160, which also shows the use of lion monopodia. Animal supports were quite often used, as in the case of a sofa at the Royal Pavilion, Brighton, made by John Marshall, which has silver crowned eagle supports.

The ottoman, introduced from Turkey at this time, consisted in its early form of a large, generously-upholstered, rectangular seat for several people, that was usually supplied with loose cushions. From this there evolved a circular type having a raised and padded centre support on which a number of people could sit, facing outwards.

A number of stools continued to be made, many of them closely based on Greek, Roman or Egyptian models. These were often of X-shape, like the example illustrated in Plate 161, and sometimes terminated in animal heads and paws. The junction of the X-form was often embellished with a lotus decoration. Low footstools were also made. The music-stool, with a revolving seat, adjustable for height, and sometimes fitted with a back, was an introduction of the early years of the century and Gillow's illustrate a typical example in their 1825 records.

TABLES

Tables possessing a central pillar support, generally with a tripod base and a round top, became very popular in the early nineteenth century. Plate 162 shows a table of the kind designed by Thomas Hope in 1807 after a Classical Greek model. It is of mahogany, inlaid with ebony and silver. Of the same type, but dating from about 1820 and generously embellished with ormolu mounts, is the table illustrated in Plate 163. It is veneered with coromandel wood and the top contains beneath a sheet of glass an engraving of the Wellington Shield commemorating the victories of the Duke of Wellington. The small table illustrated in Plate 170, which also has a central pedestal, dates from about 1810 and is of mahogany and rosewood with mother-of-pearl inlay and brass mounts. Its heavy scroll legs, carved with acanthus, are a typical Regency form. Many occasional tables were designed in this pedestal form, as well as those known as loo tables, designed for the card game of lanterloo. In general, fewer tables were made specifically for card-playing but they were designed in numerous forms.

Some occasional tables were made in sets of four known as quartetto tables, being graduated in size so that they fitted within one another in 'nests'. Of slender proportions, they had four turned baluster legs, the end pairs resting on supports with splayed feet.

Another new introduction was the sofa table, a long, narrow table designed to stand in front of a sofa, where it might serve numerous purposes. It was generally supported at the ends by slabs or lyre-forms but examples were also made in which four splayed legs supported a platform, from which rose a central pedestal. An example of this type is illustrated in Plate 164, fitted with end flaps and brass paw feet and inlaid with brass ornament. Plate 165 shows an unusual square pianoforte in the form of a sofa table, made by Broadwood and Sons in 1801. Also basically in the form of a sofa table is the 'Dressing Table', after a design by George Smith of 1805 (Plate 166). It is of mahogany, with stringing and stars inlaid in ebony and the end supports are derived from the sarcophagus; the drawers, which have no handles, are released by springs underneath. Dressing-tables with swivelled mirrors attached were made, too, a popular support for each side of the glass being a lyre.

Dining-tables mostly consisted of a series of 'pillar and claw' tables, i.e. tables with a central pillar supported on four curved legs, terminating in paw feet of brass or carved wood, resting on brass castors. Between each of the 'pillar and claw' sections a flap could be inserted and fixed with a metal strap so that the size of the table could be altered at will.

Typical side-tables of the Regency period were rectangular with supports in the form of Egyptian terms, lion monopodia or other animal supports – some of the latter, in their massiveness, strongly recalling the Palladian style. Mahogany or rosewood were usual, often with an inlay of ebony or brass.

Sideboards continued to be made either with legs or standing on pedestals; the latter type were frequently surmounted by knife-boxes, either tapered or in the shape of an urn. Mahogany or rosewood were customary, often with brass inlay and a brass rail at the back. Lion paw feet were particularly favoured for this item of furniture, and they were sometimes used even with the pedestal type (Plate 167); lion-mask handles were often used for the drawers.

As with other tables of the period, there was great diversity in the form of library tables. The traditional form, on pedestals, was still made but entirely new types were introduced, round or hexagonal, having central supports or monopodium legs, whilst other library or writing tables were of simple, rectangular shape, on turned legs, with frieze drawers (Plate 168). The circular type was sometimes made deep enough to contain rows of books in the frieze, in which case it would be called a drum table; this name was also applied to a similar type which had drawers in the frieze.

Work-tables were made with supports of 'pillar and claw' type, with end supports, especially in the form of lyres, or with four turned legs. Some incorporated a sliding panel in the back to serve as a firescreen, some were combined work- and games-tables containing chess and backgammon boards, and most were fitted with a silk work-bag suspended below them. Decoration was as varied as design and they might be made of rosewood, mahogany or satinwood, inlaid with ebony or brass, or japanned. One type,

A new introduction was the Canterbury, a small stand, usually of mahogany, for holding cutlery and plates. One end would contain three divisions, for cutlery, and the other would be rounded, to fit the plates, and enclosed within a wooden gallery with balusters; it was fitted with castors so that it could be wheeled to the table. Somewhat confusingly, the name was shortly after applied to a stand for sheet music or books, too.

A small stand consisting of three or more shelves, supported by slender balusters at the corners, and known as a what-not, appeared at this period. Sometimes the shelves were fitted with brass galleries and occasionally small drawers were included in the design. The example illustrated in Plate 174 is of rosewood.

The teapoy was a small stand on a pillar and claw support designed to contain tea caddies or jars (Plate 175). They were often highly decorative and richly inlaid with various woods.

The typical Regency convex mirror was introduced from France at about the turn of the century. These looking-glasses are generally characterised by their broad circular frames of gilded wood, having a cavetto moulding embellished with balls – often surmounted by an eagle and acanthus leaves. Some were very large, totalling about eight feet to the top of the cresting.

The other notable development in looking-glasses was that of the horizontal overmantel mirror, which commonly consisted of a large central pane of glass flanked by two smaller ones. It was set in a gilded wooden frame, with a broad frieze along the top, decorated with Classical figures. Pier-glasses often reached enormous proportions, the frames of many later examples being elaborately carved with large-scale ornament. The cheval glass retained its popularity; it was supported on various forms of splay leg, sometimes with brass paw feet.

Wall-lights and girandoles of gilded wood were frequently surmounted by an eagle. Serpentine candle branches made of glass, embellished with glass drops and strings of glass beads, became fashionable for wall-lights or lustres. In chandeliers, the tendency was for these strings of glass drops to be arranged in long, flowing lines. Oil lamps were mostly based on Classical forms and stood on pedestal bases.

The tripod pole-screen now acquired a solid base of Classical type, resting on paw feet. An alternative to the normal screen panel was a cross-bar from which was suspended a small banner of velvet with tassels.

Clock cases were decorated with motifs from the same diverse sources as other furniture, and various types were often included in the same design. Gothic motifs were specially favoured, the tops of the cases being in the shape of a pointed arch.

The first
lished du
sis placed
Machiner
veneer wa
was chiefl
increasing
their chea
Gillow an
and Mansf
Furnitu
beauty, w
styles was
of furnitu
current. T
and the G
Regency m
dining-roo
ting featur
simply des
the period
the mid-ei
handed way
was especia
a very grea
lot of furni
cut up and

G. MAHOGANY BOOKCASE, inlaid with ebony. Based on a design in Sheraton's *Encyclopaedia*, 1805. The busts, of painted plaster, represent Charles James Fox, William Pitt, Admiral Nelson and Admiral Duncan. Two of them are dated 1809. Height 8 ft. 4 in.
Victoria and Albert Museum. Copyright Fratelli Fabbri, Milan. *See page 126*

of this trade in his *Encyclopaedia of Cottage, Farm and Villa Architecture*, first published in 1833. A variation on the Elizabethan style was drawn from the furniture of the Italian Renaissance or of François I. The Gothic style continued to flourish, sometimes in the archaeological manner established during the Regency but more frequently with the carving applied to typical Victorian shapes. An attempt was made to improve standards by the architect A. W. N. Pugin, whose furniture, inspired by Gothic forms, was of sound and appropriate construction and detailing, the ornament appearing to 'grow' from it rather than to be arbitrarily imposed upon it (Plates 180 and 189). He published a book of designs, entitled *Gothic Furniture*, in 1835, and a considerable quantity of furniture in this simplified Gothic form was produced by the firm of J. G. Crace and Sons in the late 1840s and 1850s. It had a beneficial effect on the furniture trade in general. Well into the last quarter of the century, Gillow's produced what they called 'New Palace Westminster' (or 'N.P.W.'), which was largely inspired by the furniture designed for the new Houses of Parliament by Pugin and made by Crace and Sons.

A considerable amount of furniture, however, chairs and sofas in particular, was not based on historical styles, the designs being largely determined by considerations of comfort: a notable example of this was the admirably functional balloon-back chair (Fig. 19). The great importance placed on comfort resulted in the rather bulbous shapes and blurred outlines caused by very thick upholstery. Such rounded shapes, though, were not restricted to seat furniture; many other pieces such as sideboards were given elaborate, curvilinear shapes that sometimes had the appearance of being moulded rather than carved. Together with this lack of charply defined outlines, there was often a merging of separate parts into one another.

As the Rococo style waned in popularity a new type of carved decoration was evolved that satisfied the Victorians' love of elaborate detail. Known by the descriptive name of 'naturalistic' carving, it was particularly developed in centres in Warwickshire, on Tyneside and at Bath. This type of carving reached its peak in the portrayal of scenes from the chase and historical scenes, incorporated in the designs of a number of sideboards; many pieces appeared to exist chiefly in order to display the life-like creations of the carver's skill (Plate 188).

From 1845 to 1849 there were annual exhibitions of decorative arts held in London by the Society of Arts, and in the following years there were a number of important international exhibitions, all of which had a great influence on furniture design. The fine examples of craftsmanship, if not of design, that were exhibited, although not typical of general production in that they were far larger and more elaborately ornamented, nevertheless accurately portray the taste of the time. The first major international exhibition was held in London in 1851 and showed only too plainly the poverty of design in this country, in contrast to the material prosperity, the enormous over-decorated exhibits representing Victorian taste at its worst. The influence of the French exhibits there contributed to a slight improvement that was noticeable in ensuing years. That took the form of a move towards simplicity of line and away from the Rococo, which was always a dangerous influence for the Victorians. A more architectural form now became possible, and a tendency to confine ornament within panels, instead of allowing it to flow over the outlines. Elaborate pieces were still produced, however, many embellished with large carved figures and surmounted by tall mirrors. A gold medal was awarded for a typical exhibition piece of this type, made by Jackson and Graham for the Paris Exhibition of 1855; it took the form of a cabinet with an enormous looking-glass, embellished with large gilded figures, inlaid marbles, porcelain plaques and ormolu mounts.

Professional designers were almost unknown in the Early Victorian period, notable exceptions being Robert Bridgens, who published a pattern book entitled *Furniture with Candelabra and Decoration* in 1838, and A. W. N. Pugin; but a few people, such as the architect Philip Webb, and Ford Maddox-Brown, the Pre-Raphaelite painter, had already in the 1850s designed a few simple pieces of furniture in solid wood without veneer that were very advanced for their day.

As to decoration in the Early Victorian period, the main development was that carved ornament, inlay and marquetry went out of fashion – not to return until well into the 1850s. Oak, mahogany, rosewood and walnut were the most widely used woods, oak being especially favoured for historical styles. Painted decoration was no longer popular, except when used on papier-mâché or cast iron. A fresh approach to design was initiated by the development of a new technique of bending beech under the application of steam. Examples of this bentwood furniture were exhibited at the 1851 Exhibition by its inventor, Michael Thonet of Vienna, and chairs made by the process soon became very much in demand in this country, having the advantages of cheapness and strength. The process was adopted by other makers but the genuine Thonet products can be identified by the firm's label.

A number of new materials were employed as a result of the search for novelty and for methods of cheap mass-production. One of the most important was papier-mâché, which had been used in the eighteenth century for trays and small decorative objects but was now employed for the first time for furniture of various kinds (Plates 182 and 186). A certain amount of strengthening with rods of iron within the papier-mâché was necessary for articles that were subjected to considerable stress, such as chairs and tables; alternatively, wood japanned to resemble papier-mâché was used for the structural parts. It was usually painted black, given a high gloss and painted with brightly-coloured flowers; sometimes a coloured print, varnished over, would be inset in the papier-mâché. Mother-of-pearl and coloured glass imitating gems were also used to decorate these articles. The greatest producers of this type of furniture were the firm of Jennens and Bettridge of Birmingham. Gutta-percha was occasionally used for furniture and even coal was employed for at least one chair, though that was probably intended purely for exhibition purposes. Hall and garden furniture were frequently made of cast iron, (Plate 195) which was commonly painted black or grained to look like wood. Marble became widely used for the tops of such items as sideboards and washstands and was also used for tables from time to time; marbled slate was a cheaper substitute, periodically used for table tops. Composition, sometimes on a wire core, was used, as it had been in the previous century, for applied decoration. Brass inlay on a ground of red or green tortoiseshell in the manner of A. C. Boulle was popular, above all for cabinets and on writing-tables in Louis XIV style.

Machine-made screws with gimlet-pointed tips came into general use about the middle of the century.

SEATS AND BEDS

The Greek style was particularly favoured for dining-rooms, libraries and other rooms that were considered to have masculine connotations. (Bedrooms and drawing-rooms were thought of as more the province of the ladies.) Henry Whittaker chose this style when he designed chairs for the Conservative Club in 1844, as Philip Hardwicke had done ten years earlier for the Court Room and Court Dining-Room at the Goldsmiths' Hall. The style became much modified during the Early Victorian period but many dining-room chairs retained the broad, curved top-rail of *klismos* origin that sometimes terminated at each end with a volute.

The back with a broad, curved top-rail soon gave way to a completely new type, evolved by intermediate stages from it: it had a rounded shape in which the uprights merged into the top-rail without a break, the horizontal splat forming the lower edge of the curve. This type, which soon acquired the descriptive name of 'balloon-back', was very comfortable and quickly became popular not only for dining-rooms but also for drawing-rooms, whilst a lighter version was made for bedrooms of painted beech or birch, with a cane seat and double side stretchers (Fig. 19). A prototype of the balloon-back appears in Gillow's records as early as 1827. The earlier examples had straight, turned legs, sometimes splayed at the bottom, but from the middle of the century cabriole legs were often introduced, on bedroom and drawing-room chairs especially. The balloon-back retained its popularity throughout the century, even after the introduction of numerous other fashionable designs.

Another new shape appeared for a low library chair: the back and arms were in the form of a continuous, upholstered semi-circle. In early types, dating from the 1840s, this was only supported in the middle but by 1860 there was generally a line of balusters right round the semi-circle.

The Rococo style which had been revived in the late Regency period was frequently used for drawing-room and bedroom chairs, the delicacy of the elaborately carved, and often gilded, style being considered appropriate in these essentially 'feminine' rooms. Plate 178 illustrates one of the so-called 'fly' chairs designed by Hardwicke in 1834 for a room at the Goldsmiths' Hall to which ladies would be admitted. In the mid-nineteenth century many chairs were based on the Louis XV style but carving of Rococo type was also applied to chairs that were based on no particular historical style.

FIG. 19. Early Victorian bedroom chair with balloon-back

The Gothic style continued to hold interest, particularly for halls and libraries, sometimes appearing as no more than carved decoration, while in other examples it was given a far more imaginative treatment. Some excellent chairs of this type were designed by A. W. N. Pugin. Plate 180 shows one of the armchairs, of oak, upholstered in imitation leather, designed by him in about 1840 for Scarisbricke Hall, Lancashire. An outstanding example of Early Victorian design, it is neither an imitation of a medieval chair nor an ordinary Victorian shape embellished with Gothic motifs, but, rather, a completely original conception in which Gothic forms are incorporated.

Interiors based on the Elizabethan style became popular in the 1830s, the general shape of chairs and the motifs used, however, following the Charles II type though the seat and back panels were generally upholstered, usually with velvet or Berlin woolwork (Plate 179). Most examples were smaller than their seventeenth century prototypes. They retained their popularity throughout the period. There was also a revival of a folding chair of a type current in the Elizabethan period (Plate 15), and Gillow's records for 1840 refer to one as an 'Oak Glastonbury Monks Chair'.

The oval-backed armchair of the Louis XVI period served as a model for the Early Victorians, too, periodically being modified by the use of cabriole legs.

Until the middle of the century upholstery was mostly very thick and was held in place by means of deep buttoning that emphasised the rounded shape of most upholstered furniture. The framework was usually completely hidden under deep padding, and the buttons were evenly spaced and covered with the same material. The widespread use of coiled springs also contributed to the bulky appearance of the upholstery and long fringes attached to seat-rails further served to conceal the shape. Berlin woolwork in brightly-coloured silks became very fashionable and loose printed chintz covers were widely used as well. Large armchairs and sofas were sometimes upholstered with Oriental carpet. A great deal of shoddily made furniture was produced in small workshops by sweated labour, such materials as hay or wood shavings being used to stuff chair seats. Chair covers were in general fastened with tacks hidden under an edging of machine-made gimp.

From about 1850 the upholstery was so applied that the wooden framework appeared as a surround to it, becoming available for carved decoration. One chair of the kind that became very popular had a high, rounded and waisted back (sometimes called a spoon back) and short legs, often of cabriole form (Plate 183). At the same time, wooden arms with small pads came into favour and a little openwork carving or fret-work was often introduced. A particularly elaborate example of an armchair with these features is shown in Plate 181. This was designed and made for the 1851 Exhibition by Henry Eyles of Bath and incorporates a portrait of the Prince Consort in the back. It also shows the revival of marquetry decoration.

Another low-seated, upholstered chair without arms was characterised by a continuous serpentine line running from the back, through the seat-rail, into the front legs. These chairs, developed from a lighter type of Regency design, are known by some as 'Spanish' or 'fireside' chairs, though the names may not be contemporary.

The prie-dieu, or devotional chair, used for family prayers, had a low seat, too, combined with a tall back surmounted by a wide, padded top-rail on which the elbows could be rested when kneeling. The small square seat rested on short turned or cabriole legs. It was frequently upholstered in gros-point needlework or Berlin woolwork.

A large variety of chairs were designed for dining-rooms and drawing-rooms from the middle of the century, in which padded panels were set within a separate outer wooden frame.

Papier-mâché chairs were made in a wide variety of designs, some being based on historical styles, such as the 'Elizabethan', but others exploiting the possibilities offered by this moulded material. Plate 182 illustrates a chair in which an entirely new shape has been created that would scarcely have been possible in wood. It is painted in various colours on a glossy black ground and inlaid with mother-of-pearl.

A completely new shape was also made possible by the use of the technique of heating moist beechwood. Mass-produced bentwood chairs that were both cheap and strong soon became most popular in England, particularly for shops and restaurants. For such use, seats of serviceable plywood were usual but chairs made for the home were mostly cane-seated.

Large numbers of Windsor chairs were made, many by mass-production methods. These included not only the traditional hoop-back type but also a nineteenth century version with a flat, curved top-rail and sometimes shaped laths instead of spindles.

A new kind of rocking-chair appeared in the mid-nineteenth century, superseding the earlier type where rockers were attached to an ordinary chair. Made of bentwood or strips of brass or steel, these rocking-chairs were of a remarkably advanced and functional design, in which the rockers were carried on up into the arms and the back in one continuous serpentine curve; they were completely devoid of period ornament.

Hall seats, chiefly of oak or mahogany, were based on various historical styles, Gothic and Elizabethan being particularly favoured. Plate 184 shows an Early Victorian oak hall chair based on a type of writing chair that was common about 1730. This is closely similar to a design in Gillow's records for 1827, inscribed 'A Yew Tree claw with circular seat £5. 15. 0.'.

The type of sofa very common about 1830, and of Classical inspiration, that had a straight back and arms was soon replaced in popularity by the curvilinear type covered in deep, buttoned upholstery in which the back and arms merged in a continuous serpentine line. One type, known as a 'Sociable Sofa', had high rounded corners at the back that enabled two people to partly recline in opposite corners for conversation. Another innovation was the 'tête-à-tête', which had two chairlike end sections facing inwards and a small table or stand on a central support rising from the upholstery in the middle; the ends were sometimes made to swivel. A design for a similar piece, inscribed 'Conversational Sofa', is illustrated in Fig. 20; in the Gothic style, with some of its ornament apparently inspired by Pugin's chair (Plate 180), it was designed by L. N. Cottingham for Snelston Hall, Derbyshire, in 1842. Gillow's produced their own version of this item of furniture which they called a 'Medleycott'. Plate 186 illustrates a sofa of papier-mâché, where the influence of both the Louis XV and Louis XVI styles can be seen.

The ottoman was a round or rectangular seat for several people with a central padded back, its framework usually being completely concealed by the upholstery and fringes in the Early Victorian period. On some examples the seats were divided up with arms, forming individual sections, and occasionally a jardinière surmounted the back.

Many stools and footstools were designed to match a set of chairs in the traditional

FIG. 20. A 'Conversational Sofa', designed by L. N. Cottingham for Snelston Hall, Derbyshire, in 1842

way. A new introduction, however, was the hour-glass stool, in which a circular top and base were linked by a covering of pleated material, drawn together in the middle so as to resemble the shape of an hour-glass.

Four-poster bedsteads, where the bed could be completely enclosed by the curtains, were in general use in the early years of Victoria's reign but soon declined in popularity when the 'French' bed became fashionable in which the hangings were draped from a pole projecting from the wall at right-angles to the bed. The half-tester also became favoured, some being made so that the hangings could be pulled right round, enclosing the upper end of the bed. Cast iron bedsteads were common by the middle of the century and a considerable number of brass beds were made, mainly in Birmingham.

TABLES

The central pedestal table of Classical origin, popularised during the Regency, was perpetuated in many variations in the following decades for use as dining-, occasional-

and loo-table. The basic form of the tripod supporting the pedestal was often retained, though generally elaborated, but on occasion a circular base on paw feet was substituted. Another common form of table with central support had four splayed legs upholding a platform, from which rose four turned balusters. Card-tables were usually constructed in a similar fashion, with either a central pedestal or balusters rising from the platform. The simplest type were rectangular when closed; when opened they were swivelled through ninety degrees so that the opened flap rested on one half of the frame which contained a large compartment where cards and games could be stored. Tables with smaller tops, marked out for chess, were similarly constructed.

The chess-table shown in Plate 185 has a top of papier-mâché, inlaid with mother-of-pearl and enriched with painting and gilding. The tripod stand is of wood, with gilded ornament on a black ground. Some small tables were wholly made of papier-mâché, embedded with metal rods for strength.

Occasional tables were made in great numbers and were specially useful for displaying the ornaments, photographs and other bric-à-brac so beloved of the Victorians. Round and octagonal ones with central supports were much favoured and the form of the Regency sofa table with end supports also persisted.

Dining-tables were generally made with thick, turned legs, often reeded or carved in the Elizabethan or Jacobean style. They were frequently extensible by the insertion of additional leaves. Historical styles were popular for hall tables, too, Elizabethan, Gothic and Grecian all being in vogue.

Small gate-leg tables were in fashion for serving afternoon tea. Many with two gate-legs had a very narrow central section, so that when the flaps were down they would take up little room against the wall.

Another type of extensible dining-table invented at the time was known as a 'capstan table'. The circular top was divided into segments that could be withdrawn to increase the diameter, additional sections being inserted into the resulting gaps.

Work-tables with a cloth bag suspended from the top were mostly round or octagonal, with end supports either in the manner of a sofa table, or of the baluster and platform type.

A much-liked type of writing table was designed in the Louis XIV style and decorated with Boulle marquetry of brass and tortoiseshell. The pedestal type was generally of mahogany. End supports might be employed instead of pedestals or legs and oval or kidney-shapes were occasionally used.

The sideboard was an important item, now being esteemed more for its own decorative appearance than as a place to display plate. Most of the earlier examples continued the Regency tradition of two pedestal supports with a space for a wine cooler between them but this was soon superseded by a new type where cupboards filled the entire lower part. A horizontal looking-glass was usually provided at the back and the whole design given generous curves embellished with Rococo carving, all angularities being rounded off (Plate 187). After 1850 a semi-circular plan became common. Many sideboards were designed in the Elizabethan style with strapwork ornament; others were constructed from old bits of sixteenth and seventeenth century furniture comprising carved frames and drawers and turned supports.

The sideboard was an ideal subject for a display of the skills of the naturalistic school of carvers. The Victorians' love of a story, well-known from their paintings, is expressed in these sideboards in carvings of the chase or of scenes from history or literature. Plate 188 shows a sideboard carved by Gerrard Robinson of the Newcastle School of carvers depicting Robinson Crusoe and forming part of a suite of furniture made in 1857, each item of which is similarly decorated.

More practical than the sideboard was the side-table, fitted with two or more shelves in the manner of the sixteenth century court cupboard, that was often used in the dining-room for putting plates on during the serving of meals. Of similar construction was a movable dumb-waiter or dinner-wagon on wheels. The dumb-waiter shown in Plate 194 is based on the traditional eighteenth century type but the proportions, especially of the legs with their heavy carved scrolls and paw feet are typical of the Early Victorian period.

Not unlike the sideboard and frequently used as a substitute for it in smaller rooms was the chiffonier. One or more shelves were supported on brackets or balusters above the cupboard section, which was often curved in plan and flanked by open shelves. Some were made of papier-mâché.

Small tables, known as 'scrap' tables, whose tops were inlaid with pieces of different coloured marbles were popular in Early Victorian times. A considerable industry grew up in Derbyshire producing these tables, as well as vases and other ornamental pieces, from the local spars and marbles. At first mainly irregular pieces of marble were employed but in many later examples quite elaborate designs were executed, mainly of foliage and fruit. In the table shown in Plate 177, that is dated 1839 and forms part of the contents of Osterley Park, an attempt has been made to blend with Adam's interiors at that house, the marble in this instance having been collected in Italy.

CASE FURNITURE

Case furniture in the Early Victorian period largely continued to be made in the tradition established during the Regency, and was based on the usual historical styles. The very elaborate pieces made for exhibitions from the 1840s onwards were influential in causing a general increase in ornament and in size. Plate 189 shows a high quality cabinet in the Gothic style designed by Pugin for the Great Exhibition of 1851 and made by Crace and Sons.

A low cabinet with glass doors and shelves for displaying china became common in the mid-century. It often had glazed, quadrant-shaped doors at either end and was decorated with brass inlay or Boulle marquetry.

Of similar height and proportions was the dwarf-bookcase, fitted with open shelves or doors with glazed or brass trellis panels. The larger ones were mostly of break-front type. In tall bookcases of traditional form a middle stage was sometimes fitted with a drawer, the front of which let down on brass quadrants to form a writing surface – with the usual arrangement of drawers and compartments behind.

Various kinds of cupboards, like sideboards, were frequently made up from old bits of carved wood of Elizabethan or Jacobean origin.

The small, pedestal writing-desk known as a Davenport, introduced during the Regency, became widely used. In some the sloping top could be opened to reveal small drawers inside and a drawer at the front was fitted with a writing surface; further drawers and pigeon-holes rose from the top. Hidden drawers and compartments might be revealed by means of spring catches.

The chest-of-drawers was generally made in the traditional form, with two or three long drawers below two short ones, but a taller and narrower type was introduced where the drawers, all of equal width, increased in depth towards the bottom. Handles were mostly of the large round wooden knob type. Some examples stood on a solid plinth, whilst others had short turned legs.

Night-tables might be made to look like a small version of the chest-of-drawers; another type was in the form of a small pedestal cupboard, sometimes fitted with a marble top (Plate 191). 'Bed Step Night Tables' were still in production and were mentioned in Gillow's records for 1850. The euphemism 'night commode' was adopted at this time.

MISCELLANEOUS

Plate-glass was invented in 1839 by a man named James Chance. It caused a noticeable effect not only in windows but also in looking-glasses. Moreover, a new chemical method of silvering was discovered in the following year. These discoveries led to a reduction in the cost of making large mirrors that meant greater use of them for walls as well as in cabinets and sideboards. With the tendency for bay windows to be used in place of tall narrow windows, the pier-glass as such largely went out of fashion though tall mirrors were used on other walls and over the fireplace. Smaller rooms were generally furnished with a horizontal overmantel mirror, framed in gilded wood or papier-mâché.

Screens of both cheval and tripod type were popular, many being fitted with panels of embroidery or Berlin woolwork. They were made in a variety of styles, including

Elizabethan and Gothic, but Rococo ornament with naturalistic details was particularly favoured in the Early Victorian period. Plate 192 shows a gilded cheval screen of this type fitted with a panel of silk embroidered in various colours. A screen in the Elizabethan style, the panel painted with a Romantic landscape, is shown in Plate 193. The frame, which is ornamented with strapwork, is painted and gilt and inset with coloured stones.

The name 'Canterbury' that was used in the Regency for a stand for cutlery and plates, usually referred in the Victorian period to a small, rectangular stand, perhaps fitted with a drawer, above which were vertical compartments for holding sheet music or books. Some of them were made of papier-mâché. The name was used for a music stool fitted with a compartment for music sheets below the seat as well.

Another Regency introduction, the what-not, increased in popularity, being ideal for the display of small objects. At first it was similar to the Regency type, having three or more shelves supported by baluster legs at the corners, and fitted with castors. But in about 1855 a triangular version was introduced that was designed to stand in a corner.

The hat stand was an important item in the hall of the smaller Victorian house. Usually it consisted of a wooden post with branches for hats and coats, and a frame for umbrellas and sticks, that rested in a metal tray at the bottom. More elaborate examples were also produced incorporating a table and a seat, the hooks for hats and coats flanking a mirror set in the back. Many were also made of elaborately shaped cast-iron (Plate 195).

Long-case clocks, specially popular for halls, were mostly of oak or mahogany, and many of them were carved with Elizabethan or Gothic ornament.

XII

LATE VICTORIAN AND EARLY TWENTIETH CENTURY

1860 to 1914

In the second half of the nineteenth century there was an increasing reaction against the elaborate designs that were still being produced and the period is characterised by its reformist movements, mostly led by architect-designers, all of which had some effect on the general furniture trade. Another important aspect of the period was the growth in the number of large firms, particularly from the 1880s on, and the considerable export trade that was developing. The reformist firm founded in 1861 by William Morris as Morris, Marshall, Faulkner and Co., and re-formed four years later as Morris and Co., was active until the end of the century, its chief designer for most of the time being Philip Webb (1831–1915). A great deal of well-designed furniture was produced by it but Morris's approach was in some ways unrealistic as he blamed bad design on the use of machines and tried to put the clock back by returning to the making of furniture by hand. Naturally this conflicted with his intention of producing large quantities of well-designed furniture at a low price. The firm's early productions were very plain, with large flat areas for narrative painting, several pieces of the kind being exhibited at the 1862 Exhibition in London. These simply-shaped pieces, contrasting so strongly with the contorted and elaborately carved forms of much contemporary furniture, were in many cases decorated with paintings in the medieval tradition by Morris himself, by Burne-Jones or by other Pre-Raphaelite painters (Plate 210). Inevitably, such furniture was expensive, as indeed were some of the later pieces, on which fine quality marquetry was used. Throughout their existence, however, the firm also turned out considerable quantities of reasonably-priced furniture such as their rush-seated chairs selling at five shillings (Plate 196). The firm attempted to live up to Morris's ideal – 'Have nothing in your home that you do not know to be useful or believe to be beautiful' – and undoubtedly had a beneficial effect on design in general. In 1890 they bought the Pimlico workshop of Holland and Sons, by which time they had to give in to the necessity of using machinery. Their chief designer during these later years was George Jack (1855–1932), a pupil of Webb.

Two architects, William Burges (1827–1881) and Norman Shaw (1831–1912), were among the first to design furniture in a style that foreshadowed the work of the so-called 'Aesthetic Movement'. Burges's furniture, the first examples of which he exhibited in 1862, consisted basically of rectangular shapes, but most of it was generously embellished with Gothic architectural forms, as well as being painted and gilded, and containing panels of medieval scenes. Shaw made great use of turned balusters and shelves (Plate 206), features that were to be widely adopted on a somewhat smaller scale in the following years; he also made use of painted decoration in small panels.

The 'Early English' or 'Modern English Gothic' style that began in the late 1860s and remained in fashion right through the eighties, derived much of its inspiration from the work of Morris, Burges and Shaw. One of its leading exponents was the architect Charles Lock Eastlake (1836–1906), who in 1868 published *Hints on Household Taste*, a book of designs for furniture constructed in the medieval manner, of solid wood, pegged without glue. This book advocated what was considered to be honest construction and a discriminating use of Gothic forms, and it achieved wide circulation. 'Early English' pieces were large and heavy and formed of straight, rather than curved, lines with architecturally-inspired ornament. A feature of this type of furniture was the use of narrow boards, vertical or at an angle of forty-five degrees, for filling in panels. It differed from the medieval practice on which it was based in that the slats were all exactly the same size. Also very characteristic were numerous shelves and brackets supported by small balusters. Another influential designer working in the style was Bruce Talbert (1838–1881) (Plate 198), who designed for some of the leading firms such as Holland and Sons, Collinson and Locke and Jackson and Graham. His *Gothic Forms Applied to Furniture*, published in 1867–8, was followed by a second book in 1876, *Examples of Ancient and Modern Furniture*, that contained designs with a strong Jacobean flavour. Unpolished oak was used for much of the furniture based on the work of these designers.

The architect, T. E. Collcutt, carried the style a stage further, giving his furniture a lighter and more highly finished appearance with ebonised wood, often partly gilded, the numerous balusters being ornamented with incised rings. His designs became well-known through the publication of his catalogue in 1872. This style was widely adopted for overmantels as well as case furniture.

In the 1880s furniture with a Japanese flavour came into vogue. Burges, who was one of the early collectors of Japanese wood-block prints, had occasionally used Japanese motifs in some of his furniture but it was his friend, E. W. Godwin (1833–1886), who was responsible for the widespread popularity of the Japanese style. He designed a great deal of furniture both for individuals and for the general trade (including Gillow's, who made Japanese furniture for stock, Collinson and Locke, William Watt and W. & A. Smee), which, though inspired by Japanese furniture, was in fact highly original (Plates 199 and 207). It was characterised by lightness and elegance, with a marked emphasis on openwork verticals and horizontals. Many pieces were inset with panels of carved boxwood or embossed leather. Another leading designer in this style was Christopher Dresser (1834–1904). The general trade quickly took up the fashion though their products were usually much diluted versions of Godwin's designs, pseudo-Oriental motifs often being applied to ordinary European forms. Some of Godwin's work was inspired by Greek and Gothic sources, too.

As a consequence of the emphasis placed by Morris on handcraftsmanship a number of groups of designers and craftsmen were set up, working together in what they termed 'guilds', a revival of a medieval idea; under the system a number of craftsmen would work together on one piece of furniture. This development became known as the Arts and Crafts Movement and was of great importance during the last twenty years of the century. The Arts and Crafts Exhibition Society held many exhibitions in London, beginning in 1888, in which the names of both designers and craftsmen were included. Among the designers whose work was exhibited were C. R. Ashbee (1863–1942), Ernest Gimson (1864–1919), George Jack, Lewis Day (1845–1910) and W. R. Lethaby (1857–1931). The first and most important of the guilds to be established was the Century Guild founded by the architect A. H. Mackmurdo (1851–1942) and Selwyn Image. Most of their furniture was in a light-coloured wood, such as satinwood, and decorated with inlay – a marked characteristic of many of their simply-designed pieces being a surmounting cornice. Also important was the Guild of Handicrafts, established by C. R. Ashbee in 1888 in the East End of London and later removed to Chipping Campden, Gloucestershire. Some of their later work, particularly that designed by the architect M. H. Baillie Scott (1865–1945), had a strong Art Nouveau flavour. Baillie Scott, whose furniture and interiors were distinguished by a striking use of coloured ornament, designed a number of interiors with built-in furniture and partly sub-divided areas that foreshadowed many twentieth century ideas of open planning and fitted furniture. His work was well-known in Germany and he was responsible for decorating and furnishing, among other places, the palace of the Grand Duke of Hesse at Darmstadt.

There were already in the 1880s a few isolated appearances of the sinuous curves of the Art Nouveau style, some of Mackmurdo's work incorporating such forms, but it did not become really established until about 1890. Thereafter, for about a decade, this country played a leading part in the new movement, and many articles on English Art Nouveau appeared in Continental magazines; at the same time a considerable export trade in furniture developed. (In Italy the style was even named after the firm of Liberty's, who pioneered a great deal of Art Nouveau design.) The architect, C. F. A. Voysey (1857–1941), is generally considered to have been one of the leading designers in the style. His work is characterised by strongly accentuated horizontals and verticals (rather than by the swirling curves that developed in most Continental Art Nouveau furniture), and so is in consequence of far sounder construction. His furniture is a simple yet sophisticated interpretation of traditional forms of English furniture, the Art Nouveau curves mostly being restricted to the decoration on a basically rectangular shape (Colour Plate H). Voysey's ideas were widely copied and adapted both here and on the Continent. Attenuated female figures, curvaceous tulips, and tall rose-trees were all popular motifs for Art Nouveau furniture, which was also embellished with painted ornament, mounts of plain or embossed metal and inlay of wood, glass, metal, ivory and mother-of-pearl.

The most striking designer of the Art Nouveau movement in Britain, however, was the Glasgow architect, Charles Rennie Mackintosh (1868–1928), well-known for his interiors and furniture for the Glasgow School of Art and for tea-rooms in the same city. His work was particularly original, much of it, such as his chairs with high backs, being very mannered and conveying a feeling of tension (Plate 203). He made great use of oak, stained dark brown, purple or green or finished with a white, high-gloss paint. He did not use veneers but some of his furniture is inlaid and some embellished with repoussée copper or pewter.

Another architect producing good, simple furniture designs in the Art Nouveau idiom was George Walton. In addition, a number of commercial firms were making furniture of progressive design in the late nineteenth and early twentieth centuries, among them William Birch Ltd., of High Wycombe (Plate 202). A further leading firm producing simple furniture, often decorated with a little inlay, was Heal and Sons, who worked from 1893 to the designs of Sir Ambrose Heal (1872–1959). Liberty's and J. S. Henry were also noted for their advanced designs, exporting a great deal of furniture to the Continent. Wylie and Lockhead pioneered the new ideas in Glasgow.

The general furniture trade was influenced by all the successive reform movements, though inevitably many of the new ideas were misunderstood or adopted in debased form. However, the over-elaborate carving and decoration so typical of the Early Victorian period was to a great extent replaced by simpler forms and a more restrained use of ornament, with marquetry and inlay replacing carving in popularity. Nevertheless, a considerable amount of furniture with carved decoration was still made, particularly in the 1870s and 1880s, and most of it was now produced by steam-powered machinery and finished by hand. A cheap way of imitating carving was invented, using steel dies, but this was not entirely satisfactory as the end of the grain rather than its length was revealed.

In the 1870s there was a revival of interest in the style of Chippendale that led to the production of furniture based on designs in the *Director*. The Adam revival, heralded by the appearance of a large satinwood cabinet in the Adam style, exhibited by Wright and Mansfield at the 1867 Exhibition, quickly achieved popularity; Holland's and

H. OAK WRITING-CABINET with copper mounts. Designed in 1896 by C. F. A. Voysey. The simplicity of the design, with its pronounced verticals and horizontals, is characteristic of Voysey's work. The large copper hinge, incorporating a pastoral scene, forms an attractive decorative feature. Height 5 ft. 6 in.

Victoria and Albert Museum. Copyright Fratelli Fabbri, Milan. *See pages 144 and 153*

typical of much of his work and of the slightly austere approach sometimes adopted by Arts and Crafts designers. George Jack designed simple rectangular cabinets of walnut or mahogany, decorated with high quality marquetry of foliage forms, which appear to been inspired by Morris's textile and wallpaper designs. Ernest Gimson and C. R. Ashbee worked in a similar manner.

In the writing-cabinet designed by C. F. A. Voysey in 1896, illustrated in Colour Plate H, all decoration has been eliminated except for the elaborate ornamental copper hinge, incorporating a pastoral scene. This is typical of Voysey's rather austere style that relies for its pleasing appearance on subtle shaping and the relationship of the various parts. As in much of his furniture, the tapering shafts, imparting strong verticality to the design and here carried through to the top of the cabinet, are opposed by the pronounced horizontality of the wide projecting flat cornice. The long strap hinges, terminating in heart shapes, are characteristic features of Voysey's work, too.

Cabinet furniture designed by C. R. Mackintosh was in general basically rectangular, and might have Art Nouveau curves introduced along one edge, or in a pierced panel. On other pieces the Art Nouveau character was imparted by the mounts of brass, coloured glass or of beaten pewter or copper. Some of his cabinet work was stained a dull brown or green; other pieces were given a white enamel finish.

All these ideas were adapted for popular taste by the general furniture trade. Heal and Son gave a lead by producing good quality cabinet furniture of simple outline, sometimes of plain wood, inlaid, or painted. They were particularly noted for their bedroom furniture.

Some writing-cabinets with fall-fronts of eighteenth century type were produced by such leading firms as Holland and Sons. Bookcases based on the designs of Chippendale and Adam, with glazed fronts above panelled doors, were widely made and china cabinets of similar inspiration were popular. Those designed in the Adam style were generally of inlaid satinwood. A combined sideboard bookcase was introduced at this time, in which the lower stage consisted of cupboards with panelled doors and the upper part had a glass-fronted book compartment, flanked by brackets and shelves.

The Elizabethan style persisted alongside the more progressive designs right up to the end of the century, sideboards and bureaux being made of dark, stained oak, coarsely carved with Renaissance-type ornament.

Dressing-tables in the late nineteenth century were usually fitted with a pivoted glass, sometimes flanked by sets of drawers. The lower part might be in the form of two pedestals of drawers or simply a table with drawers. They were mostly designed *en suite* with wardrobes, washstands, chests-of-drawers and bedside cupboards. These suites of furniture were generally in light-coloured woods and decorated with banding or other simple inlay in a darker wood.

Wardrobes were rectangular, commonly having a broad, central door fitted with a looking-glass and narrower flanking sections, that might also be fitted with doors. Three drawers were usual below and there was often an architectural cornice.

Chests-of-drawers tended to be of traditional form but an alternative, less common type consisted of a pedestal of drawers decreasing in size from bottom to top. Some had a plain plinth but bracket feet or stout turned feet were common, too; handles were mostly in the form of large wooden knobs. Mahogany was still widely used for chests-of-drawers and many were considerably larger than had been customary hitherto.

Owing to improvements in the water closet, the bedside commode of the Early Victorian period was largely superseded by the pedestal cupboard, frequently made in pairs.

The washstand, an important item in the bedroom, was supplied with a marble top that often had a hole in it for the basin. The back would be fitted with tiles and below the marble top there might be drawers or small cupboards. Occasionally a cistern with a tap was incorporated in a superstructure.

MISCELLANEOUS

The hall stand became an obligatory item of furniture in the smaller Late Victorian house, and it was made of oak or mahogany. In addition to hooks for hats and coats and a rack for umbrellas and walking-sticks, it often incorporated a small table, seat and mirror.

What-nots were frequently triangular in shape, so that they fitted into a corner. Balusters and spindles were much used in their design, and the plain oak or other wood of the shelves was commonly inlaid with scrolling arabesques based on the Adam style. Some were made with bamboo supports, their shelves being japanned with a red or black ground.

The long-case clock, generally of oak or mahogany, was often fitted with Westminster chimes. Some were carved with a rather coarse imitation of Elizabethan decorative motifs. Unpolished oak was used on some table clocks, too, and their carved decoration might be derived from both Classical and Gothic sources.

An example of the adoption of the surmounting flat cap and the heart motif favoured by Voysey can be seen in the barometer and thermometer illustrated in Plate 213. The traditional rounded form has also been converted into a basically rectangular shape.

Plate 211 shows a piano designed in accordance with the reformist Gothic principles of designers such as Norman Shaw. Dating from about 1865, it was possibly designed by Charles Bevan, a commercial designer who worked for such firms as Marsh, Jones and Cribb of Leeds and London. It is of satinwood, inlaid and gilded, with three silk panels at the front.

Mirrors tended to become incorporated in other pieces of furniture and in the elaborate overmantels fitted with numerous small shelves, but those that were made as separate items were generally given fairly plain moulded frames of oak or mahogany.

XIII

MODERN FURNITURE

Britain, which had held a leading position in the field of design at the beginning of the century, played no significant part in the development of the new movement that grew up between the two World Wars, and it is necessary to look briefly at developments on the Continent in order to understand how modern design evolved here.

Whereas Art Nouveau had been typified by an entirely new type of ornament, the new style sought to dispense with decoration altogether, relying rather on a clear expression of the structure to give a pleasing design. An early appearance of the new style was in 1917, when a Dutchman named Gerrit Rietveld, a member of the 'de Stijl' group, designed several pieces of furniture that were strongly influenced by Cubist principles. Notable among these was an armchair in which there were no joints, the method of connecting the various wooden members by screws being clearly visible.

The most important influence on modern design was undoubtedly that of the Bauhaus, a school of design set up in Germany in 1919 by the architect Walter Gropius. When it was closed down in 1933 by the Nazis, some of its leading members fled to Britain and America, where they continued to expound its principles. An important new technique, developed at the Bauhaus, was the use of steel tubing for the framework of furniture, the earliest chair in this form being that designed in 1925 by Marcel Breuer. This formula was developed by other designers, notably Mies van der Rohe. In 1928 Breuer designed a chair of tubular steel, with back and seat panels of bentwood and cane, which was produced in large numbers by the firm of Thonet and proved to be extremely influential. Stainless steel, in the form of subtly curving bars, was used for the supports for the 'Barcelona chair', a classic of modern design created by Mies van der Rohe for the 1929 International Exhibition at Barcelona. Steel was also adopted for the frames of tables, which were generally fitted with glass tops.

Tubular steel furniture of Continental design was sold by progressive British firms, such as Heal's, during the 1930s and leading designers in this country, including Serge Chermayeff, Wells Coates and Betty Joel, were influenced by the new ideas.

The 1933 Exhibition of British Industrial Art in Relation to the Home, held in London, also served to bring the most advanced designs to the notice of the public. Metal furniture was well suited for contract work and was popular for offices, public halls and canteens but it met with some resistance for domestic use from a public accustomed to reproduction furniture and to the traditional material, wood – to whom its clean, functional lines appeared 'clinical' and cold.

There had been a marked improvement in the technique of making plywood during the First World War, which included the development of laminated wood, where thicker layers are used, the grain of all of them running in the same direction. Impregnated with synthetic resins to strengthen and set it, it is considerably stronger than ordinary plywood, yet slightly springy, an attribute that makes it particularly suitable for the supports of chairs. A notable example, obviously inspired by the tubular steel-framed chairs, was the reclining chair with curving supports of laminated wood designed in 1936 by Marcel Breuer for the Isokon Furniture Company Ltd. of London. New methods by which plywood could be bent with electricity were introduced, too, enabling it to be bent in two directions, a technique of practical use for such things as chair seats.

There was little training in the new techniques in Britain between the wars and the general standard of design was low. Even so, a consistently high standard was maintained by Heal and Son Ltd., whose designs were considerably influenced by the new movement. Plate 214 shows a chair of chromium-plated steel and leather designed in 1933 by Ambrose Heal (1872–1933), the son of the founder. Also of good quality and design, though less influenced by Continental ideas than by traditional English forms, was the furniture produced by Gordon Russell Ltd., of Broadway, Worcestershire, much of which was still made by hand. The walnut writing desk illustrated in Plate 225 was designed in 1927 by Sir Gordon Russell, the founder of the firm. It has panels of burr elm and a chased silver lock-plate embossed with the date.

Art Deco is the name given to the 'modernistic' style that arose in the 1920s in which the ideas of the Cubists and the Bauhaus play a large part. An excellent example of the style is the writing-table designed by Edward Maufe for the 1925 Paris Exhibition of Decorative and Industrial Arts (Plate 217). This style became widely adopted by the furniture trade although the general standard was inevitably much lower. A jazz-modern idiom was adopted for new kinds of furniture, such as cocktail cabinets, wireless sets and radiograms, as well as for the popular three-piece suite of sofa and two easy chairs. Mirrors were made in jagged, angular forms that were often composed of several pieces of glass joined together, and sometimes tinted. Wood was generally stained and finished with a high gloss in contrast to the more natural finish used by the progressive firms. At the same time 'Tudor', 'Jacobean', 'Queen Anne' and other reproduction furniture was still produced by the general furniture trade – often embellished with machine-made ornament, fixed with glue.

During the Second World War government-controlled 'Utility Furniture' was introduced. This inexpensive furniture designed to make the most economical use of materials in short supply, though rather austere, had the salutary effect of introducing the general public to designs with clean lines and plain surfaces that were free of heavy stains and applied ornament. In 1948 another factor in the improvement of design in this country was the founding of the Council of the Royal College of Art, in which Sir Gordon Russell was instrumental in creating a closer link between the school and industry.

The Scandinavian countries, especially Denmark, began to exercise a strong influence in Britain shortly after that. A tradition of good design had been built up there, making use of both machines and handcraftsmanship, wood being almost exclusively employed. The British public, having become accustomed to the simplicity of line of Utility Furniture, were now ready to accept this same virtue in the better quality Scandinavian furniture and the substantial quantity imported had a beneficial effect on British design. In addition, the principles expounded by the Bauhaus have been followed in the best furniture produced here since the last war.

In the early post-war years, pale woods such as oak and beech were mainly favoured; these retain their popularity but have been joined by other richly-grained woods such as teak and rosewood. Ebonising was sometimes introduced in the 1950s, particularly for the tapering, splayed legs that were almost ubiquitous throughout that decade and it is still occasionally used to give contrast. During the 1960s brightly coloured lacquers became popular as an alternative to a natural wood finish, followed by the re-introduction of coloured stains that allow the natural grain of the wood to show through.

From early developments in America in the 1940s plastics have come to play an increasingly important part in the making of furniture. In particular, moulded shapes fitting the human body are now made, obviating the need for thick upholstery and resulting in lighter designs. A new technique for shaping chairs, known as injection moulding, was made possible by the development in Britain of a new, tough plastic, polypropylene, that was discovered in 1954 by Professor Natta while working for the Shell Chemical Company. This new plastic not only costs far less than glass-fibre moulding but is also proof against staining and chipping. It has been used for the stacking chairs shown in Plate 216, which were designed in 1962 by Robin Day for Hille of London Ltd. The frame of these is of tubular chrome steel but the same moulded seat is used for a number of types of chair. The stacking chair is itself an important innovation. A metal swivel base is frequently used as a support for moulded plastic seats of the type pioneered by Charles Eames in America and Arne Jacobsen in Denmark. In the late 1960s legless chairs of rigid polyurethane foam moulded in sculptural shapes were introduced by Max Clendinning for Aerofoam and by Peter Murdoch for Hille.

Metal has been much used for furniture, mainly in conjunction with wood or plastic, since the Second World War, and especially for the legs of chairs and tables. In addition to the swivel base for chairs mentioned above, a similar central support is fitted to some tables – often with a spiral thread – allowing the height to be adjusted. Such parts are generally produced for the furniture industry by firms specialising in precision metal products. An early post-war use of tubular metal supports was for the storage units designed by Robin Day and Clive Latimer, which won a prize in the 1948 International Competition for Low Cost Furniture sponsored by the Museum of Modern Art in New York. The plywood units, fitted with sliding glass doors or wooden flaps, were slung from the supports well above the floor level. Another landmark in British post-war design was the 'Antelope' chair designed by Ernest Race for the 1951 Festival of Britain, which had a frame of metal rods and a plywood seat (Plate 215). Square section stainless steel tube has been used for the legs of an easy chair designed in 1962 by Robin Day for Hille (Plate 218). The table shown in Plate 219, by the same designer and maker, is fitted with chromium-plated steel legs with a satin finish, and is demountable for packing. Chromium-plated steel has also been used for the legs of the dining-chair illustrated in Plate 220, designed by Richard H. Young for Merrow Associates Ltd. A further use for steel is in the form of a wire mesh, painted or given a plastic finish, for seat furniture. In the late 1960s there was a revival of interest in the tubular steel furniture of the 1930s and several notable pieces were designed by Richard Young for Merrow Associates. An improvement in both the strength and the appearance of this type of furniture has been effected by a newly developed method of fixing the steel parts together with an internal screw.

Unit furniture, hardly known in this country before the last war, has been widely developed since then, and it reflects the current tendency for furniture to become an intrinsic part of architecture. Storage units, at first mainly developed for kitchens and in the form of room dividers for the fashionable open-plan interiors, now embrace innumerable ingeniously contrived types. Those designed for bedrooms incorporate drawers, shelves, cupboards, hanging space and even folding beds, whilst living room units comprise shelves for books and ornaments, writing bureaux, drinks cabinets and compartments for television sets and record players. Some are free-standing and are made entirely of wood or having metal supports, whilst others are screwed to the wall or completely built-in. Unit seating is now common, consisting of square-seated chairs that can be used singly or in a row, and is expecially useful for reception rooms and airport lounges. Tables are often made to the same module so that they can be placed in line or used as corner units. Rectangular cushions of latex foam are used as an alternative to fixed upholstery, and they can serve to convert a table of this type into a seat. An example of this type of furniture is the 'Maxima' system of units designed by Max Clendinning for Race Furniture Ltd. in 1966; the lacquered plywood sections of which they are built up are used for the sides and backs of chairs and as supports for tables and other items. A system of interlocking units has also been devised by Christien Sell and Associates Ltd. in which a limited number of sections can be assembled very quickly in numerous combinations to make furniture of all kinds. Another firm specialising in this so-called knock-down furniture, designed to be sent through the post for assembly at home, is Lupton-Morton Mail Order Ltd.; Plate 221 illustrates one of their side-chairs, in natural beech. A further example of stacking chairs is shown in Plate 222, these being made in oak or beech by Conran and Company Ltd.

The concept of built-in obsolescence is perhaps responsible for the appearance of the paper chair in America. This venture, which makes possible interesting new sculptural shapes, has also been developed here. Plate 223 shows a chair, designed in 1966 by David Bartlett and made by the Thames Board Mills Ltd., which is composed of two pieces of fibreboard that are laminated on both sides with a white Kraft lining paper coated with extruded 'flamed' polythene. It is delivered flat for home assembly.

Another recent introduction is inflatable furniture that has the advantage of being easy to deflate and stow away, as well as being less expensive than more conventional furniture. The 'blow-up' chairs shown in Plate 224 were designed in 1966 by Paul Wood for Goods and Chattels Ltd., and made of polished P.V.C. laminate; the transparent type, an example of which can be seen in the foreground, has the added advantage of making a room appear extra spacious.

The years since the last war have seen a steady rise in the standard of design in this country. The work of architects such as Sir Basil Spence and Sir Hugh Casson, in the contract field, has had a beneficial effect on design in general. The lead given by the most progressive high-class firms like Hille and Archie Shine has been taken up by Gomme of High Wycombe (G-Plan) and others in the more popular market to bring well-designed furniture at reasonable prices to an ever-wider public, and properly trained designers are now employed by most reputable firms. The Council of Industrial Design, with its awards and its constantly changing exhibitions at the Design Centre in London, has played a considerable part in encouraging good design and making the public design-conscious. The general standard of furniture design in Britain is probably higher now than at any time since the eighteenth century, and the best of it can stand comparison with any furniture in current production abroad.

GLOSSARY

ACANTHUS A stylised, carved ornament, based on the leaves of the acanthus plant. Used in the capitals of the Corinthian and Composite orders of architecture and in numerous variations on furniture.

ACROTER A block, often with a relief carving of anthemion, used on the ends or top of a Classical pediment.

AMBRY, AUMBRY A medieval term for various types of cupboard, including a wall recess closed by wooden doors.

ANTHEMION A stylised ornament, based on the leaves and flower of the honeysuckle.

APRON A decorative member attached to the lower edge of a seat-rail or the frieze of a table or stand.

ASTRAGAL (Also called a bead.) A small, plain, semi-circular moulding.

AURICULAR CARVING A form of carving, popular in the Restoration period the fleshy appearance of which suggests the human ear.

BACKSTOOL Originally a stool with a back fitted to it – hence a sidechair. The term was still current in the second half of the eighteenth century, in addition to the word 'chair'.

BALL-AND-CLAW FOOT A termination mainly used on cabriole legs in the first half of the eighteenth century (though earlier examples occur), representing a bird's or dragon's claw clutching a ball. Of Oriental derivation.

BALL FOOT A spherical foot, used mainly on tables and case furniture in the second half of the seventeenth century.

BALUSTER One of the turned and shaped units supporting a balustrade or stair-rail; also, a member of similar form used on a piece of furniture.

BANDING A border of contrasting wood inlaid into the veneer on a panel or drawer front.

BEAD See ASTRAGAL.

BENTWOOD Wood bent by steam and pressure. The term is generally used to refer to furniture of the type made by the firm of Thonet, who perfected the technique in the mid-nineteenth century.

BERGÈRE, BARJAIR, BURJAIR A term used in the mid-eighteenth century for an upholstered armchair with a deep seat. Later in the century it came to mean an armchair with cane panels in the back and arms and sometimes in the seat.

BOBBIN-TURNING A form of turning in common use in the early and mid-seventeenth century, resembling a series of bobbins.

BOLECTION An ogee-shaped moulding used where two members with surfaces at different levels meet.

BOMBÉ A term used for commodes of three-dimensional serpentine form in the eighteenth century. Occasionally used for other types of case furniture.

BOSSI WORK Marble inlaid with composition: named after an Italian craftsman who specialised in this technique in Dublin.

BRACKET FOOT A foot shaped like a bracket, in common use on case furniture in the first half of the eighteenth century.

BUHLWORK A nineteenth century name for the technique of decorating furniture with a veneer of brass, pewter, tortoise-shell, etc., in the manner of A. C. Boulle (1642–1732).

BUN FOOT A flattened form of the ball foot, used contemporaneously with it.

BURR A growth on the trunk or root of a tree, producing wood with a striking mottled appearance.

CABLE MOULDING A spiral moulding resembling twisted ropes.

CABOCHON A gem-like carving, generally convex and surrounded by carved foliage, frequently used on the knees of chair legs in the Early Georgian period.

CABRIOLE A type of leg with a double curve, convex above concave, introduced about 1700. Also the name given to certain upholstered chairs in the late eighteenth century (see page 107).

CARD-CUT FRET A low relief fretted ornament, based on Chinese latticework and used in the mid-eighteenth century. Also employed in a 'Gothic' version during the same period.

CARTOUCHE A term of architectural origin for a tablet, roughly oval or shield-shaped with curled edges, used particularly as a central motif for broken pediments, when it often bears a coat of arms.

CARYATID A sculptured female figure used in place of a column or (in furniture) as a leg.

CAVETTO A concave moulding forming in section a quadrant of a circle, used mainly on cornices of case furniture.

CELURE The medieval name for the hanging at the head of the bed. Sometimes interchanged with TESTER (q.v.).

CHEVAL SCREEN A firescreen in which the panel is supported by a pair of short legs at each of the lower corners. Sometimes called a horse-screen.

CHIP-CARVING A simple form of decoration used on chests in the thirteenth to fifteenth centuries, consisting usually of roundels with geometrical ornament chiselled out.

CLAW An eighteenth century term for a tripod base to a table, firescreen, etc., which suggested the form of claws.

CLAW-AND-BALL FOOT See BALL-AND-CLAW FOOT.

CLOSE STOOL A box or stool containing a chamber pan.

CLUB FOOT A plain circular foot used to terminate the cabriole leg, particularly in the early eighteenth century.

CONSOLE TABLE A side-table fixed to the wall at the back and supported at the front on scrolling legs or, occasionally, an animal form, such as an eagle.

CROSS-BANDING Banding which is cut so that the grain is at right-angles across it.

CUIR BOUILLI Leather softened by boiling that is impressed with a design.

CUP-AND-COVER A name given to the bulbous form used for late sixteenth century and early seventeenth century table legs, bedposts, etc., which strongly resembles a large cup with a cover. The term is not contemporary.

CYLINDER FRONT The curved front, a quadrant in section, introduced in the late eighteenth century for bureaux.

DORCER, DOSSER A medieval term for a textile draped over the back of a chair or hung on the wall behind a seat.

DORMANT TABLE A term, used mainly in the sixteenth and early seventeenth centuries, for a table with fixed supports, to distinguish it from the then more common trestle table.

DOVETAIL A fan-shaped projection at the end of a member, forming a joint with a slot of the same shape cut out of an adjoining member.

DOWEL A wooden peg used to join two members together.

DROP HANDLE A handle introduced in the second half of the seventeenth century in which a strip of metal, usually brass, is suspended from a single fixing. In early examples this frequently resembled a strap while later ones suggest a drop of water.

DROP-IN SEAT A seat that consists of a separate, upholstered frame fitting into the seat-rail.

DRUM TABLE A tripod table introduced in the late eighteenth century with a deep, circular top containing drawers.

DUCHESSE A piece of furniture consisting of two easy chairs with a stool between.

EGG-AND-DART, EGG-AND-TONGUE A convex moulding in which a motif resembling an egg alternates with one resembling a dart or tongue (Fig. 2 on page 30).

ENDIVE MARQUETRY See SEAWEED MARQUETRY.

FALL-FRONT A hinged vertical or angled flap closing the interior of a bureau. When opened, it falls to a horizontal position, thus forming a writing-surface.

FEATHER-BANDING Banding consisting of two strips, each with the grain running at forty-five degrees to the edge but at right-angles to each other in a manner suggesting a herring-bone or feather.

FIELDED PANEL One in which the centre part is raised, having bevelled edges.

FLEMISH SCROLL A name sometimes given to the double scroll form used for the front legs of some chairs in the second half of the seventeenth century. Not a contemporary term.

FLUTING A series of parallel, concave grooves used mainly to decorate legs and friezes, especially in the second half of the eighteenth century.

FRENCH FOOT A slender, outward-curving bracket foot sometimes used in the late eighteenth century, particularly on commodes.

FRENCH SCROLL FOOT (Also called a whorl foot.) A foot in the form of a delicate upturned scroll, widely used in the Rococo period.

FRONTISPIECE See TABERNACLE FRAME.

GADROONING (Also called nulling.) A moulding with alternate grooves and convex sections used round a flat surface, such as a table top, being carved at an angle to it (Fig. 3 on page 30).

GESSO A composition of whitening, size and linseed oil applied to a wooden surface as a ground for carving and gilding.

GIRANDOLE A decorative wall-light for one or more candles, often incorporating a small mirror.

GREEK KEY A low relief ornament used on friezes consisting of a repeating pattern of right-angles.

GUILLOCHE A low relief ornament consisting of interlocking circles with additional enrichment.

INLAY A form of decoration consisting of small pieces of contrasting woods or of other decorative material, such as ivory or mother-of-pearl, let into the surface of the carcase wood.

JAPANNING The European imitation of Oriental lacquer. In the late eighteenth century it came to be used for any type of over-all painted decoration.

JOINT STOOL, JOYNED STOOL A stool with a rectangular top, having four turned legs jointed into the seat-rail and secured by four stretchers near the base.

KLISMOS An ancient Greek chair, widely copied in the early nineteenth century, with a broad, curved top-rail and curved legs.

KNOB-TURNING Turning in the form of a series of knobs or swellings.

KNURL FOOT A scroll foot in use in the mid-eighteenth century in which the scroll turns under, towards the back.

LINENFOLD A type of carved decoration suggestive of the folds into which hanging textiles fall, used on panels, mainly in the early sixteenth century.

LOOP HANDLE One in which the curved grip is suspended from two points.

LOPER A wooden rail made to slide out from a bureau to support the fall-front. Generally fitted with a round brass knob at the end by which it can be drawn out.

MITRE The junction of two mouldings of panelling at an angle of forty-five degrees, where the rail and stile are jointed at right-angles.

MONOPODIUM A support in the form of a lion's leg surmounted by a lion's head, widely used in the early nineteenth century for legs of tables, chairs, etc., or to embellish cabinet furniture.

MORTISE A rectangular recess in a piece of wood, made to receive the corresponding tenon, to form a mortise and tenon joint.

MULE CHEST A term used for a chest with a base containing two or more drawers. Not a contemporary term.

T.E.F.

NULLING See GADROONING.

OGEE A moulding having in section a concave curve above a convex one. Also known in architecture as *cyma recta*.

ORMOLU Gilded bronze or gilded brass.

OYSTERWORK Thin transverse cuts from the smaller branches of trees (particularly walnut and laburnum), applied as a decorative veneer, the growth rings suggesting oyster shells.

PAD FOOT Similar to the club foot but resting on a disc.

PALMETTE A low relief carving based on the palm leaf and used particularly on the knees of chair and table legs in the Early Georgian period.

PARQUETRY A pattern (usually geometrical) formed of small pieces of veneer. It differs from ordinary marquetry in being non-representational.

PATERA A small circular or oval ornament that may be carved, inlaid or painted.

PEG FOOT A turned, tapering foot (or short leg).

PEMBROKE TABLE A small table with two flaps supported on hinged brackets, introduced in the third quarter of the eighteenth century.

PIE-CRUST EDGE The name given to the carved rim of some tripod tea-tables of the mid-eighteenth century.

PIER-GLASS A looking-glass designed to go on a pier between two windows.

PIETRE DURE A type of mosaic work in which hard stones such as jasper and agate are used.

RAIL A horizontal member of a piece of furniture, e.g. a seat-rail.

REEDING The opposite of fluting, consisting of a series of parallel, convex mouldings.

RIBBAND BACK The name used by Chippendale for a type of chair in which the carving of the back represents interlaced ribbons.

RIBBON AND ROSETTE A moulding consisting of alternating rosettes and ribbons.

ROCAILLE Delicate ornament derived from the rockwork and shells used in grottoes.

ROMAYNE WORK Carved profiles in medallions, derived from Italian Renaissance ornament, introduced in the early sixteenth century.

SABRE LEG A leg of rectangular section, curving in a manner suggesting the form of a sabre; widely used in the early nineteenth century.

SCAGLIOLA An imitation marble, introduced from Italy in the third quarter of the seventeenth century, composed of small particles of marble, plaster of Paris and glue. Table tops with intricate patterns imitating those produced in *pietre dure* were executed in this medium.

SCROLL-OVER ARM One in which the support rises in a concave curve from the seat-rail, breaking forward in a convex curve and levelling out for the arm-rest. Used in the Queen Anne and Early Georgian periods.

SEAWEED MARQUETRY (Also called endive marquetry.) A type of marquetry introduced in the late seventeenth century consisting of delicate scrolling leaves and arabesques.

SPADE FOOT (Also called therm foot.) A foot in the form of a tapered, square block, much used in the second half of the eighteenth century.

SPANISH SCROLL A late seventeenth century type of foot in which the scroll turns under, towards the back.

SPATULATE FOOT A square-ended termination sometimes used with cabriole legs of square section.

SPIRAL TURNING See TWIST TURNING.

SPLAT The central upright member of a chair-back. (Occasionally horizontal from the end of the eighteenth century.)

SPOON BACK The name sometimes given to an early eighteenth century chair in which the back has a gentle double curve designed to fit the back of the sitter. Also a mid-nineteenth century chair with a rounded, waisted back and short legs.

SQUAB A thick loose cushion. The term also used occasionally to denote a large padded seat.

STILE A vertical member of a piece of furniture, e.g. the corner uprights of a panelled chest.

STRAPWORK A type of decoration in low relief (occasionally openwork), in which forms suggesting curving and interlacing straps figure prominently.

STRETCHER A horizontal member used to brace the legs of chairs, tables, etc..

STRINGING Decorative inlay consisting of very thin strips of wood or other material.

STUFFED-OVER A term used for a seat that is completely covered with upholstery, in contrast to the drop-in seat.

STUMPWORK Needlework in which parts of the design are padded so that they stand up in relief; sometimes enriched with small coloured beads. Used particularly on mirror frames during the Restoration period.

TABERNACLE FRAME An architectural term for a decorative frame surrounding a niche or recess. Occasionally used as a decorative form on furniture. Also called a 'frontispiece'.

TAMBOUR FRONT A flexible front, used on bureaux and night-tables, consisting of parallel strips of wood glued to a canvas backing and running in grooves.

TENON A rectangular projection at the end of a member, made to fit into a similarly shaped recess in an adjoining member so as to form a mortise and tenon joint.

TERM A terminal figure ornamenting the stile of a piece of furniture and generally consisting of a human head or bust merging into a freely-treated columnar form. Also used in a free-standing form as a pedestal in the eighteenth century.

TESTER A wooden canopy, sometimes covered with a textile, especially that over a bed.

THERM FOOT See SPADE FOOT.

TRIFID FOOT A tripartite termination sometimes used with the cabriole leg in the early eighteenth century.

TRUCKLE A name sometimes given to a small wheel, as in truckle bed – a small bed on wheels.

TRUSSING COFFER A medieval travelling chest.

TURKEY-WORK A method of knotting woollen pile developed by English weavers in the sixteenth century in imitation of Turkish carpets. Used to cover chair seats.

TWIST TURNING Turning in the form of a continuous spiral, mainly used in the Restoration period.

VITRUVIAN SCROLL A decoration used mainly on friezes, resembling a series of waves; named after the Roman architectural writer, Vitruvius.

VOLUTE A spiral scroll.

WAINSCOT The panelling of a room. Up to the seventeenth century, it also means 'oak'.

WHORL FOOT See FRENCH SCROLL FOOT.

X-FRAME A term used to describe a stool or chair in which the form of the legs approximates to a letter X.

SELECT BIBLIOGRAPHY

ASLIN, Elizabeth, *Nineteenth Century English Furniture*, London, 1962

COLERIDGE, Anthony, *The Chippendale Period in English Furniture*, London, 1966

CONNOISSEUR PERIOD GUIDES: *Tudor Period, 1500–1603; Stuart Period, 1603–1714; Early Georgian Period, 1714–1760; Late Georgian Period, 1760–1810; Regency Period, 1810–1830; Early Victorian Period, 1830–1860*, London, 1956–1958

EDWARDS, Ralph, *Georgian Furniture*, Victoria and Albert Museum, 3rd ed., revised, London, 1970

EDWARDS, Ralph, *The Shorter Dictionary of English Furniture from the Middle Ages to the Late Georgian Period*, London, 1964

EDWARDS, Ralph, *English Chairs*, Victoria and Albert Museum, 2nd ed., London, 1965

EDWARDS, Ralph, and JOURDAIN, Margaret, *Georgian Cabinet-Makers c. 1700–1800*, London, 1955

FASTNEDGE, Ralph, *English Furniture Styles from 1500 to 1830*, London, 1962

FASTNEDGE, Ralph, *Sheraton Furniture*, London, 1962

GLOAG, John, *A Short Dictionary of Furniture*, London, 1966

GLOAG, John, *A Social History of Furniture Design*, London, 1966

GLOAG, John, *The Englishman's Chair*, London, 1964

HARRIS, E., *The Furniture of Robert Adam*, London, 1963

HAYWARD, Helena, *Thomas Johnson and English Rococo*, London, 1964

HAYWARD, Helena, (ed.), *World Furniture*, London, 1965

HAYWARD, John F., *Chests of Drawers and Commodes,* Victoria and Albert Museum, London, 1960

HAYWARD, John F., *Tables,* Victoria and Albert Museum, London, 1961

HAYWARD, John F., *English Cabinets,* Victoria and Albert Museum, London, 1964

HAYWARD, John F., *English Desks and Bureaux,* Victoria and Albert Museum, London, 1968

HEAL, Sir Ambrose, *London Furniture Makers from the Restoration to the Victorian Era,* London, 1953

JERVIS, Simon, *Victorian Furniture,* London, 1968

JOURDAIN, Margaret, *Regency Furniture, 1795–1820,* 2nd ed., London, 1948. Revised edition by Ralph Fastnedge, 1965

JOY, E. T., *English Furniture, A.D. 43–1950,* London, 1962

JOY, E. T., *The Country Life Book of English Furniture,* London, 1964

MACQUOID, Percy, and EDWARDS, Ralph, *The Dictionary of English Furniture,* 2nd ed., revised by Ralph Edwards, 3 vols., London, 1960

MOLESWORTH, H. D., (ed.), *A Treatise of Japanning and Varnishing, 1688, by John Stalker and George Parker.* Reprint with introduction by H. D. Molesworth, London, 1960

MOODY, Ella, *Modern Furniture,* London, 1966

MUSGRAVE, Clifford, *Regency Furniture,* London, 1961

MUSGRAVE, Clifford, *Adam and Hepplewhite and Other Neo-Classical Furniture,* London, 1966

PEVSNER, Nikolaus, *High Victorian Design,* London, 1951

SYMONDS, R. W., and WHINERAY, B. B., *Victorian Furniture,* London, 1962

TOMLIN, Maurice, *Furniture of the Adam Period,* Victoria and Albert Museum, London, 1972

WARD-JACKSON, Peter, *English Furniture Designs of the Eighteenth Century,* London, 1958

WILLS, Geoffrey, *English Looking-glasses,* London, 1965

1. OAK BOX CHAIR (also known as a 'joyned chair'). First half of the sixteenth century. This chair is basically in the Gothic tradition and has several panels of linenfold carving but the top panel in the back shows the influence of the Italian Renaissance. Height 3 ft. 7 in. *Victoria and Albert Museum.* *See pages 22 and 24*

2. OAK STOOL with slab ends. About 1500. This was a common form of construction for both stools and benches. Height 1 ft. 10 in.
Victoria and Albert Museum
See page 23

3. OAK DRAW-TABLE AND BENCH. Early sixteenth century. This is an unusually early example of a table fitted with a draw-top. Apart from this advanced feature, this dormant table and bench, with their ogee-shaped mouldings, are of typical fifteenth-century type. Table length 5 ft. $2\frac{1}{2}$ in. Bench length 5 ft. 5 in.
Victoria and Albert Museum
See pages 23 and 25

4. OAK RENT-TABLE. First half of the sixteenth century. The top is hinged to give access to the interior. Length 3 ft. $7\frac{1}{2}$ in. *Victoria and Albert Museum.* *See page 25*

5. OAK CHEST with wrought-iron straps and hinges. Anglo-Scottish (Border); late fifteenth or early sixteenth century. The central panel depicts the Fall and is flanked by roundels of Gothic tracery. Length 6 ft. $11\frac{1}{2}$ in. *Victoria and Albert Museum.* *See page 26*

6. OAK CHEST. Thirteenth century. Such chip-carved roundels were a common form of decoration on chests. (The lock is a later addition.) Length 3 ft. 7 in. *Victoria and Albert Museum.* *See page 26*

7. OAK CHEST. First half of the sixteenth century. Inscribed *Fere God T. Love God.* The profile heads, though somewhat crude, show the influence of the Renaissance. Length 4 ft. 1 in.
Victoria and Albert Museum. *See page 27*

8. TRUSSING (OR TRAVELLING) COFFER. Oak, covered with tooled leather. Mid-sixteenth century. There are two long, and two short drawers, with the main compartment above. The interior was originally completely lined with crimson silk. Height 1 ft. 9 in. *Victoria and Albert Museum.* *See page 27*

9. OAK HUTCH. Early sixteenth century. This example, ornamented with openwork panels at the front, which serve to ventilate it, and linenfold at each end, is fitted with a hinged lid. Length 5 ft. 6 in.
Victoria and Albert Museum. *See page 27*

10. OAK CHEST, inlaid with various woods. Late sixteenth century. Such chests, elaborately decorated with architectural perspectives, are commonly known as 'Nonsuch chests', owing to their supposed resemblance to Henry VIII's Palace of Nonsuch, near Cheam, Surrey. Length 6 ft.
Victoria and Albert Museum. *See page 36*

11. OAK JOINT STOOL, with fluted baluster legs. About 1600. Height 1 ft. 9 in.
Victoria and Albert Museum. See page 32

12. OAK ARMCHAIR of *caquetoire* type. Mid-sixteenth century. The back panel is carved with Renaissance ornament incorporating a profile head. Height 4 ft.
Victoria and Albert Museum. See page 32

13. OAK ARMCHAIR, inlaid with various woods. Mid-seventeenth century. The inlaid decoration of a conventional flowering plant within a carved arch is typical of the period. Height 4 ft.
Victoria and Albert Museum. *See page 33*

14. ARMCHAIR of X-frame construction and matching footstool, upholstered with faded crimson velvet fastened with brass-headed nails. Early seventeenth century. Height 4 ft. 2 in.
Victoria and Albert Museum. *See page 33*

15. OAK ARMCHAIR with folding framework fastened with wooden pins. About 1600. The carved ornament of the back appears to have been the standard type of decoration for this kind of chair. Height 3 ft. 5 in.
Victoria and Albert Museum. See pages 33 and 134

16. ARMCHAIR. The wooden frame is painted with flowers on a gilded gesso ground. The back and arms are still covered with their original crimson velvet upholstery. About 1600. Height 3 ft. 3 in.
Victoria and Albert Museum. See page 33

17. OAK GATE-LEG TABLE. Third quarter of the seventeenth century. This simple table is supported by a slab at either end and takes up very little room when closed. Length 4 ft. 11 in. *Ham House, Surrey.* *See page 36*

18. ARMCHAIR of X-frame construction, upholstered with appliqué of cloth of gold on a red satin ground. About 1610–20. (The shield-shaped escutcheon has been inverted.) Height 4 ft. 2 in. *Knole Park, Kent.* *See page 33*

19. OAK BEDSTEAD. About 1600. The importance now placed upon the bedstead itself can be clearly seen in this example, with its elaborately carved headboard and posts. Height 8 ft. *Athelhampton, Dorset.* *See page 35*

20. SETTEE. Beech, upholstered in crimson velvet. About 1610–20. The ends can be adjusted by means of ratchets. Length 5 ft. 8 in. *Knole Park, Kent.* *See page 34*

21. OAK DRAW-TABLE, inlaid with various woods. About 1600. The legs are of typical cup-and-cover form, surmounted by an Ionic capital. Length 5 ft. 11 in. *Victoria and Albert Museum.* *See pages 21 and 35*

22. CHEST-OF-DRAWERS. Oak, inlaid with ivory and mother-of-pearl and embellished with split baluster ornament. Dated 1653. The drawers are enclosed by doors. Height 4 ft. 4 in.
Victoria and Albert Museum.
See page 37

23. OAK CHAIR-TABLE. Mid-seventeenth century. The back of the chair is pivoted, enabling it to swing over onto the arms so as to form a table top. Height 4 ft. 5 in.
Victoria and Albert Museum. *See page 34*

24. WALNUT ARMCHAIR with cane seat and back panels. About 1675. The low relief carving of scrolling foliage was a common form of decoration for chairs of this type. Height 3 ft. $8\frac{1}{2}$ in.
Ham House, Surrey. See page 44

25. WALNUT ARMCHAIR with cane seat and back panels. About 1680. This richly carved chair is a particularly fine example of its type. Height 4 ft. 3 in.
Victoria and Albert Museum. See page 45

26. GILDED ARMCHAIR with frame carved with dolphins. The upholstery is of satin tissue in pink, yellow and white on a crimson ground, trimmed with crimson and gold thread. About 1665. This sumptuous chair forms part of a set of six armchairs and six sidechairs mentioned in the Ham seventeenth-century inventories. Height 3 ft. $4\frac{1}{4}$ in. *Ham House, Surrey.* *See page 45*

27. STOOL OF GILDED WOOD. One of a pair. About 1675. The cushions are modern reproductions. Such low stools often formed part of the seating, together with chairs, in an important bedroom. Height, with cushions, 1 ft. 6 in.
Ham House, Surrey
See page 46

28. WALNUT STOOL. About 1680. The stool has been re-covered with French early eighteenth-century tent stitch embroidery. Height 1 ft. 7 in.
Victoria and Albert Museum. *See page 45*

29. CHAIR of japanned beech in pseudo-Oriental form. Third quarter of the seventeenth century. The top-rail is decorated with the cypher and coronet of Elizabeth, Countess of Dysart. Height 4 ft. 2 in. *Ham House, Surrey.* *See pages 45 and 51*

30. SIDE-TABLE, decorated with incised japanning in red, green and white on a black ground. About 1675. Although inferior to the Oriental product, the quality of the japanning on this table is high. Length 3 ft. $1\frac{3}{4}$ in. *Ham House, Surrey.* *See page 47*

31. SIDE-TABLE, decorated with floral marquetry in various woods and ivory, some stained green. About 1675. A vase-shaped or straight section at the base of the legs is a feature of many English tables made at this time.
Length 3 ft. 3 in.
Ham House, Surrey. *See pages 40 and 46*

32. SIDE-TABLE, decorated with scagliola. About 1675. Formerly at Warwick Castle. The design of the scagliola closely resembles that surrounding the fireplace in the Queen's Closet at Ham House and was probably made in Holland or by Dutch craftsmen working in London. Length 3 ft. 10 in.
Victoria and Albert Museum
See page 47

33. WALNUT CABINET ON STAND, decorated with floral marquetry of stained ivory and various woods. Last quarter of the seventeenth century. Height 5 ft. $4\frac{1}{2}$ in.
Victoria and Albert Museum. *See pages 40 and 48*

34. FOOT from a bedstead of about 1675. Carved and gilded wood. The head of a cherub, a popular motif of the Restoration period, is here used to surmount each of the three scroll supports. Height $6\frac{3}{4}$ in.
Ham House, Surrey. *See page 46*

35. JAPANESE LACQUER CABINET on an English stand of gilded pine. About 1675. Gilded or silvered stands of this type were made for both Oriental and home-produced cabinets.
Height 5 ft. 5 in. *Rijksmuseum, Amsterdam.* *See pages 42, 48 and 49*

36. WRITING-CABINET or SCRIPTOR, decorated with kingwood oysterwork and fitted with mounts of embossed silver. About 1675. Height 4 ft. 5½ in.
Ham House, Surrey. *See pages 41, 44 and 48*

37. CEDAR WRITING-CABINET with brass handles. About 1675. This cabinet is unusual in that it is a fixture, being built into the library bookshelves. Height 6 ft. 4 in.
Ham House, Surrey. *See page 49*

38. WALNUT CHEST with handles of gilded wrought iron. About 1675. Such chests were widely used for the storage of bedding, spare wall hangings and clothing. Height 2 ft. 4½ in.
Ham House, Surrey
See page 49

39. CLOSE-STOOL, japanned in gold on a black ground, with mother-of-pearl inlay. About 1675. (The handle is later.) The corners are carved and gilded in imitation of the brass mounts on lacquer cabinets. Height 1 ft. 8¼ in.
Ham House, Surrey. *See page 49*

40. BEDSTEAD, hung with blue-green silk velvet, trimmed with a ball fringe. About 1680. The canopy is enriched with gilded carving, including a lion and unicorn at each of the front corners. Height 11 ft.
Knole Park, Kent. *See page 46*

41. OAK BOOKCASE. About 1675. This bookcase, which comes from Dyrham Park, Gloucestershire, resembles those in the Pepys Library at Magdalene College, Cambridge, which were ordered in 1666 from 'Sympson the Joiner'. Height 8 ft. $1\frac{3}{4}$ in.
Victoria and Albert Museum. *See page 49*

42. MIRROR, decorated with floral marquetry of various woods and ivory, some stained green. About 1675. *En suite* with the table shown in Plate 31. Height 5 ft. 3 in.
Ham House, Surrey. See pages 40 and 50

43. MIRROR with a frame of silvered wood containing a painted escutcheon. About 1670. The arms are those of Gough of Old Falling Hall and Perry Hall, Staffordshire. Height 5 ft. $9\frac{1}{2}$ in.
Victoria and Albert Museum. See page 50

44. BRASS FIRE-DOG. About 1675. This very sumptuous piece of chimney furniture, one of a pair, is elaborately embossed and stands on paw feet. Height 1 ft. 9 in. *Ham House, Surrey.*

45. PICTURE FRAME of carved limewood in the style of Grinling Gibbons. About 1675. The portrait signed 'DOU'. Height 1 ft. $10\frac{1}{4}$ in. *Ham House, Surrey.* *See pages 41 and 50*

46. GLOBE ON WALNUT STAND. Third quarter of the seventeenth century. The original covers of embossed leather still survive for this globe and its pair. Height 2 ft. 9 in. *Ham House, Surrey. See page 51*

47. PICTURE FRAME, carved and gilded. Third quarter of the seventeenth century. The auricular style of carving, of which this is a fine example, was widely used for picture frames at this time. The painting, after Van Dyck, is of Lucy, Countess of Carlisle (1599–1660). Height 5 ft. 6 in. *Ham House, Surrey. See page 50*

48. TABLE CLOCK in a case veneered with kingwood, having a brass basket top. About 1685. The movement is by John Fromanteel. Height 1 ft. 3 in.
Victoria and Albert Museum. *See page 51*

49. BOOK-REST, japanned with gold and various colours on a black ground and inlaid with mother-of-pearl. About 1675. The cresting is decorated with the coronet and cypher of Elizabeth, Countess of Dysart. Height 1 ft. 8 in.
Ham House, Surrey. *See page 51*

50. TULIP-POT STAND. Walnut. About 1675. Height 2 ft. *Hampton Court Palace*. Reproduced by gracious permission of Her Majesty the Queen. *See page 51*

51. LONG-CASE CLOCK. Walnut, decorated with floral marquetry. About 1680. Signed on the face *Wm Clement Londini fecit*. Height 6 ft. 7 in.
Victoria and Albert Museum. *See page 50*

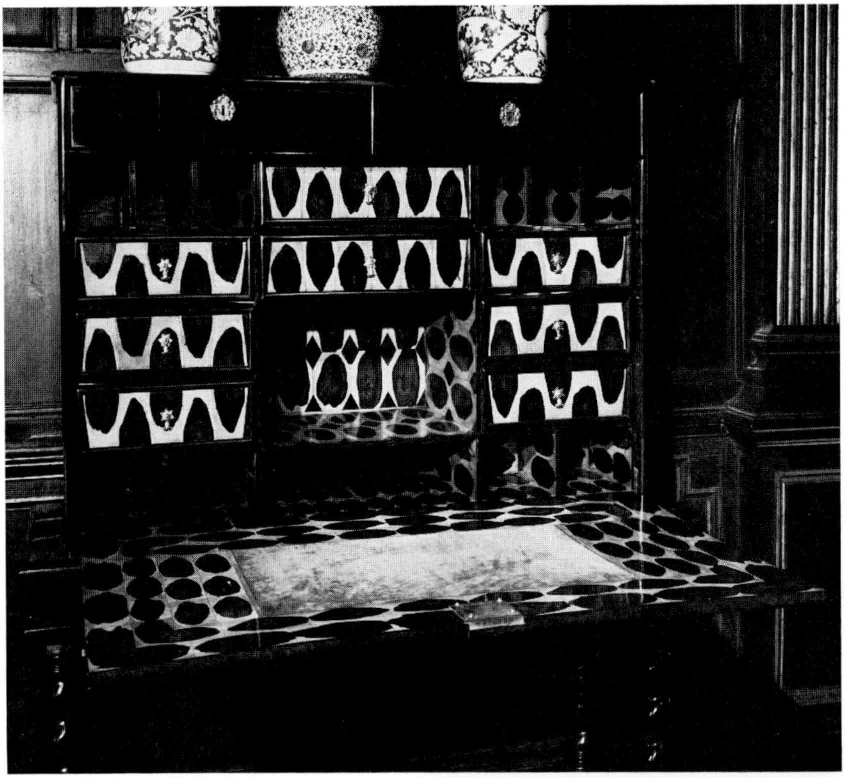

52. WRITING-CABINET, veneered with kingwood. About 1675. In the interior of this cabinet the light outer wood of the kingwood oysterwork has been retained, giving a very striking effect. Height 5 ft. 0½ in.
Ham House, Surrey. *See page 49*

53. WALNUT SETTEE, upholstered in cross-stitch needlework, with ball fringe. About 1690. Formerly at Hampton Court, Herefordshire. Height 4 ft. 6½ in.
Victoria and Albert Museum
See page 54

54. CHAIR of stained beech. The seat covered with petit-point embroidery in silk and wool. About 1690. The tall, narrow back, surmounted by an arched cresting resting on baluster uprights is typical for chairs made during the last decade of the seventeenth century. Height 4 ft. 4½ in.
Victoria and Albert Museum. *See page 54*

55. CHILD'S HIGH CHAIR of stained beech. About 1690. The holes in the front legs are for attaching a foot-rest. As in many chairs of the period, the arched top-rail echoes the form of the front stretcher. Height 3 ft. 9½ in.
Victoria and Albert Museum. *See page 54*

56. BED, with hangings of Chinese white silk and crimson velvet with a tasselled fringe. The elaborately shaped decoration round the top is of carved pine, covered with velvet, and the corner hangings, or cantons, are supported on curved iron bars. The influence of Daniel Marot is seen in this exceptionally splendid state bed, made for the 1st Earl of Melville between 1692 and 1707. Height 15 ft. 2 in. *Victoria and Albert Museum.* *See pages 52 and 56*

57. WALNUT STOOL, upholstered with contemporary silk velvet with voided pile and metal thread. Late seventeenth century. The inverted cup shape is a striking feature of the legs of this stool; they are linked by curving X-shaped stretchers. Height 1 ft. 8 in. *Victoria and Albert Museum.* *See page 54*

58. WALNUT CARD-TABLE. About 1695. Two of the back legs swing open to support the flap, forming a circular table top. The tapered legs are linked by curving, flat stretchers and supported on stylised hoof feet. Width 2 ft. $8\frac{1}{2}$ in. *Victoria and Albert Museum.* *See page 55*

59. JAPANNED CABINET with stand and cresting of silvered pine. Late seventeenth century. Japanned in imitation of tortoiseshell and decorated in gold and silver. Stand and cresting in the style of Daniel Marot. The serpentine stretchers would originally have been surmounted by carved finials. Height 7 ft. 2 in. *Victoria and Albert Museum.* *See pages 52 and 56*

60. MIRROR with frame of blue and gold *verre églomisé*, surmounted by a cresting of carved and gilded pine. About 1700. The shaped top section is fitted with a separate piece of glass, as was usual. Height 6 ft. 8 in.
Victoria and Albert Museum. *See page 57*

61. LONG-CASE CLOCK. Walnut, with seaweed marquetry. About 1695. Straight columns at the corners of the hood have superceded the twisted columns of the Charles II period. Height 7 ft. 3 in.
Victoria and Albert Museum. *See pages 53 and 58*

62. GATE-LEG WRITING TABLE. Walnut, decorated with seaweed marquetry. Late seventeenth century. The tapered legs, linked by straight stretchers, are supported on ball feet. Length 3 ft. 0½ in.
Victoria and Albert Museum
See pages 53 and 55

63. WALNUT CHEST-OF-DRAWERS of the type commonly known as a 'bachelor's chest'. About 1710. The writing surface unfolds towards the front to rest on the pair of lopers flanking the top drawer. The mottled grain of the burr walnut veneer on the drawer fronts and the top can be clearly seen. Length 2 ft. 6 in.
Victoria and Albert Museum
See pages 59 and 64

64. WALNUT ARMCHAIR. The seat upholstered with petit-point embroidery. Early eighteenth century. One side stretcher and the cross stretcher are missing. The joints between the various parts can be clearly seen. Height 3 ft. 6 in.
Victoria and Albert Museum. *See pages 59, 61 and 62*

65. WINGED ARMCHAIR of walnut, with gros- and petit-point embroidery in coloured wools. Early eighteenth century. Club feet were often built up with small pieces of wood at the sides and two of these pieces have become broken off. Height 3 ft. 11 in.
Victoria and Albert Museum. *See pages 61 and 62*

66. BED. The canopy and bedhead covered with the original crimson worsted, trimmed with braid. Early eighteenth century. Height 9 ft. $0\frac{1}{2}$ in.
Victoria and Albert Museum. *See page 62*

67. BUREAU-CABINET, veneered with burr walnut. About 1710. The arching of the top is characteristic of many cabinets dating from this time. The cresting is of carved and silvered pine. Height 7 ft. 3 in.
Victoria and Albert Museum. See page 64

68. CABINET ON STAND. Walnut, with ash feather-banding. Early eighteenth century. A particularly attractive grain has been selected for the veneer of the doors. The legs, square in section, terminate in spatulate feet. Height 5 ft. $5\frac{1}{2}$ in.
Victoria and Albert Museum. See pages 61 and 64

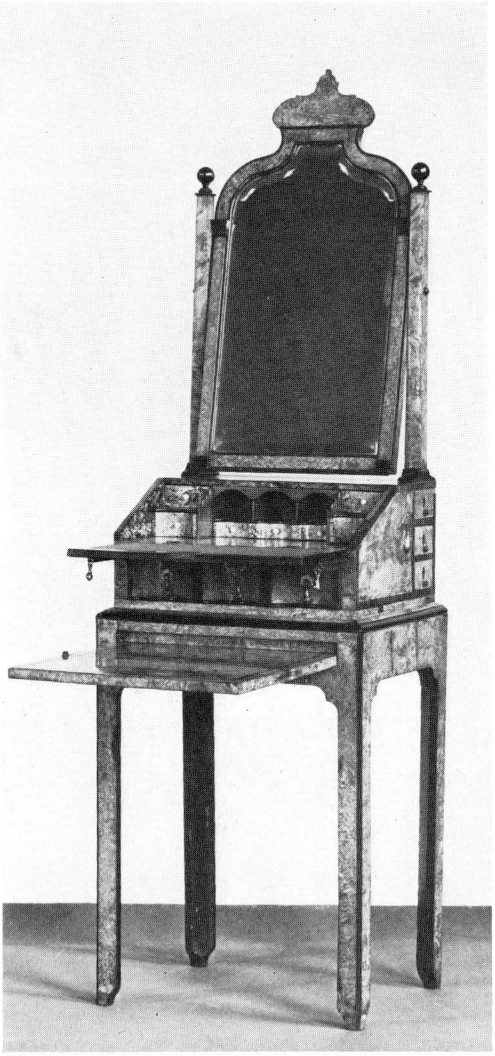

69. DRESSING-GLASS ON STAND. Veneered with amboyna, kingwood and rosewood. Early eighteenth century. The influence of Oriental forms is seen in the legs, which are chamfered on the inside.
Height 5 ft. $0\frac{1}{2}$ in.
Victoria and Albert Museum. *See page 65*

70. OAK LIBRARY STEPS with leather castors. Second quarter of the eighteenth century. Fitted with a book-rest and a hinged, collapsible seat. The flight of steps is also hinged to make for easy moving. Height 6 ft. 9 in.
Ham House, Surrey. *See page 75*

71. GILDED CHAIR with X-frame construction. About 1735. The influence of the style of William Kent is clearly visible (cf. Plate 72) but the design has been greatly simplified. Height 3 ft. $4\frac{1}{4}$ in. *Ham House, Surrey.* *See page 69*

72. GILDED ARMCHAIR, designed by William Kent in about 1730. Kent has revived the traditional X-frame construction for the front legs of this chair, embellishing the design with large-scale scrolling acanthus. Height 3 ft. 4 in. *Devonshire Collection, Chatsworth.* Reproduced by permission of the Trustees of the Chatsworth Settlement. *See pages 68 and 69*

73. ARMCHAIR of carved walnut. About 1745. The legs are enriched with acanthus carving and terminate in paw feet. Height 3 ft. 3 in.
Victoria and Albert Museum
See pages 68 and 69

74. OAK HALL CHAIR. About 1735. Made for the 4th Earl of Dysart and painted with his arms and coronet. Hall chairs, introduced about this time, were often made in this form, based on an Italian Renaissance type of chair. Height 3 ft. $5\frac{1}{2}$ in.
Ham House, Surrey. *See page 70*

75. MAHOGANY BED. About 1740. The strong architectural influence favoured by the Palladian school is seen in the use of Corinthian columns at the corners and the Palladian window motif superimposed on the headboard. Height 9 ft. 3 in. *Victoria and Albert Museum.* *See pages 66 and 71*

76. MAHOGANY SETTEE with partial gilding. About 1740. From Wroxton Abbey, Oxfordshire. This type of scroll leg, much favoured by Palladian designers, is decorated with a scale motif, while the uprights of the back are carved with falling coins and the seat-rail with a Vitruvian scroll. Height 6 ft. 11½ in. *Victoria and Albert Museum.* *See page 70*

77. 'LOVE-SEAT'. Fruitwood, with upholstery of red and green cut velvet (probably Spitalfields). About 1730. The plain, uncarved leg and simple pad foot, typical of the Queen Anne period, were sometimes retained for later designs. Height 3 ft. 4 in. *Ham House, Surrey.* *See page 71*

78. TRIPOD TEA-TABLE, japanned in red and gold on a black ground. About 1740. This table is fitted with a 'bird-cage' under the top, enabling it to be swung into a vertical position when not in use. Diameter 2 ft. 7 $\frac{1}{4}$ in. *Ham House, Surrey.* *See page 72*

79. SIDE-TABLE of painted and gilded wood, with a marble top. Designed by Matthias Lock for Ditchley House, Oxfordshire, in about 1740. Unlike most of Lock's work, which was in the Rococo style, this table has the monumental quality of much Palladian furniture. Length 4 ft. 6 in. *Temple Newsam House, Leeds.* *See page 72*

80. MAHOGANY SIDE-TABLE with a top of veined green marble. About 1735. This table, though less monumental than that illustrated in Plate 79, still has a heaviness and largeness of scale. Length 5 ft. $0\frac{3}{4}$ in. *Ham House, Surrey*. *See page 73*

81. w
featu
Victor

84. BOOKCASE of pine, painted brown and partly gilded. About 1730. The glass-fronted doors of this strongly architectural piece of furniture are in the form of a Palladian window.
Height 7 ft. 1½ in. *Victoria and Albert Museum.* *See pages 66 and 73*

85. BUREAU-CABINET, japanned in gold on a red ground. About 1730. The fronts of the doors are fitted with plates of looking-glass. Height 7 ft. 8 in. *Victoria and Albert Museum.* *See page 74*

86. MAHOGANY BUREAU-CABINET, decorated with brass, some inlaid; the pediment veneered with tortoiseshell. About 1735. Attributed to John Channon. The three small plinths originally supported gilded statuettes. Height 8 ft. 3 in. *Victoria and Albert Museum.* *See pages 68 and 74*

87. BUREAU, veneered with walnut and yew and, in the interior, with amboyna; ivory mounts. About 1720. The drawer fronts are framed with feather-banding and cross-banding, surrounded by a bead. Height 3 ft. 5 in. *Victoria and Albert Museum.* *See page 74*

88. CHEST of carved and gilded gesso on wood. About 1720. From Shobden Court, Herefordshire. Elaborately carved chests, sometimes of sarcophagus form, were designed for many Palladian interiors, where they were more for ornament than for use. Length 4 ft. 9 in.
Victoria and Albert Museum. *See page 74*

89. PIER-GLASS with frame of gilded wood. About 1735. One of a pair. The strongly architectural frame is surmounted by a broken scroll pediment. Height 6 ft. $10\frac{1}{4}$ in. *Ham House, Surrey*. *See page 75*

90. PIER-GLASS with frame of painted wood. About 1735. The plinth in the middle of the broken pediment supports an eagle, the crest of the Child family. Height 4 ft. 2 in. *Osterley Park, Middlesex*. *See page 75*

91. CHANDELIER of gilded wood, with branches for eight lights. About 1730. This remarkably fine chandelier, showing strong French influence, is decorated on the branches with fish-scale ornament. Height 3 ft. 3 in.
Victoria and Albert Museum
See Page 75

92. CHANDELIER of gilded brass with branches for eight lights. About 1730. On the central section, between the candle branches, are eight small plaques embossed with Classical figures, each surmounted by a cherub. Height 1 ft. 4 in.
Ham House, Surrey. *See page 75*

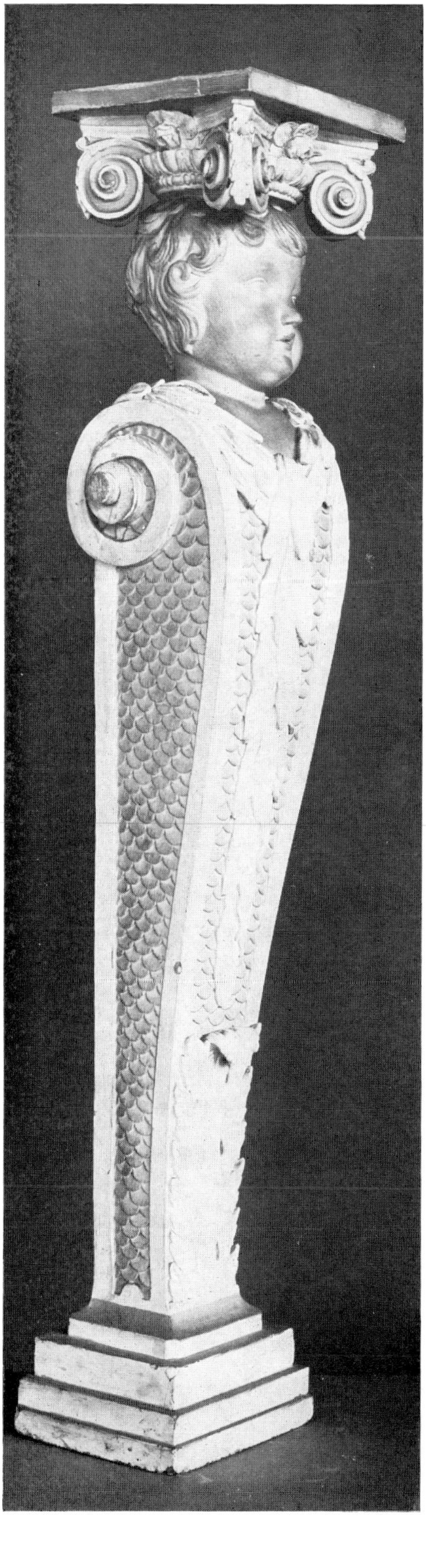

94. TABLE CLOCK. The case decorated with pieces of looking-glass, ormolu mounts and corner columns of clear glass. First quarter of the eighteenth century. The movement is by Joseph Windmills & Son of London. Height 1 ft. 10 in.
Victoria and Albert Museum. See page 75

93. CANDLESTAND, painted grey and white. About 1730. In the form of a term, with a cherub's head surmounted by an Ionic capital, a type that was particularly popular at the time. Height 3 ft. 9½ in. *Victoria and Albert Museum. See page 75*

95. WINDSOR CHAIR in 'Gothic Taste'. Back and legs of yew, with an elm seat. Mid-eighteenth century. Height 3 ft. $5\frac{1}{2}$ in.
Victoria and Albert Museum. See pages 78 and 81

96. MAHOGANY ARMCHAIR. Third quarter of the eighteenth century. Straight lines have been entirely eliminated in this chair and the curving framework is enriched overall with delicate Rococo carving. Height 3 ft. $4\frac{3}{4}$ in.
Victoria and Albert Museum. See pages 77 and 82

97. ARMCHAIR of gilded wood. Third quarter of the eighteenth century. This chair is a slightly more restrained essay in the Rococo style than the one illustrated in Plate 96. Height 3 ft. $4\frac{3}{4}$ in.
Osterley Park, Middlesex. *See page 82*

98. MAHOGANY ARMCHAIR ('Burjair Chair'). Upholstered with green and red cut silk velvet (probably Spitalfields). Third quarter of the eighteenth century. Height 3 ft. 6 in.
Ham House, Surrey. *See page 82*

99. MAHOGANY SETTEE in the 'Chinese Taste'. Mid-eighteenth century. The back, of double-chair form, is mainly composed of Chinese fret and there is a recurring motif derived from the pagoda roof. Height 3 ft. $2\frac{1}{2}$ in.
Victoria and Albert Museum. See pages 77 and 82

100. MAHOGANY SETTEE in the form of a double 'Ribband-back' chair. About 1760. Closely based on a design (Plate XV) in Chippendale's *Director*, 3rd edition, 1762. Height 3 ft. $3\frac{1}{2}$ in.
Victoria and Albert Museum. See pages 81 and 82

101. CONSOLE-TABLE of gilded and painted wood, with a marble top. Mid-eighteenth century. The inclusion of motifs symbolising the chase – in this case, the hound – was often a feature of English tables of this type. Length 3 ft. 3 in.
Victoria and Albert Museum. *See page 83*

102. SIDE-TABLE of mahogany, with a white marble top. Mid-eighteenth century. A design for a table of this type, described as a 'Sideboard Table', appears in Chippendale's *Director*, 1st edition, 1754, Plate XXXV. Length 5 ft.
Ham House, Surrey. *See pages 78 and 83*

103. MAHOGANY CABINET ON STAND in the 'Gothic Taste'. Mid-eighteenth century. The doors are based on the form of a Gothic window and are surmounted by ogee arches with finials. Height 8 ft. 6 in.
Victoria and Albert Museum. *See pages 78 and 85*

104. MAHOGANY CABINET ON STAND in the 'Chinese Taste'. Mid-eighteenth century. Made to house a small Chinese cabinet with drawers. The model temple on the top is an unusual feature. Height 5 ft. 11½ in. *Victoria and Albert Museum.* *See pages 77 and 85*

105. MAHOGANY TRIPOD TEA-TABLE. Mid-eighteenth century. The central shaft and the legs, which terminate in a version of the French scroll foot, are carved with very delicate Rococo ornament.
2 ft. 8¼ in. square.
Victoria and Albert Museum
See page 84

106. COMMODE in the French manner. Veneered with various woods, fitted with a marble top and mounted with ormolu. Attributed to Pierre Langlois. About 1765. This very fine commode is decorated with the newly re-introduced marquetry. Length 4 ft. 4¼ in.
Victoria and Albert Museum. *See pages 78, 80 and 88*

107. MAHOGANY BREAKFAST-TABLE. Mid-eighteenth century. This table corresponds with Plate XXXIII in Chippendale's *Director*, 1st edition, 1754. Length (open) 3 ft. $3\frac{1}{4}$ in. *Victoria and Albert Museum.* *See pages 78 and 84*

108. MAHOGANY LIBRARY TABLE. Mid-eighteenth century. Attributed to William Vile. The front can be unlocked and pulled forward to reveal a writing-desk. The oval forms, clasped by Rococo acanthus leaves, are typical of Vile's work. Length 5 ft. *Victoria and Albert Museum.* *See pages 79 and 85*

109. PIER-GLASS and SIDE-TABLE in the 'Gothic Taste'. Gilded and ebonised wood. Mid-eighteenth century. Maximum use has been made of the pointed arch motif in the design of these two pieces.
Pier-glass height 5 ft. 10 in. Table length 4 ft. 3 in.
The Vyne, Hampshire. *See pages 78 and 89*

110. MIRROR with frame of gilded and bronzed wood. Designed and made in about 1743 by Matthias Lock for Hinton House, Somerset. Though of high quality, this frame is unusually heavy for the Rococo style. Height 8 ft. 7 in. *Victoria and Albert Museum.* *See pages 79 and 89*

111. CANDLESTAND of stained and gilded pine, with metal candle branches. Designed by Thomas Johnson in about 1760. One of a set of four from Hagley Park, Worcestershire.
Height 5 ft. 2½ in. *Victoria and Albert Museum.* *See pages 79 and 89*

112. MIRROR in the 'Chinese Taste', with frame of gilded wood. Mid-eighteenth century. One of a pair.
Height 11 ft. 1 in.
Victoria and Albert Museum
See pages 77 and 89

113. MIRROR with frame of gilded wood. Mid-eighteenth century. The broken outline of the frame is composed of scrolls, foliage and Rococo shellwork, surmounted by a winged horse, the crest of the Tollemache family.
Height 5 ft. *Ham House, Surrey.* *See page 89*

114. MAHOGANY CHEVAL SCREEN with a panel of Chinese painted paper. About 1740.
Height 4 ft. $5\frac{3}{4}$ in. *Ham House, Surrey.* *See page 90*

115. MAHOGANY ARMCHAIR, veneered with rosewood, satinwood and other woods; brass medallion in the back and brass feet and swags. About 1775. Attributed to John Linnell. Height 2 ft. $11\frac{1}{4}$ in. One of a set of eight from the *Library, Osterley Park, Middlesex.* *See pages 80, 94 and 95*

116. ARMCHAIR of gilded wood. Probably an early design in the Neo-Classical style, dating from shortly after 1760. (The use of a columnar form for the splayed back legs appears somewhat experimental.) Height 3 ft. 2 in. *Victoria and Albert Museum.* *See page 95*

117. ARMCHAIR of gilded wood. About 1775. Originally from the Drawing Room at Northumberland House, London. The maker's name, I. CULLEN, is inscribed under the seat rail. Height 3 ft. *Syon House, Middlesex.* *See page 95*

118. ARMCHAIR of gilded wood. About 1770. The carving of this chair, which is of very high quality, includes a portrait medallion in the top-rail. Classical urns are incorporated in the design of the seat-rail. Height 3 ft. 5 in.
Victoria and Albert Museum. *See page 95*

119. SATINWOOD BED, inlaid with green-stained wood, the canopy surmounted by gilded carving. Designed by Adam in 1779 for the Taffeta Bedroom at Osterley. The hangings are of Chinese painted taffeta. Height 11 ft. $0\frac{1}{2}$ in.
Osterley Park, Middlesex. *See pages 97 and 99*

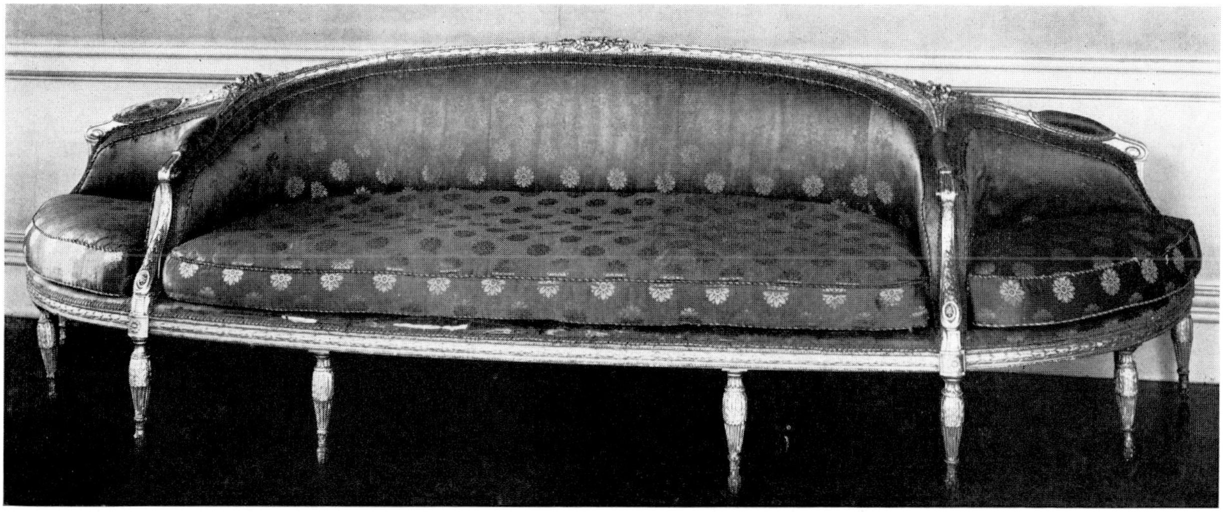

120. 'CONFIDANTE' of gilded wood. About 1775. Originally from the Drawing Room at Northumberland House, London. *En suite* with the armchair in Plate 117. Height 3 ft. 3 in. *Syon House, Middlesex.* *See page 96*

121. SIDE-TABLE of gilded wood with a white marble top, inlaid with composition. About 1775. Originally from the Drawing Room at Northumberland House, London. Height 2 ft. 6 in. *Syon House, Middlesex.* *See pages 93 and 97*

122. PICTURE FRAME of gilded wood, incorporating a carved plaque depicting Minerva and Cupid. About 1766. This is a particularly fine example of a picture frame in the Neo-Classical style. Height 7 ft. 10 in.
Victoria and Albert Museum. See page 101

123. CABINET ON STAND, made to display landscape panels in coloured marble. Inlaid satinwood, with marble and ormolu mounts. Designed by Adam in about 1771 for Kimbolton Castle, Huntingdonshire. Height 6 ft. $2\frac{1}{4}$ in.
Victoria and Albert Museum. See page 99

124. COMMODE in transitional style, decorated with marquetry in various woods and ormolu mounts. Attributed to John Cobb. About 1770. This commode has a Rococo bombé shape but is decorated with marquetry of Classical character. Length 3 ft. 8 in.
Victoria and Albert Museum. See pages 79 and 98

125. COMMODE, veneered with harewood, satinwood, rosewood and other woods and enriched with ormolu mounts. One of a pair designed by Adam in 1773 for the Drawing Room at Osterley. Length 5 ft. 2 in.
Osterley Park, Middlesex. See pages 98 and 99

126. DETAIL of the left-hand panel of the Commode shown in Plate 125. *See page 98*

127. HALL CHAIR. Beech, painted with dark green decoration on a white ground. One of a pair from the villa of David Garrick, the actor, at Hampton, Middlesex, probably supplied by Thomas Chippendale in 1770. Height 3 ft. $2\frac{1}{2}$ in.
Victoria and Albert Museum. See page 96

128. CHIMNEY-BOARD. Painted canvas on a wooden frame. Designed by Adam in 1778 for the State Bedchamber at Osterley. These boards were used to block the opening when the fireplace was not in use. Height 3 ft. 10 in.
Osterley Park, Middlesex
See page 102

129. CHEST-OF-DRAWERS. Satinwood, banded with rosewood and inlaid with green-stained wood. Designed in about 1780 for the Taffeta Bedroom at Osterley, this is a remarkably handsome piece in a less ornate style than the furniture designed for the State Rooms. Length 4 ft. 2 in.
Osterley Park, Middlesex
See page 99

130. CANDLESTAND of carved pine, painted green and white. One of a pair designed by Adam. Height 3 ft. 11¼ in.
Osterley Park, Middlesex
See page 100

131. PIER-GLASS with a frame of gilded wood. Designed by Adam in about 1770 for the Eating Room at Osterley. One of a pair. An oval frame was very seldom used by Adam for his pier-glasses. Height 12. ft 9 in.
Osterley Park, Middlesex. *See pages 93 and 100*

132. CHIMNEY-GLASS with a frame of gilded wood, incorporating a painted plaque representing Venus and Cupid. Designed by Adam in about 1775 for the State Bedroom at Osterley. The surmounting eagle with an adder in its beak is the crest of the Child family. Height 10 ft. $1\frac{1}{2}$ in.
Osterley Park, Middlesex. *See page 100*

133. PIER-GLASS with a frame of gilded wood in tri-partite form. One of a pair designed by Adam in 1777 for the Breakfast Room at Osterley. The excessive attenuation of some of Adam's later work is already visible in this glass.
Height 7 ft. 10 in.
Osterley Park, Middlesex. *See pages 93 and 101*

134. TRIPOD POLE-SCREEN, painted in grey, black and terra-cotta, the panel containing silk embroidery. Designed by Adam in 1779 for the Etruscan Room at Osterley. Height 5 ft. 6 in.
Osterley Park, Middlesex. *See page 102*

135. MARBLE CLOCK with figures of Derby porcelain and ormolu mounts, on a plinth veneered with satinwood and mahogany. The clock movement is contained within the fluted marble half column, on the ormolu base of which is engraved *Vulliamy London 1787*.
Height 6 ft. 1 in. *Victoria and Albert Museum.*

136. URN ON STAND. Wood, painted white and partly gilded; brass mounts. Designed by Adam in about 1770 for the Eating Room at Osterley. The pedestal door is open to show the compartment inside and the brass tap is visible in the frieze. Height 5 ft.
Osterley Park, Middlesex. *See page 101*

137. DRESSING-TABLE, veneered with harewood and other woods. About 1780. Fitted with an adjustable glass and numerous compartments in the top and a brushing slide at the front. Width 2 ft. 1 in.
Victoria and Albert Museum
See page 113

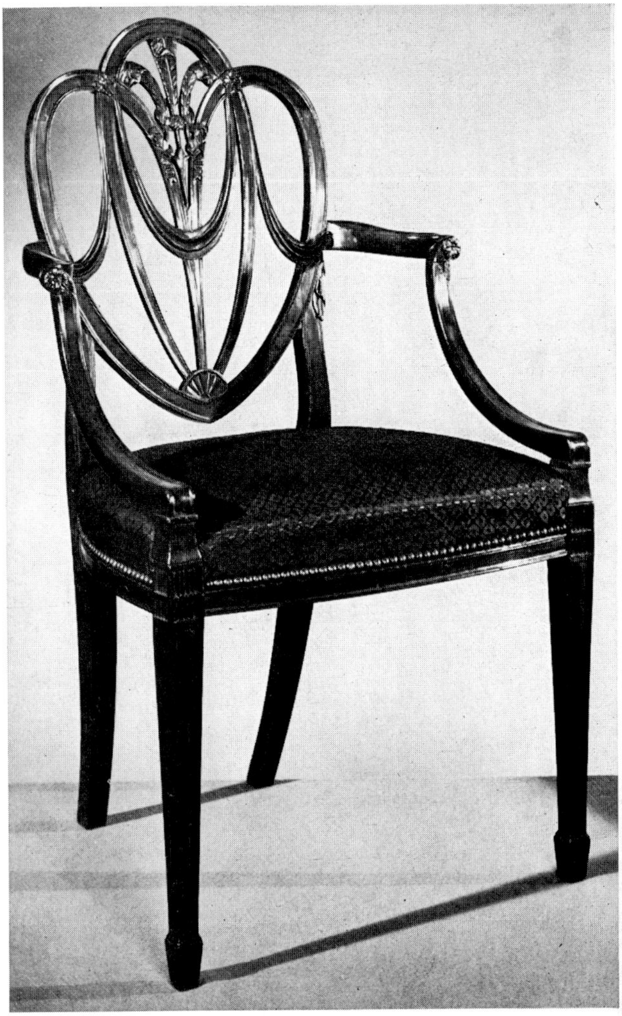

138. MAHOGANY ARMCHAIR with heart-shaped back. About 1780. The Prince of Wales's feathers are a prominent feature of this design in the Hepplewhite style. Height 3 ft.
Victoria and Albert Museum. *See pages 106 and 107*

139. ARMCHAIR of painted and gilded wood. About 1780. The oval back is filled with a large anthemion motif. Height 3 ft. $0\frac{3}{4}$ in.
Ham House, Surrey. *See page 106*

140. BED, painted green and white, with hangings of Indian painted cotton. Made by Thomas Chippendale for David Garrick, the actor, in about 1770. (The chairs and wardrobe belong to the same suite.) Height 7 ft. 10 in. *Victoria and Albert Museum.* *See page 110*

141. SETTEE with painted decoration on a black ground, fitted with cane seat, back and arm panels. About 1790. The back would also originally have had cushions. Height 3 ft. 1 in. *Victoria and Albert Museum.* *See pages 109 and 110*

142. MAHOGANY DINING-TABLE with gate-leg. About 1780. Two or more of these tables could be put together for dining and when not required for use they would serve as side-tables. Width 3 ft. 9 in. *Victoria and Albert Museum.* *See page 111*

143. SATINWOOD PEMBROKE TABLE, banded with rosewood and inlaid with various other woods. About 1780. Width (open) 3 ft. $2\frac{1}{2}$ in.
Victoria and Albert Museum. *See page 112*

144. WORK-TABLE of beech, painted white and decorated with gilded composition; fitted with a bag of green silk. About 1770. Height 2 ft. $6\frac{1}{4}$ in.
Osterley Park, Middlesex. *See page 112*

145. BUREAU-CABINET, veneered with satinwood inlaid with various woods. The front of the top drawer lets down on brass quadrants to form a writing surface. About 1785. Height 6 ft. 10 in. *Victoria and Albert Museum.* *See page 114*

146. BUREAU-CABINET, veneered with satin-wood and rosewood, fitted with a cylinder front. About 1790. Height 7 ft.
Victoria and Albert Museum. See page 114

147. CABINET ON STAND, veneered with harewood inlaid with floral marquetry. About 1785. The cabriole legs of the stand are of the very attenuated type often used in the late eighteenth century. Height 4 ft. $4\frac{1}{4}$ in.
Victoria and Albert Museum. See page 105

148. COMMODE DRESSING-TABLE of mahogany inlaid with satinwood and ebonised wood. About 1785. The top drawer is fitted with an adjustable glass and a number of compartments. Width 3 ft. 8½ in. *Victoria and Albert Museum*
See page 115

149. SATINWOOD COMMODE with painted decoration. About 1785. Length 3 ft. 6 in. *Victoria and Albert Museum.* *See page 115*

150. CORNER WASH-STAND of painted wood. About 1790. The folding top, when opened, serves to protect the wall from splashes. Height 2 ft. 7½ in.
Victoria and Albert Museum. *See page 115*

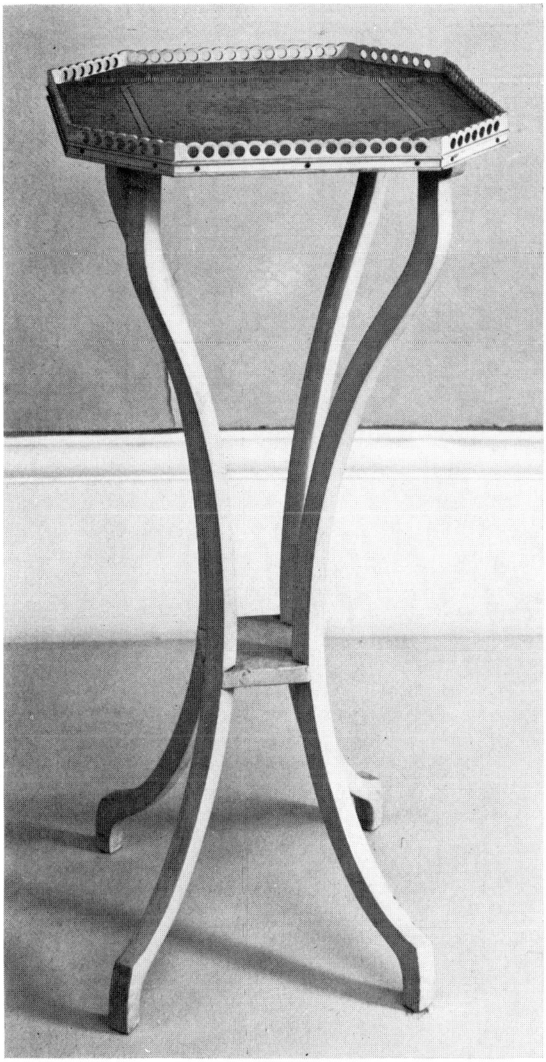

151. STAND of painted beech. About 1780. This very delicate piece of furniture might equally well serve as a stand for an urn or as an occasional table.
Height 2 ft. 6 in. *Osterley Park, Middlesex.* *See page 116*

152. MAHOGANY READING-STAND. About 1780. Such stands, having an adjustable book-rest and sometimes fitted with an extensible shaft, were popular for libraries.
Height 3 ft. $0\frac{3}{4}$ in.
Osterley Park, Middlesex. See page 116

153. KNIFE-CASE in the form of an urn, with marquetry of chestnut and harewood. About 1780. The lid is fixed to a central shaft and is held in an open position by means of a spring. Height 1 ft. $6\frac{3}{4}$ in.
Victoria and Albert Museum. See page 117

154. MAHOGANY KNIFE-CASE, fitted with silver mounts. About 1785. Knife-cases were generally made in pairs, to stand on sideboards. Height 1 ft. $3\frac{1}{2}$ in.
Victoria and Albert Museum. *See page 117*

155. CHAIR of *klismos* type, painted with Grecian decoration in terra-cotta on black. Based on a design by Thomas Hope. About 1807. The broad, curved back and curving legs are features of this type of chair. Height 2 ft. 9 in.
Victoria and Albert Museum
See pages 119 and 122

156. MAHOGANY ARMCHAIR with leopard-skin seat. About 1820. A more restrained use has been made of the *klismos* form in this chair. The carving is of very high quality.
Height 3 ft. $7\frac{1}{2}$ in.
Victoria and Albert Museum. See page 122

157. CHAIR, painted black and partly gilded, fitted with a cane seat. The large anthemion motif and the top-rail mount are of lacquered brass. First quarter of the nineteenth century. An example of rope moulding can be seen in the back. Height 2 ft. 10 in.
Victoria and Albert Museum. See page 122

158. ARMCHAIR, painted black and partly gilded. Based on a design dated 1804 (Plate 56), from George Smith's *Household Furniture and Interior Decoration*, 1808. The monopodium form has been used for both back and front legs. Height 3 ft.
Victoria and Albert Museum. See pages 121 and 122

159. ARMCHAIR in the Gothic style. Mahogany, partly gilded. Made for the Drawing Room of Eaton Hall, Cheshire, about 1823, probably to a design of William Porden. The Gothic details have been applied to a typically Regency shape. Height 3 ft. 1 in.
Victoria and Albert Museum. See page 122

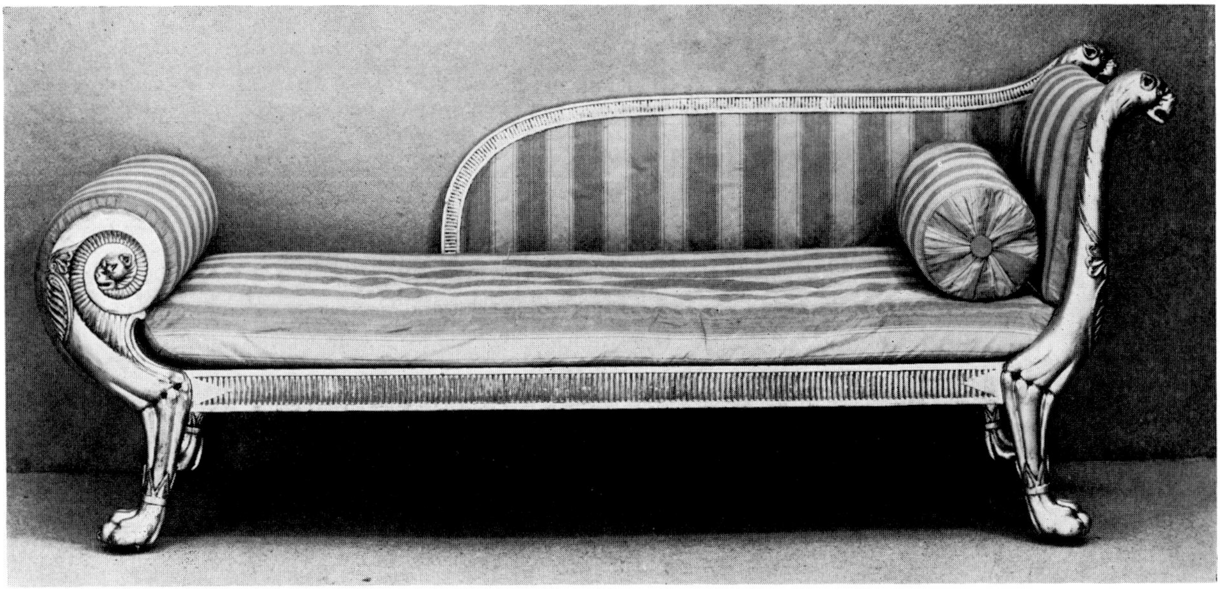

160. SOFA of gilded beech, with lion-headed monopodium supports. Made by Gillow and Sons in about 1805. Length 6 ft. 8 in. *Victoria and Albert Museum.* *See pages 121 and 124*

161. STOOL of X-form. Mahogany, partly gilded, with ormolu mounts. About 1820. A design for a similar stool in Ackermann's *Repository of the Arts* for 1809 is described as a 'window seat'. Height 1 ft. 11¼ in. *Victoria and Albert Museum.* *See page 124*

162. MAHOGANY PEDESTAL TABLE, inlaid with ebony and silver. Made exactly to a design (Plate 39) in Thomas Hope's *Household Furniture and Interior Design*, 1807. Formerly at Deepdene, Hope's house near Dorking, Surrey. Diameter 3 ft. 6 in. *Victoria and Albert Museum.* *See page 124*

163. PEDESTAL TABLE of coromandel wood, with ormolu mounts. About 1820. The top contains under glass an engraved design for the Wellington Shield, which is now at Apsley House, Hyde Park Corner. This table is of the same type as that shown in Plate 162 but far more richly ornamented. Diameter 4 ft. *Osterley Park, Middlesex.* *See page 124*

164. SOFA TABLE, veneered with amboyna and kingwood, having brass inlay and brass paw feet. One of four made in 1816 for Princess Charlotte, only daughter of George IV, on her marriage to Prince Leopold. Length (extended) 4 ft. $9\frac{1}{2}$ in.
Victoria and Albert Museum. *See page 125*

165. SQUARE PIANO in the form of a sofa table. Mahogany and rosewood, inlaid with various woods. Made by John Broadwood and Sons in 1801. This is a most unusual design for a piano. Length 6 ft. $9\frac{1}{2}$ in. *Ham House, Surrey.* *See page 125*

166. MAHOGANY DRESSING-TABLE, inlaid with ebony stars and stringing. Based on a design dated 1805 (Plate 72) in George Smith's *Household Furniture and Interior Decoration*, 1808. The drawers have no handles and are released by spring catches. Length 3 ft. 10 in. *Victoria and Albert Museum.* *See page 125*

167. ROSEWOOD SIDEBOARD, inlaid with brass. About 1820. The sarcophagus-shaped knife-boxes are attached to the top with brass fixings. Length 6 ft. 2 in. *Victoria and Albert Museum.* *See page 125*

168. MAHOGANY WRITING-TABLE, inlaid and mounted with brass. About 1800.
Length 4 ft. $7\frac{3}{4}$ in.
Osterley Park, Middlesex
See page 125

169. DETAIL of the writing-table illustrated in Plate 168, showing the quarter-round bead that began to be used in the construction of drawers about this time.
Osterley Park, Middlesex. *See page 121*

170. PEDESTAL TABLE. Mahogany and rosewood, inlaid with mother-of-pearl and enriched with brass mounts. About 1820. The central pedestal, supported on four scroll or splayed legs, became widely used for many kinds of table. 2 ft. square. *Victoria and Albert Museum* *See page 124*

171. HANGING CABINET. Mahogany, inlaid with brass. About 1800. The cabinet is ornamented with motifs drawn from Egyptian, Greek, Roman and Gothic sources. Height 6 ft. $2\frac{1}{2}$ in. *Victoria and Albert Museum.* *See page 126*

172. CABINET or CHIFFONIER. Pine, decorated with penwork and fitted with ivory handles. About 1815. The background is inked in, allowing the design to appear in the natural colour of the wood. Height 4 ft. 3 in. *Victoria and Albert Museum.* *See pages 120 and 126*

173. BUREAU-CABINET, veneered with zebrawood and satinwood. The handles, the Egyptian masks and the feet are of brass. About 1808. The watercolour drawings behind the Gothic style glazing are signed 'J. Baynes, 1808'. Height 5 ft. 2½ in. *Victoria and Albert Museum.* *See page 126*

174. ROSEWOOD WHAT-NOT, with brass gallery. About 1810. Height 3 ft. 6 in.
Victoria and Albert Museum. *See page 128*

175. ROSEWOOD TEAPOY with parquetry decoration in various woods (Tunbridge ware). About 1820. Fitted with two lidded compartments and two cut-glass bowls for different varieties of tea. The semi-circular section covered with pleated silk is a drawer. Height 2 ft. 7 in.
Victoria and Albert Museum. *See page 128*

176. NIGHT-TABLE in the form of bedside steps. Gilded wood and cane panels, with treads covered in green velvet. About 1820. Height 2 ft. 3½ in.
Osterley Park, Middlesex. See page 127

177. 'SCRAP' TABLE. Painted wood, with a top inlaid with variously coloured marbles. Inscribed round the edge: *Fragments collected in 1839; Terme di Tito; Terme di Caracalla; Monte Palatino & Tempio dei Cesari*. An attempt has been made to blend with the Adam style. Length 2 ft. 4½ in.
Osterley Park, Middlesex. See page 138

178. CHAIR of painted and gilded wood in the revived Rococo style. Designed by Philip Hardwicke in 1834 for the Goldsmiths' Hall, London. Height 2 ft. 9 in.
Victoria and Albert Museum. See page 133

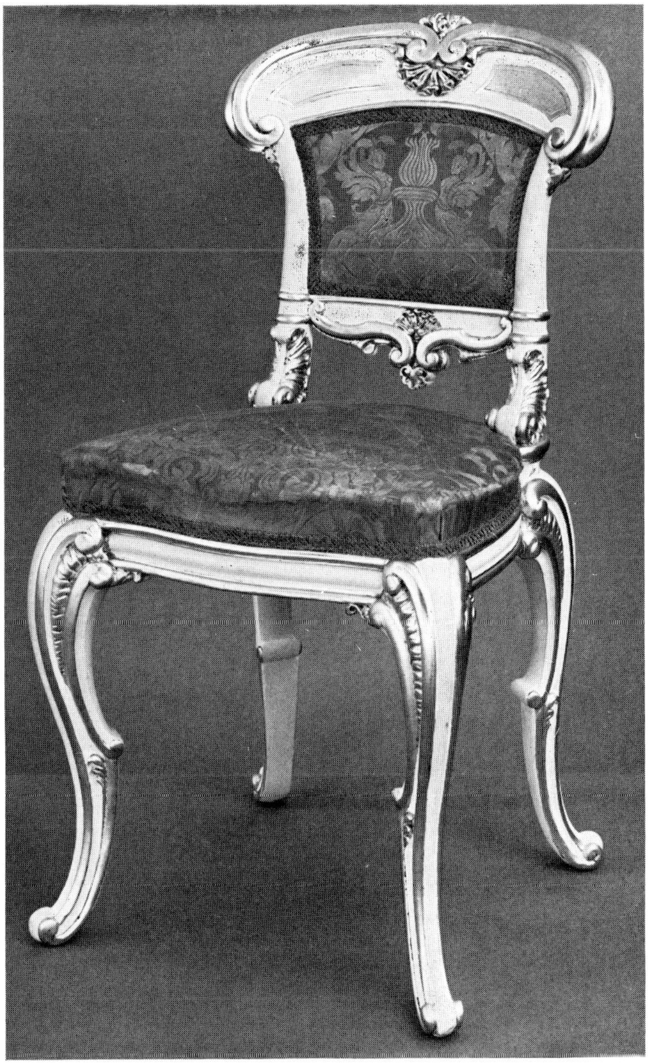

179. 'ELIZABETHAN' CHAIR. Mahogany, with upholstery of Berlin woolwork. Mid-nineteenth century. The derivation from chairs of the Charles II period is obvious but the chair is unmistakably nineteenth century. Height 3 ft. 4 in.
Victoria and Albert Museum. See pages 129 and 133

180. MAHOGANY ARMCHAIR with seat and back upholstered with imitation leather. Designed by A. W. N. Pugin in about 1840 for Scarisbricke Hall, Lancashire. A completely new use has been made of Gothic forms, rather than their grafting onto a typical nineteenth-century shape. Height 3 ft. $8\frac{1}{2}$ in. *Victoria and Albert Museum.* *See pages 130, 133 and 135*

181. MAHOGANY ARMCHAIR with marquetry decoration and a painted panel of the Prince Consort. Made by Henry Eyles for the Great Exhibition, 1851. Height 3 ft. $8\frac{1}{2}$ in.
Victoria and Albert Museum. *See page 134*

182. PAPIER-MÂCHÉ CHAIR, painted in various colours on a black ground and inlaid with mother-of-pearl. About 1840. The moulded shape of this chair foreshadows twentieth-century plastic forms.
Height 2 ft. $8\frac{1}{2}$ in.
Victoria and Albert Museum. See pages 131 and 134

183. MAHOGANY CHAIR, upholstered with Berlin woolwork. Mid-nineteenth century. This type of chair was sometimes known as a spoon back.
Height 3 ft. $1\frac{3}{4}$ in.
Victoria and Albert Museum. See page 134

184. OAK HALL CHAIR. About 1830. Based on a common type of Early Georgian writing-chair. The back is carved with the crest and coronet of the Earl of Jersey. Height 3 ft. *Osterley Park, Middlesex.* *See page 135*

185. CHESS-TABLE. Wooden base with gilded decoration on a black ground; papier-mâché top, similarly ornamented and inlaid with mother-of-pearl. About 1825. Length 2 ft. $1\frac{1}{2}$ in. *Victoria and Albert Museum.* *See page 137*

186. PAPIER-MÂCHÉ SETTEE painted in various colours on a black ground and inlaid with mother-of-pearl. Mid-nineteenth century. The influence of both the Louis XV and Louis XVI styles can be seen in this piece. Height 3 ft. 7 in.
Victoria and Albert Museum. *See pages 129, 131 and 135*

187. MAHOGANY SIDEBOARD with marble top. About 1840. The curving plasticity is typical of many pieces of furniture made at this time. Height 5 ft. $4\frac{1}{2}$ in.
Victoria and Albert Museum. *See page 138*

188. OAK SIDEBOARD, carved with scenes depicting Robinson Crusoe. Made in 1857 by Gerrard Robinson. The naturalistic school of carvers exercised their skill with narrative carving on many mid-century sideboards. Height 6 ft. 4 in. *Victoria and Albert Museum.* *See pages 130 and 138*

189. OAK CABINET in the Gothic style, embellished with wrought iron. Designed by A. W. N. Pugin for the Great Exhibition of 1851 and made by Crace and Sons. Height 8 ft.
Victoria and Albert Museum. *See pages 130 and 138*

190. MAHOGANY DAVENPORT. Early nineteenth century. The top section slides forward for use. The left-hand side is fitted with dummy drawers. Height 3 ft. 6 in.
Victoria and Albert Museum. See page 127

191. PEDESTAL CUPBOARD, veneered with Hungarian ash and fitted with a marble top. About 1840. Such cupboards were made in pairs for bedside use. Height 2 ft. 10½ in.
Osterley Park, Middlesex. See page 139

196. ARMCHAIR. Stained ash, with rush seat. Based on a traditional type of Sussex chair, this is one of many similar designs produced by Morris and Co. from about 1865 onwards. Height 2 ft. $8\frac{3}{4}$ in.
Victoria and Albert Museum. See pages 141 and 145

197. MAHOGANY ARMCHAIR with cane panels. Made by Morris and Co., probably after a design by George Jack, about 1895. The cushions are covered with Morris's 'Tulip' chintz. Height 3 ft. 1 in.
Victoria and Albert Museum. See page 145

198. CHAIR of ebonised beech, with inlaid decoration. Probably designed by Bruce Talbert in about 1865. Basically a balloon-back chair into which ornament derived from Gothic architecture has been introduced.
Height 2 ft. 11¼ in.
Victoria and Albert Museum. See pages 142 and 147

199. OAK ARMCHAIR, covered with leather upholstery, ornamented with Japanese motifs in gold. Designed by E. W. Godwin and made by the Art Furniture Company, London, in 1867 for Dromore Castle, Ireland.
Height 3 ft. 6¾ in.
Victoria and Albert Museum. See pages 143 and 147

200. ARMCHAIR, veneered with harewood, banded with rosewood. Designed by Owen Jones in about 1872. This shows a remarkably fresh approach to chair design, owing nothing to traditional form and ornament. Height 2 ft. $8\frac{1}{2}$ in.
Victoria and Albert Museum. *See page 148*

201. MAHOGANY CHAIR with rush seat. One of a pair made for the use of the Earl and Countess of Jersey at the Coronation of Edward VII in 1902, as recorded on a metal plaque attached to the back of the seat-rail. Attributed to Ernest Gimson. Height 3 ft.
Osterley Park, Middlesex. *See page 148*

202. OAK ARMCHAIR, inlaid with ebony and fitted with rush seat and back panels. Made by William Birch Ltd of High Wycombe in 1901, this chair shows a discriminating use of Art Nouveau ornament, in which it is strictly subordinate to form. Height 2 ft. 9½ in.
Victoria and Albert Museum. See pages 144 and 148

203. ARMCHAIR of oak, finished with a dark stain. Designed in about 1897 by C. R. Mackintosh. TABLE of stained oak. Designed in about 1906 by C. R. Mackintosh. Chair height 4 ft. 6 in.
Table 2 ft. 1½ in. square.
Glasgow School of Art
See pages 144, 148 and 149

204. EBONY DINING-TABLE. Designed in 1913 by A. Randall Wells and made by Ernest Gimson. This is an original method of increasing the size of a table. Circumference 4 ft. 3 in., increased to 6 ft. 4 in. when expanded. *Victoria and Albert Museum.* *See page 150*

205. CHIFFONIER veneered with Hungarian ash, having stringing and balusters of ebonised wood. About 1880. Height 4 ft. 3½ in. *Victoria and Albert Museum*
See page 151

206. OAK CABINET, with inlaid and painted ornament. Designed by Norman Shaw and shown at the 1862 International Exhibition in London. This cabinet represents an attempt to return to what was felt to be honesty of medieval construction and craftsmanship. Height 9 ft. 3 in. *Victoria and Albert Museum.* *See pages 142 and 150*

207. SIDEBOARD of ebonised wood, inset with panels of embossed leather and mounted with silver-plated handles and hinges. Designed in about 1867 by E. W. Godwin, this remarkably advanced design was very influential, many pieces of furniture in the 'Anglo-Japanese' style being derived from it. Height 5 ft. 11 in.
Victoria and Albert Museum. *See pages 143 and 151*

208. CABINET, decorated with marquetry in various woods and mounted with ormolu. Late nineteenth century. The decoration is based on that of the Adam period but the shape is quite untypical of that time. Height 4 ft. 8 in.
Victoria and Albert Museum. *See pages 145 and 151*

209. CABINET, veneered with satinwood and decorated with marquetry in various woods; ormolu mounts. Made by Holland and Sons in 1868, this cabinet shows the influence of the late eighteenth-century styles of both England and France. Height 3 ft. 7½ in. *Victoria and Albert Museum.* *See pages 145 and 209*

210. PAINTED AND GILDED WARDROBE. Designed by Philip Webb in 1858/59, with painted panels illustrating Chaucer's 'Prioress's Tale' by Edward Burne-Jones. Made as a wedding present for William Morris. Height 7 ft. $3\frac{3}{4}$ in.
Victoria and Albert Museum. *See page 141*

211. SATINWOOD PIANO decorated with Gothic ornament. Inlaid and gilded, with silk panels at the front. About 1865. Possibly by Charles Bevan. Height 4 ft.
Victoria and Albert Museum. *See page 154*

212. OCCASIONAL TABLE in the Anglo-Moresque style, inlaid with mother-of-pearl, ivory and pewter. About 1880. It was fashionable to have furniture and interiors in the Moorish style about this time. Height 1 ft. $7\frac{1}{2}$ in.
Osterley Park, Middlesex. *See page 145*

213. BAROMETER AND THERMOMETER. Mahogany case, inlaid with harewood. About 1900. The influence of English Art Nouveau can be seen in the popular heart motif and the flat surmounting cornice. Height 2 ft. $1\frac{1}{2}$ in.
Osterley Park, Middlesex. *See page 154*

214. ARMCHAIR of chromium-plated steel and leather. Designed by Ambrose Heal in 1933 and made by Heal and Sons Ltd. Height 2 ft. 6 in.
Victoria and Albert Museum. *See page 157*

215. 'ANTELOPE' CHAIR. Frame of enamelled steel rods and seat of enamelled plywood. Designed by Ernest Race, R.D.I., F.S.I.A., for the Festival of Britain, 1951, and made by Race Furniture Ltd, London. Height 2 ft. 8 in. *See page 159*

216. STACKING CHAIRS. The injected-moulded polypropylene shell, mounted here on a tubular steel frame, can be married to a variety of bases. Designed in 1962 by Robin Day and made by Hille of London Ltd. Height 2 ft. $5\frac{1}{4}$ in. *See page 158*

217. WRITING-TABLE faced with white gold and fitted with tassel handles. Designed by Edward Maufe for the Paris Exhibition of Decorative and Industrial Arts, 1925. Height 4 ft. *Victoria and Albert Museum. See page 157*

218. ARMCHAIR with frame of square section stainless steel tube. Upholstered with rubber webbing, plastic and latex foam, covered in fabric. Designed in 1962 by Robin Day and made by Hille of London Ltd. Height 2 ft. $4\frac{1}{2}$ in. *See page 159*

219. OCCASIONAL TABLE with legs of chromium-plated steel having a satin finish. Designed in 1958 by Robin Day and made by Hille of London Ltd. Length 4 ft. *See page 159*

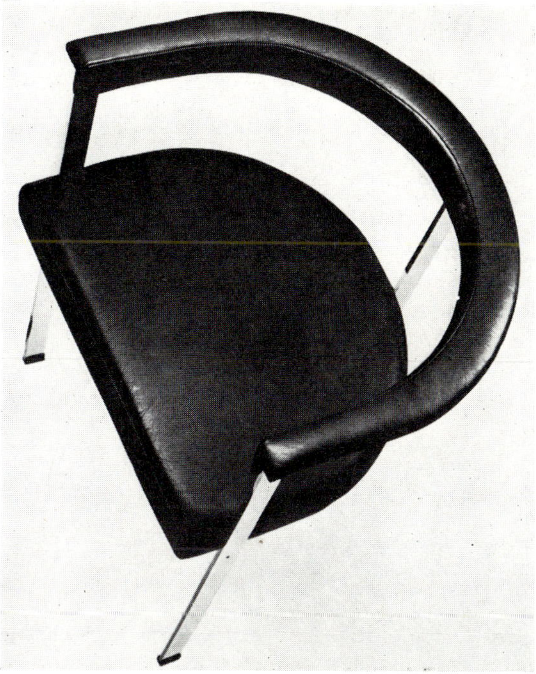

220. DINING-CHAIR with chromium-plated steel frame and latex and polyether foam upholstery, covered with P.V.C. Designed in 1968 by Richard C. Young and made by Merrow Associates Ltd, Merrow, Surrey. Height 2 ft. 2 in. *See page 159*

221. DINING-CHAIR of natural beech. Designed by Lupton–Morton Design Development Ltd in 1966 and made by Lupton–Morton Mail Order Ltd, Wallingford, Berks.
Height 2 ft. 4 in. *See page 160*

222. OAK STACKING CHAIRS with foam rubber upholstery covered in fabric or leather. Designed in 1963 by Conran Design Group Ltd and made by Conran and Co. Ltd, Thetford, Norfolk.
Height 2 ft. 4 in. *See page 160*

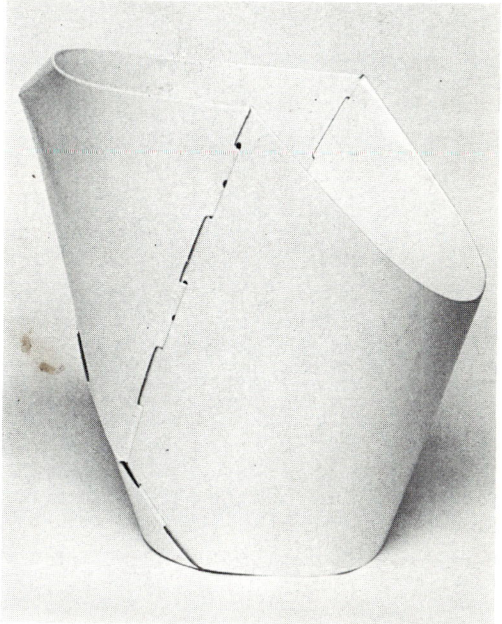

223. PAPER CHAIR. Designed in 1966 by David Bartlett and made by Thames Board Mills Ltd, it is composed of two pieces of fibreboard, laminated on both sides with a white Kraft lining paper, coated with extruded 'flamed' polythene.
Height 2 ft. $2\frac{1}{2}$ in. *See page 160*

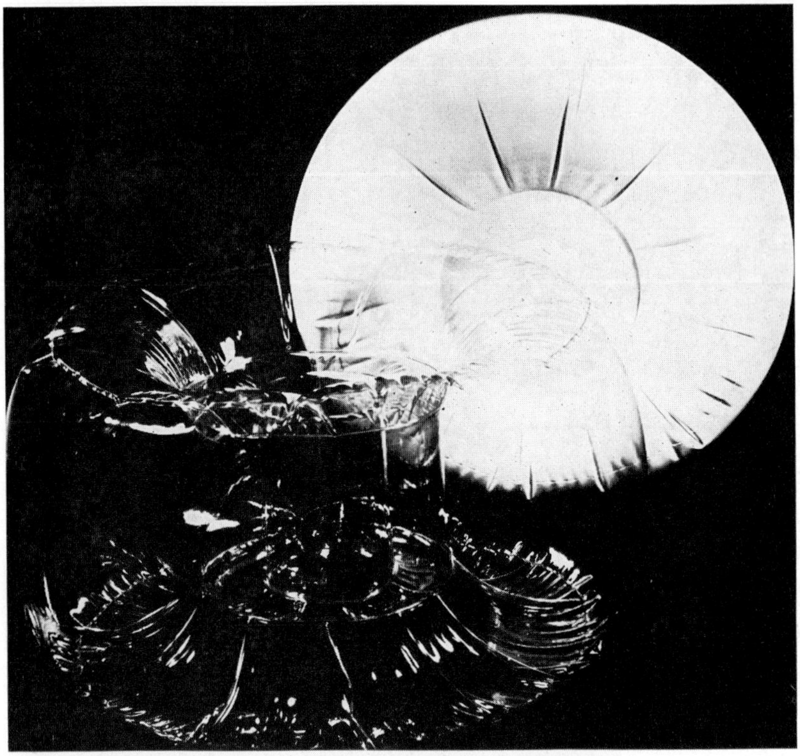

224. INFLATABLE CHAIRS made of polished extruded P.V.C. Designed in 1966 by Paul Wood and made for Goods & Chattels Ltd, London. Diameter 3 ft. 2 in.
See page 160

225. WALNUT WRITING-CABINET, with panels of burr elm and a chased silver lock-plate having a rosebush design, dated 1927. Designed by Sir Gordon Russell. Height 5 ft.
Victoria and Albert Museum. *See page 157*